C000067885

The London Palladium

THE STORY OF THE THEATRE AND ITS STARS

CHRIS WOODWARD

Published by Northern Heritage Publications
an imprint of Jeremy Mills Publishing Limited

www.jeremymillspublishing.co.uk

First Published 2009
Text © Chris Woodward 2009

Every effort has been made to trace the copyright holders of
the posters, programmes and other items used in this volume.
It is the belief of both the publisher and the author that the
necessary permission has been obtained. However, should
there be any omissions in this respect, we can only apologise
and shall be pleased to make the appropriate acknowledgements
in future editions.

All rights reserved. No part of this book may be reproduced
in any form or by any means without prior permission in
writing from the publisher.

ISBN: 978-1-906600-39-6

THIS STORY IS DEDICATED TO
MY LATE PARENTS,
BILL AND VERA

AND

TO MY FAMILY,
NADINE, NATALIE AND NATHAN,
WHO ASKED SO MANY TIMES,

'HAS THE POSTMAN BROUGHT YOU
ANY MORE PROGRAMMES TODAY?'

CONTENTS

FOREWORD

All artists require a platform, a showcase for their talents. For Da Vinci, it is now the Louvre, for Nureyev and Fonteyn it was the Royal Opera House Covent Garden, for Olivier it was the National Theatre. For the entertainers of the twentieth century, be it Danny Kaye, Judy Garland, Jack Benny or home-grown favourites like Norman Wisdom, Tom Jones, Bruce Forsyth or Morecambe and Wise, there was only one perfect arena for them – the stage of the London Palladium, in the heart of London's theatre district.

It was billed as 'The Ace Variety Theatre' – a quaint claim in this day and age, but to play the Palladium for any act, top of the bill or opening Tiller girl, meant something. It meant you were considered the best and worthy of being given so many minutes on THE stage in a variety bill. The reason it earned this status was architectural as well as geographical.

The man who drew the plans and conceived the theatre, its proportions and ambience, was the great theatrical architect Frank Matcham. His genius was to create a huge auditorium with 2,300 seats and yet at the same time preserve the essential intimacy that performers need in order to make contact with their audience. Every twitch of Marlene Dietrich's eye, a tiny move of the toe by Danny Kaye, every tear from Judy Garland; they all had to be capable of being picked up by every sector of the audience, even at the back of the 'gods' (upper circle). When standing centre stage, as I have done (happily for them without an audience!), what strikes you is how close the seats feel from up there.

The Palladium is a masterpiece of theatre building. It also proved to be photogenic. When Val Parnell opened its doors for that famous Sunday night series of television events, *Sunday Night at the London Palladium*, the theatre looked glamourous, gorgeous, and warm and inviting. A happy accident – there was no such thing as TV (or Bruce Forsyth!) when the theatre was designed and built.

It is a magical edifice. My memories of it are magical, too. If I can end on a parochial note, perhaps I saw its stage used to maximum advantage in the heyday of Ken Dodd, the last great 'front cloth comic'. Standing under the royal box, watching Doddy milk his audience for laughs and feeling the place rocking, was what the theatre was all about. An intimate comedian at one with 2,300 people. The London Palladium is truly a temple of popular culture.

MICHAEL GRADE CBE

DEFINITION

OED **London:** The capital of the United Kingdom
Palladium: The chemical element of atomic number 46, a rare silvery-white metal resembling platinum.

QED **The London Palladium:**
The greatest variety theatre.
All the stars say so!

ACKNOWLEDGEMENTS

*T*his book might never have been written in its present form, but for a chance discussion in 1977 with Percy Press Senior, the famous Punch and Judy operator. Percy had a collection of over 1000 theatre programmes to dispose of on behalf of the widow of a 'Gallery First Nighter'. It took me some time to decide to purchase this collection, as my shelves were already overflowing at that time with over 5000 magic books and magazines from around the world.

In this collection of theatre programmes from all over Britain, the majority relating to any one particular theatre was, as chance would have it, from the London Palladium. Being an avid collector and realising almost immediately that it was going to be an impossible task to collect every programme from every theatre, I decided to specialise and to concentrate on the London Palladium. This was a theatre where my parents had taken me as a child, from which I had the unforgettable memory of seeing Judy Garland sitting on the edge of the stage and dangling her legs over the footlights. It was a stage that one day I was determined to stand on myself.

Following successful negotiations with Percy, I was able to acquire the collection and in the years that followed I have added to my then small but growing collection of Palladium programmes and memorabilia.

To list all those who have helped would be virtually impossible, but my thanks are due to my publisher Jeremy Mills, to my editor Natasha Roberts, my designer Paul Buckley, to David Drummond, and to so many other friends and colleagues. Every possible attempt has been made to contact those artists who designed the theatre posters and programme covers, and whose valuable and colourful contributions I rightly acknowledge here.

I am also most grateful to the following: Stan Allen, Richard Baker, Jennie Bisset, David Budd, Mike Caveney, Nick Charlesworth, David Cheshire, Raphael Djanogly OBE, Ken Dodd OBE, Matt Field, Michael Freedland, The Grand Order of Water Rats, Tony Gulliver, Bryan Hammond, Alex Hepworth, Alan Howard, David Hibberd, Evelyn and Maurice Karstadt, Paul Kieve, Virginia King, Peter Lane, The Lord Chamberlain's Office, Tony Mabbutt, Michael McGiveney, Doug McKenzie, The Magic Circle, Tony Michaels, Dennis Norden CBE, Patrick Page, Tim Reed, David Smith, Christopher Stone, Jack Seaton, Howard Swinson, Max Tyler, Michael Roberts, The Royal Archive, Derek Nichol of Flying Music Ltd, Toye, Kenning & Spencer, Vaudeville Post Cards, Frankie Vaughan CBE, John Wade, Peter Warlock, Bryn Williams BEM, and Peter Wood.

I must not forget to mention Michael Young MD for his help along the way, Annette Koslover for her guidance, film researcher Cy Young for enabling me to see first-hand old film footage of early shows, and Emeritus Professor Gerald Dworkin, for his direction, help and encouragement.

I am also grateful to Lord Lloyd Webber, Mr Gareth Parnell, the General Manager, and all the staff at the London Palladium. Also, very special thanks are due to Brenda Thomas, the then Advertising Manager for Stoll Moss Theatres, and her successor Mark Fox. My gratitude also goes to the producer John Fisher, former Head of Entertainment at Thames Television Ltd. John is also a respected writer on popular entertainment and it was he who gave me the inspiration never to give up until this book was written and published.

Thanks must also go to the late Dr John M. Turner, whose extensive knowledge on the history of the Hengler family was second to none. The chapter relating to Hengler's Circus could never have been written without his help and advice. I must also mention Daphne Coutts-Smith and her late husband James, better known as Jim Smith. Jim was the ATV Senior Floor Manager who invented and tested almost all of the games on *Beat the Clock*.

My thanks to Ian Bevan and Patrick Pilton, whose books, *Top of the Bill* and *Every Night at the Palladium* respectively, told different stories about the same subject, and inspired me to bring forward my own interpretation.

My sincere appreciation to Michael Grade CBE for his foreword.

Finally, my eternal thanks to my ever patient wife, Nadine. Many's the time I have been called for a meal, only to be found typing away on the computer.

So read on and enjoy! I hope that you feel my efforts have been justified.

'Curtain Up' on the world famous

London Palladium

For the concert of life, no one has a programme...

Chapter One

NUMBER 7
ARGYLL STREET

The heavy, gold-fringed, red plush curtains meet with a resounding whoosh, the applause dies down and the first half comes to a close. The music is over for the time being, and the 'boys in the band' leave the orchestra pit eagerly for their well-earned break. The conversation noise level in the audience rises, as they discuss the merits of what they have just seen.

Due to the fire and safety regulations, the safety curtain must be lowered at this point. This 'curtain', weighing nearly half a ton, is specially constructed to act as a barrier in the unlikely event there is a fire outbreak either backstage or in the auditorium. In the centre of this curtain there is depicted a large painting of the front elevation of Hengler's Circus. It is painted by the artist Kewley and portrays how the building looked some 130 years earlier. I wonder, though, how many Palladium patrons realise how fascinating this early history is.

Argyll Street was first developed in the early 1730s on land belonging to John Campbell, the 2nd Duke of Argyll, one of the leading generals of the Duke of Marlborough.

Originally, Argyll House occupied the site on which the Palladium now stands on the east side of Argyll Street. It was first built in 1737 by Archibald Campbell, the 3rd Duke of Argyll, and then enlarged in 1742 for Lord Ilay. During the period 1750–62 the Duke's mistress, Mrs Shireburn, occupied Argyll House. Later, in the early 1800s, it became the London home of the Earl of Aberdeen. Coincidentally, it was during this period that the precious metal *palladium* was discovered in 1803 by UK chemist Dr W. Hyde Woolaston.

The Earl of Aberdeen had been Conservative Prime Minister of Great Britain from 1852 to 1855, and whilst in office it was he who had persuaded the Americans to accept the 49th Parallel as the rightful boundary with Canada. He resigned as Prime Minister in 1855 after criticism of his mismanagement of Britain's involvement in the Crimean War. When he died in 1860 aged seventy-six, his home was put up for auction by his son and was sold for the sum of £18,500.

In 1863 it was resold for a lesser sum of £15,500 to George Haig, a firm of wine and spirit merchants. With a commercial eye for business Haig had little or no interest in the house. It was the site that attracted him. So, in 1865, Number 7 Argyll Street – a building of little architectural merit – was demolished. Haig excavated the entire 23,000 square feet of extensive gardens to a depth of 25 feet below pavement level to provide much needed bonded wine cellars. Groined arches that were constructed of blue lias and Portland cement supported the cellar roof. These arches remain to this very day. The walls are thick enough to support the weight of the heavy building erected above and the roof of the cellars is 8 feet below pavement level in Argyll Street.

In 1868 the majority of the site was covered by a large, rectangular one-storey structure over the cellars. This was called the Corinthian Bazaar and Exhibition Rooms and was designed by Owen Lewis. The building took its name from the Corinthian columns that formed part of the classical front to Argyll Street. This elegant façade still remains to this very day, albeit with a slightly altered form to the middle two columns. This was simplified to allow for a wider entrance to the main vestibule.

A gutta-percha merchant acquired the property, and in 1870 a new temporary wooden structure, originally entitled the Palais Royal Exhibition Rooms, was erected at the rear. This was intended to be a diorama and a bazaar. It was run as a place of general entertainment and was the home of talking machines, wizards, panoramas and other kindred exhibitions.

In 1871 the building was remodelled and reopened as the Palais Royal. The gutta-percha merchant introduced equestrian entertainments, but sadly these were not successful. The whole building was again remodelled under the supervision of the architect Jethro Thomas Robinson to provide 'one of the handsomest as well as the most comfortable places of entertainment'.

Frederick Charles Hengler, the son of a famous tightrope walker, was the manager of the family circus business. George Haig approached him and a temporary lease was granted to Hengler. Plans were drawn up to provide the public with quality equestrian entertainment not seen since the days of Ducrow (1793–1842).

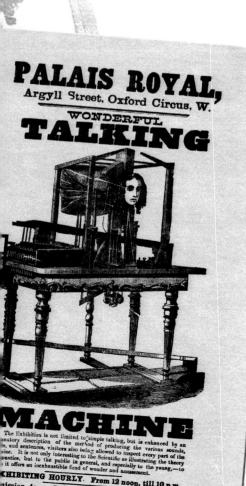

HENGLER'S GRAND CIRQUE,
PALAIS ROYAL,
ARGYLL STREET, REGENT STREET, LONDON,
Will Open on Saturday Evening, September 16.

ALLEY & CO., Printers by Steam, 9, Ryder's Row, Capel Street, Dublin.

Following a preview on Thursday, 31 August for the press and for Charles Hengler's close friends at the Palais Royal, his new Cirque opened to the public two weeks later on 16 September 1871.

The Palais Royal venture was Charles Hengler's third attempt to establish a presence in London. Some seven years earlier he had been responsible for providing the circus entertainment at the reopened Agricultural Hall in Islington. A year later he had been responsible in a similar capacity at E.T. Smith's Cremorne Gardens in Chelsea.

Frederick Charles Hengler was born in 1820 and came from a long line of circus performer managers whose earliest family record can be traced back to 1783. Printed in the programme for 18 November 1882 was a very interesting statement:

> Hengler's Cirque has achieved during the last thirty years greater success than has ever been known in the annals of circus history. Its name is a household word. HENGLER'S has become an institution in the principal cities and towns of the kingdom; having been established in Liverpool 26 years, in Glasgow 22 years, in Dublin 22 years, in Hull 19 years, in Bristol 18 years, in Birmingham 17 years and in London 12 years. The last named being the longest period on record of a *circus proper* retaining its popularity in the Metropolis.

Due to fire regulations the wooden structure of the Cirque had to be demolished and, following the acquisition of a new thirty-year lease by Hengler at an annual rental of £1300, a new building of a more substantial nature was constructed in 1885. Mr C.J. Phipps FSA, the noted and well-respected architect of

Charles Hengler

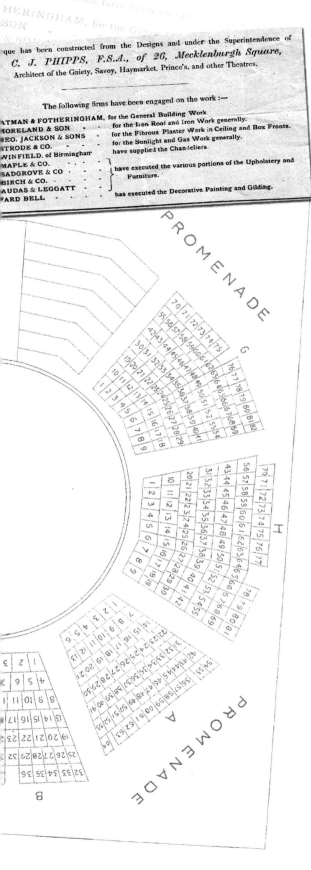

que has been constructed from the Designs and under the Superintendence of

C. J. PHIPPS, F.S.A., of 26, Mecklenburgh Square,

Architect of the Gaiety, Savoy, Haymarket, Prince's, and other Theatres.

The following firms have been engaged on the work :—

ATMAN & FOTHERINGHAM, for the General Building Work.

MORELAND & SON . . for the Iron Roof and Iron Work generally.

GEO. JACKSON & SONS . for the Fibrous Plaster Work in Ceiling and Box Fronts.

STRODE & CO. . . . for the Sunlight and Gas Work generally.

WINFIELD, of Birmingham . have supplied the Chandeliers.

MAPLE & CO. . . . }

SADGROVE & CO . . . } have executed the various portions of the Upholstery and Furniture.

BIRCH & CO. . . . }

AUDAS & LEGGATT . . }

WARD BELL . . . has executed the Decorative Painting and Gilding.

26 Mecklenburgh Square, was given the job of creating the new building. His previous works had been the Savoy, Haymarket and Gaiety Theatres, so his track record was well known to provide all the superlatives necessary. The company in charge of construction was Messrs Patman & Fotheringham. The sunlight and gasworks were provided by Strode & Company and the programmes also noted that the chandeliers had been provided by Winfield of Birmingham – all craftsmen of the highest quality.

The opening night's performance included Whimsical Walker, Chirgwin the Clown, and Miss Jenny O'Brien, and top of the strong bill was 'The Stud of Highly Trained Trachene Horses in a Surprising Performance', trained and introduced by M. Lorenz Wulff. It was a night to remember!

One of the early Hengler's programmes states that:
Mr Charles Hengler's Popular Equestrian Manoeuvres, Quadrilles and brilliant Scenes of Pageantry, for which this establishment stands, form a constant succession of charming varieties. Comprising the most talented artistes in the country; a complete and finished entertainment; organised as only can be by long experience and a perfect knowledge of the art that is so essential to know how to place before an audience An Equestrian Entertainment, Refined and Charming.

Other notices in the programme stated that:
The greatest vigilance is exercised in Messrs Henglers' Establishments at all times to secure the comfort and safety of the audience.

Visitors to the Stalls, Boxes and Reserved Chairs and Parterre are at liberty to view the stables during the interval only.

Visitors wishing to leave the Cirque before the performance terminates, are respectfully requested to do so between acts. It is otherwise annoying to the audience generally and dangerous to the artists.

Constantly searching for new ideas to attract his discerning public, in May 1887 Hengler presented a *Grand Chromoplastic Tableau*, 80 feet by 35 feet, representing Jerusalem and Calvary, with groups modelled after the famous *Oberammergau Passion Play*.

The handbill stated that it was the only place large enough to exhibit it. Admission was one shilling. The tableau had previously been exhibited at the Royal Crystal Palace in Munich and was visited by every member of the Royal Family.

The previous year a Command Performance had taken place at Windsor Castle and Charles Hengler had lived long enough to be proud of his wonderful achievements and to be awarded this honour. Unfortunately, ill health caught up with him and on 28 September 1887 he passed away aged sixty-seven. Under the terms of his will, his circus empire had been left in trust to his two sons Frederick and Albert. Frederick, the elder brother, died

HENGLER'S

Grand Cirque,

ARGYLL STREET, W.

Licensed by the Lord Chamberlain to ALBERT HENGLER, Sole Lessee and Manager.

Re-open for the Winter Season on Boxing Day, Dec. 26,

With Mr. HENGLER'S UNRIVALLED

CIRCUS TROUPE,

The best of RIDERS, GYMNASTS, ACROBATS, LEAPERS, JUGGLERS, &c., &c., and the

FUNNIEST OF CLOWNS,

STUD OF THOROUGH-BRED

HORSES AND PONIES.

Also, for the first time in London, an entirely new and original Grotesque

➤ PANTOMIME, ◄

Entitled, THE

VILLAGE WEDDING,

In Three Scenes and numerous Tableaux.

Invented, Designed, and Produced by

MR. ALBERT HENGLER.

NOTICE !—Mr. HENGLER desires to publicly acknowledge his indebtedness to **Mr. ALFRED POWELL, Sen.,** for his most valuable assistance in the Engineering Department of this production.

HENGLER'S GREAT

REAL WATER SPECTACLE.

A Marvellous Transformation. Must be seen to be believed.

23,000 GALLONS OF REAL WATER

Poured into the Arena in the incredibly short time of **35 seconds.**

At Every Representation, the Great Water Novelty.

SCENE 1.—
THE VILLAGE GREEN.
SCENE 2.—
THE FOUR-WHEELED CAB.
SCENE 3.—
A FETE ON THE RIVER.

NOTE.—In this Scene an absolute and unequalled Novelty will be presented to the astonished gaze of the Public:—In the incredibly short space of 35° SECONDS the large Arena is flooded with **23,000 GALLONS** of

REAL WATER,

And on this huge Lake will be introduced a Series of **SCREAMINGLY COMIC INCIDENTS AND MISHAPS.** The sight of this Mighty Torrent of Water

➤ RUSHING ◄

Into the Arena, should of itself be sufficient to

ATTRACT ALL LONDON,

Forming as it does a view in Miniature of the Gigantic

WHIRLPOOL OF NIAGARA

Notwithstanding the great amount of labour entailed by this Production, it will be performed at

EVERY REPRESENTATION.

DOORS OPEN FOR THE

DAY PERFORMANCES

AT 1-30.

EVENINGS AT 7-30.

Commencing Half-an-hour Later.

HENGLER'S.

TWO PERFORMANCES

— DAILY —

At 2 o'clock, Doors open at **1-30**; and 8 o'clock, Doors open at **7-30.**

◆ COMMENCING ✛ BOXING ✛ DAY, ◆

DECEMBER 26.

PRICES : Private Boxes, 40s. & 30s. ; Stalls, 4s. ; Reserved Chairs, 3s. ; Parterre, 2s. ; Amphitheatre and Promenade, 1s.

Children under 10 Years of age Half-price to all parts.

Box Office open daily at the Cirque, Argyll Street, from 10 till 5 on December 8th and onwards. Seats may also be secured at the City and West End Libraries.

HENGLER'S CIRCUS.

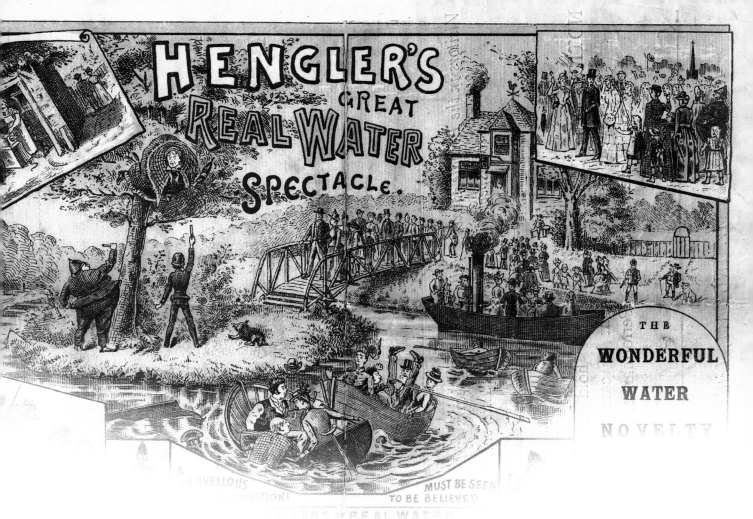

two years later and the mantle of responsibility for the running of the family business fell solely on the shoulders of Albert. He was just twenty-six years of age.

In 1891 and in an endeavour to lift himself out of the financial doldrums (for he still had to pay ground rents and other outgoing charges for the rates, taxes and ancillary expenses), Albert Hengler presented item thirteen on the programme 'for the first time in London'. He staged a grotesque pantomime entitled *A Village Wedding, or Tramps Abroad* in three scenes, and numerous tableaux introducing the Hengler's Great Water Novelty.

The final scene, 'an absolute and unequalled novelty, was presented to the astonished gaze of the public. In the incredibly short space of thirty-five seconds the large arena was flooded with 23,000 gallons of real water'. A notice in the programme stated that 'The Management will not hold themselves responsible for any damage that might be caused by the splashing of water during the performance.' Albert had spoken to his father many times before – and to other members of the family – of this dream of a great water spectacle, but all they did was laugh, saying it would never succeed. However, succeed it did, and more, earning him sufficient money to buy out his late brother's share in the family business and for Albert to own all four family circuses outright. Today the water spectacles in Las Vegas and other venues must surely have had their origins here.

Over the years many additional novelties were introduced to attract the public. Today we might be entertained watching *The Strongest Man on Earth* or *Gladiators* on television, but Hengler was there first. One such act from America was The Gilfort Brothers. Their Herculean feats became the talk of the town. Other different features that Hengler introduced were Promenade Concerts, the Royal Italian Opera Grand Ballet and the Marionette Company. Who dared to argue that variety was not offered in Argyll Street!

In 1893 the newspaper *Tit Bits* had an enquiry column. One of the questions raised was 'Which circus proprietor has held in-hand at one time the greatest number of horses?' Always willing to advise its readers, it stated that it was

> Herr Edward Wulff, who in February 1893 surprised the audiences attending one of his performances of his Continental Circus in Argyll Street. He controlled no less than fifty horses moving in circles in different directions. This display was certainly the greatest example of skill in training ever manifested. Every horse had to be taught his particular share of the performance.

The circus arena setting was like a huge tiered wedding cake. Ponies walked around the platform edge of the ring, whilst another troupe trotted around the inside of the ring in a different direction. A further three tiers, all with horses trotting, rose to the top with Edward Wulff sitting astride his own steed. A most spectacular sight indeed, as the inside of his programmes showed. By 1894 the programme stated that the number of horses had been increased to sixty! Can you begin to imagine how much hay it took to keep them all in the best possible health, bearing in mind this was only one item on the programme?

HENGLER'S
GRAND CIRQUE
EVERY EVENING

GRAND HENGLER'S CIR

Argyll Street,
REGENT STREET LONDON.
Patronised by Royalty and the Nobility
of Great Britain.

Licensed by the Lord Chamberlain to
CHARLES HENGLER

EVERY EVENING
Doors open at 7.
Commence at 7·30.

MORNING PERFORMANCES.
Doors open at 2
Commence at 2·30.

Carriages may be ordered for
Day Performance at
4·15
Evening at 10·20

HENGLER'S
GRAND CIRQUE
Open every Evening at 7, commence at 7·30.

PRICES OF ADMISSION:
Stalls, 4s.; Reserved Chairs, 3s.; Parterre, 2s.;
Amphitheatre and Promenade, 1s.
Private Boxes - - - £1 10 0
Children under Ten, Half-price to all parts.

	Mr. G. CLEMENTS.
Musical Director	Mr. L. EGERTON.
Ring Master	Mr. F. FURNESS.
Box Bookkeeper	Mr. A. H. HENGLER.
Secretary and Treasurer	Mr. ALF. POWELL
Business Agent	

Proprietor and Director,
Mr. C. HENGLER.

NATIONAL
SKATING
PALACE
REAL ICE
HENGLER'S CIRCUS
REGENT
STREET.W

.. National Skating Palace, ..

HENGLER'S GRAND CIRQUE,

ARGYLL STREET, REGENT STREET, W.

◁ **GRAND NATIONAL** ▷

FANCY DRESS

SKATING CARNIVAL

Monday, January 20th, 1896.

EVENING DRESS or FANCY DRESS

IS ABSOLUTELY DE RIGUEUR

TICKETS LIMITED TO 500.

Each Ticket includes admission for One Gentleman
and One Lady. No Ladies' Tickets.
Tickets, including Recherché Supper for Two
(Wines not included), TWO GUINEAS.

Commencing at 11 p.m. Supper at 1 a.m. Carriages at 3 a.m.

TWELVE DIAMOND and OTHER PRIZES

For the Winning Costumes worn by Ladies :

Diamond Star, Diamond Bracelet, Diamond Corsage Watch, and
Nine Pairs of the Special " Palace " Skates.

In addition to which, as a SOUVENIR of this CARNIVAL, every Lady Visitor will be
Presented with a copy of the

NEW WALTZ SONG, ENTITLED " SKATING,"

By THEO. BONHEUR, composer of " Love's Golden Dream."

**TICKETS CAN BE OBTAINED AT THE OFFICE IN THE ENTRANCE
HALL.**

PATRONS

H.R.H. THE PRINCE OF WALES.
H.R.H. THE DUKE OF YORK.
H.R.H. THE DUCHESS OF YORK.
H.R.H. THE DUKE OF SAXE-COBURG AND GOTHA.
H.M. THE KING OF BELGIANS.

H.R.H. THE DUKE OF YORK.
W. HAYES FISHER, ESQ., M.P.

PRESIDENT

Programme of the Competition

FOR THE

World's Championship in Figure Skating for 1898

(Under the auspices of the International Skating Union),

TO BE HELD AT

THE NATIONAL SKATING PALACE,

ARGYLL STREET, LONDON, W.,

ON TUESDAY, FEBRUARY 15TH, 1898,

Commencing at 3.0 and 8.0 p.m.

Referee :—

R V. G. BALCK, Stockholms Allmänna Skridskoklubb, President of the International Skating Union.

Judges :—

F. ADAMS, The Skating Club.
E. BELL, Davos Skating Club.
FILLUNGER, Wiener Eislauf Verein.
F. JENKIN, Wimbledon Skating Club.

COUNT VON ROSEN, Stockholms Allmänna
Skridskoklubb.
CAPT. J. H. THOMSON, The Skating Club and
Wimbledon Skating Club.

Competitors :—

1. G. FUCHS, Münchener Eislauf Verein.
2. C. HOLT, N.S.A.
3. G. HÜGEL, Wiener Eislauf Verein.

4. H. GRENANDER, Stockholms Allmänna
Skridskoklubb and N.S.A.
5. L. WIIK, Helsingfors Skridskoklubb.

Winner of the Championship for 1897; G. HÜGEL, Wiener Eislauf Verein

Hengler was very much a family man and observed the Sabbath with his entire cast. In his book *Acrobats and Mountebanks*, Le Roux stated that

> I remember entering the arena one Sunday morning in London and was considerably surprised to find the whole company in morning dress assembled in the ring. A black-coated individual, Bible in hand, was addressing the acrobats. It was a Clergyman. I have been told since that Mr Hengler exacts punctual attendance at the Sunday service from every one of the troupe.

By 1895 Hengler had leased the building to the National Skating Association, who turned it into an ice rink with 'real' ice. It was the second such rink to open in London. Early in 1896 a Grand National Fancy Dress Skating Carnival was presented in Argyll Street: 'Evening Dress or Fancy Dress absolutely de rigeur with tickets at Two Guineas [£2.10] including a Recherché Supper for two, [wines not included!] and with a limited admission to 500.' It must surely have been a grand affair. Then, on the Lord Mayor's Day, a Grand Fancy Dress Carnival was announced and the tickets were twenty-five shillings each (£1.25) – quite expensive in those days. However, the prizes on offer were five guineas (£5.25), so perhaps it was worth entering!

On Saturday, 6 November 1897, in between the music for skating, the famous French magician and illusionist Buatier de Kolta made an appearance with his *Disappearing Man* presentation. Mr Nelson Reed, the General Manager of the NSA, announced in the press that, 'if you have nothing better to do, you might drop in and see this marvellous disappearance in mid-air.' De Kolta possibly holds the record for the first magician to appear in Argyll Street!

Such was the considered importance of the venue that in February 1898, the National Skating Association of Great Britain held the World Figure Skating and Combined Figure Skating Championships at the National Skating Palace.

On 4 February 1904, an ice hockey match was played at Hengler's on the occasion of the Union Jack Carnival, and was the first to be witnessed by royalty in Britain. The following June at 10.30pm and in aid of the St Helena Hospital Home, a game of 'Living Bridge' was played, where all the cards were human.

Public taste was slowly beginning to change. The idea of going to the circus or even ice-skating was not at the top of the list of activities of the paying public. Although the building continued to be known as Hengler's, the Royal Italian Circus took a lease on the Hengler site in the hope of trying to make a success of it. The publicity certainly had the edge on all that had gone before:

> It is the most wonderful show of its kind that the world has seen and is absolutely unique. There is Fasolin the Flying Trapeze Monkey. If you have not seen his performance you will never credit to what perfection a monkey may be trained. There is Madame Batavia. Do you know that the press speculated that people would not believe that a bear could do such things? Men have even gone so far as to wager that it is a man dressed up! This mistake is not as ridiculous as it seems. Go and see for yourself, then you will understand.

HENGLER'S CIRCUS,
ARGYLL STREET, W.

A
"LIVING BRIDGE" FÊTE
WILL BE HELD ON
MONDAY, JUNE 27th, at 10.30 p.m.
(DOORS OPEN AT 10)
UNDER THE IMMEDIATE PATRONAGE OF
H.R.H. PRINCESS CHRISTIAN OF SCHLESWIG-HOLSTEIN.
H.R.H. THE DUCHESS OF CONNAUGHT.
H.R.H. THE DUCHESS OF ALBANY.
IN AID OF ST. HELENA HOSPITAL HOME.
President—H.R.H. PRINCESS CHRISTIAN.

FÊTE COMMITTEE:
THE COUNTESS OF RECTIVE, *President*.
THE COUNTESS OF LATHOM.   MRS. CHARLES NEEDHAM.
MRS. WINDHAM BARING.   MR. A. LINDSAY LISTER.
MRS. ANDREW HICHENS.   BARONESS ARILD ROSENKRANTZ,
Hon. Sec.

MR. HERBERT BEERBOHM TREE has kindly consented to assist in the representation of the game.
The details for cutting, shuffling, dealing, and playing the game without using cards will be arranged by MR. LINDSAY LISTER, who is known to Bridge players as "BADSWORTH."
The game will be played with the living cards by four well-known players.

SEATS, Numbered and Reserved, £1 1s. and 10s. 6d.
Unreserved Seats and Promenade, 1st Circle, 7s. 6d.; 2nd Circle, 5s.
Buffet Supper by Gunter—Tickets, 5s. each.

Tickets may be had from the Ladies of Committee, or from THE SOCIAL BUREAU, Ltd., 30, New Bond Street, and at Hengler's Circus, Argyll Street.

HENGLER'S CIRCUS,
Argyll Street, W.

Under the Immediate Patronage of
H.R.H. PRINCESS CHRISTI...
OF SCHLESWIG-HOLS...
H.R.H. THE DUCHESS
OF CONNAU...
H.R.H. THE DUCHESS OF ALB...

LIVING
BRIDGE

In Aid of
ST. HELENA
HOSPITAL HOME.

MONDAY, JUNE 27th,
1904.

ROYAL ITALIAN CIRCUS

Sig. B Volpe & Madame Batavia

Prior to their London season when the circus had been in Birmingham, the Chairman of the Society for the Prevention of Cruelty to Animals visited the show and, unbeknown to the trainers, saw the animals at practice (which the paying public could also do in London any day). He was absolutely satisfied with the method of training and found the animals in the very pink of condition.

15

On 23 June of that year, Signor Volpi had the honour of taking all his circus equipment to Buckingham Palace to present his latest circus marvels by command of His Majesty King Edward VII.

In 1907, Beketow, the Russian circus owner, brought his marvels to Argyll Street twice daily, and *Pierrot in Fairyland* – a grand Christmas pantomime, enacted by over a hundred juvenile performers – was offered to the patrons; 'Introducing all the popular fairy stories and nursery rhymes and his Grand Circus Company: 200 first class artists and 100 highly trained horses, marvellous acrobats, *screamingly* funny clowns, performing animals, plus "specialities" such as the famous Konyot Family.'

M. Beketow was also the first person to bring to Argyll Street the Great International Wrestling Tournament for the Championship of the World. With Prizes of £500 and the 'Diamond Belt', offered by Mr Frank C. Bostock, it was a competition that would have been worth entering! Prior to the Wrestling Tournament M. Beketow provided added thrills with Staig's Steeplejack Cyclists' *Motoring in the Chimney* (Laurie Staig would go on to appear during World War Two as a member of the Australian Air Aces and later still with his *Wall of Death* at Battersea Pleasure Gardens in the 1950s.)

By 1908, Austin Fryer was the new lessee at Hengler's, presenting twice daily *another* circus with an additional finale offering of *Cinderella*. On reflection, the rags to riches story might have been considered appropriate for this 'Cinderella', an establishment which had worked so hard for some thirty-seven years and was about to be transformed into the most beautiful creature in theatrical history.

On 15 June 1908 the Argyll Street doors finally closed and the freehold was sold.

The transformation scene was about to begin.

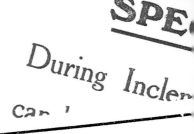

SPECIAL NOTI

During Inclement Weather can be obtained from the Clo depositing **3**s. If the Umbrel within **7** days **2**s. **6**d. will

HENGLER'S CIRCUS,
Argyll Street, W.

Manager - - FOSTER C. MARNER

CINDERELL

TWICE DAILY AT 2.3

Doors Open Thirty Minutes before
Commencement of the Performance

NOTICE.

M. BEKETOW RUSSIAN CIRCUS,

TWICE DAILY at **2** and **8** p.m.

ARGYLE ST (HENGLERS) Oxford Circus W.

200 ARTISTS. 100 HORSES.

SPECIAL XMAS ATTRACTIONS.

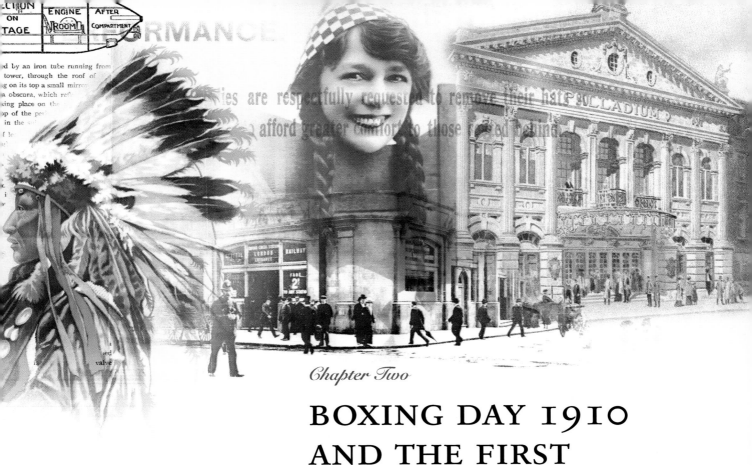

Chapter Two

BOXING DAY 1910 AND THE FIRST DECADE

t was 26 December 1910, the Christmas festivities were well under way and there was an immense air of expectancy in Argyll Street; a brand new theatre was about to come to life. It was almost like being at the birth of a child. A horse and carriage pulled up at the kerb, dropping off its passengers outside the beautiful edifice. The street was already thronged with specially-invited patrons eagerly awaiting their first performance. Immaculately attired guests jostled in the queues to enter. Having known the earlier successes and failures, they stood in anticipation and wonderment at the bright lights beckoning them inside to take their seats. Little did they know that they would not be disappointed.

The old Corinthian façade still stood proud, with its elegant columns seemingly reaching to the stars. Nothing of the old tawdry bazaar image remained. In its place was a brand-new building that had been designed by renowned theatre architect Frank Matcham and built at a cost of £250,000. It was in fact standing on nearly a third more ground than Hengler's had originally occupied. This was to allow for the perfect layout of the building – with the sumptuous carpets and plush red seats housing nearly 3,000 people, the circle and grand circle had been constructed on a cantilever principle so that no pillar or obstruction interfered with the view from even the most distant seat. It was the first theatre of its kind in London at the time, and remains so to this very day. The most important design feature of the house was that the back rows were not remote from the stage – even from the farthest point of the circle the line of sight was excellent. This feature still stands and though the seating capacity of the Palladium is still great – some 2,300 plus seats, the second largest capacity in London – no member of the audience should have any difficulty in appreciating the more delicate work of the actor or singer.

The Daily Telegraph reported,

> In comfort and convenience of design and in beauty of decoration it is no less distinguished. Already it is clear that the quality of the entertainment provided will be worthy of the structure. The site is served by two tube railways, which together tap every quarter of London. There are besides these all the omnibuses of Oxford Street and Regent Street.

Theatre ticket prices ranged from 6*d.* and 1*s.* (2p and 5p) for numbered reserved seats in the circle, right up to 2*l.* 2*s.* 0*d.* (£2.10) for a box seating four persons. Should you wish to add an extra member of your family or take along a guest, it was only an extra 7*s.* 6*d.* (37p) for an extra chair to be added! With seats in the popular orchestra stalls at 2*s.* 6*d.* (12p), no one could have any excuse not to attend.

The stage had a depth of 40 feet and the proscenium opening was 47 feet wide. Although sadly now gone, at either side of the stage was a large illuminated sign that would indicate by numerical value the artist that corresponded with the number in the programme. At precisely 7.30pm, the number '1' appeared in the light box to indicate the overture. The Musical Director, James Sale, raised his baton and proceeded to conduct the London Palladium Orchestra. As one might expect, the piece of music was entitled the 'Palladium March', and

THE PALLADIUM.

NEW VARIETY THEATRE.

A magnificent addition to London's places of entertainment will be made on Boxing Day. That afternoon is to see the doors of the Palladium open for the first time. For mere size the Palladium claims a place in the forefront. In comfort and convenience of design and in beauty of decoration it is no less distinguished. Already it is clear that the quality of the entertainment provided will be worthy of the structure.

And where is the Palladium? Many of us remember where Hengler's Circus stood. For those who have forgotten or never knew, the best direction is across the road from the Oxford-circus Tube Station. The site is thus singularly convenient, being served by two Tube railways, which together tap every quarter of London. There are, besides these, all the omnibuses of Oxford-street and Regent-street. The space occupied by Hengler's was, however, not enough for the enterprise of Mr. Walter Gibbons. By the acquisition of adjoining property he obtained a site of no less than 37,000 square feet. This has enabled him to provide ample accommodation for as many as 1,300 people in the stalls, and though there are only two tiers above—grand circle and circle—the Palladium will seat 5,000 people. The tiers are constructed on the cantilever principle, so that no pillar or other obstruction interferes with the view from the most distant seat. Even from the farthest point of the circle the line of sight is excellent. The most important feature in the design of the house is that even the back rows are not remote from the stage. Though the seating capacity of the Palladium is so great, none of the audience will have difficulty in appreciating the more delicate work of actor or singer. How much additional pleasure that means it is superfluous to explain. The prices of seats will range from 5s for a stall to 6d for the back rows of the circle. Every seat in the house, including the cheapest, can be booked. Booking, it may be noted, has already been considerable. Until Dec. 7 the box-office is to be found at the Holborn Empire.

From The Daily Telegraph, 1st December 1910

That after-
m open for
ium claims
convenience
it is no less
the quality
orthy of the

of us remem-
or those who
st direction is
Tube Station.
, being served
her tap every
ides these, all
Regent-street.
s, however, not
Walter Gibbons.
erty he obtained
e feet. This has
commodation for
alls, and though
grand circle and
,000 people. The
lever principle, so
on interferes with
at. Even from the
ne of sight is excel-
re in the design of
rows are not remote
ting capacity of the
e audience will have
ore delicate work of
litional pleasure that
plain. The prices of
all to 6d for the back
n the house, including
Booking, it may be
derable. Until Dec. 7
t the Holborn Empire.

ph, 1st December 1910

was specially commissioned by James Sale and dedicated to Walter Gibbons Esq. It is perhaps apposite to mention here that Sale had been employed by Hengler to provide the music for *Cinderella*, his last pantomime in Argyll Street. Sale was to remain in that important Argyll Street role as Musical Director until finally laying down his baton in 1916, with Horace Sheldon following on in this role and filling his shoes admirably.

A very full opening bill ensued, and ran for over four hours, well into the next day. What an exciting evening it must have been! Following the rousing overture, opening the show was item number '2' in the light box, Stacey and Williams – 'The Immaculate Pair'. They were followed by popular instrumentalists The Three Keltons, the clever character comedienne Nellie Wallace, and the Frank L. Gregory Troupe, 'the World's Greatest Jugglers and Hoop Manipulators'. The popular Lancashire comedian George Gilbey was followed by The March Hares in *Merry Vaudeville Variations*. Whit Cunliffe then entertained, before Sir Martin Harvey, together with his full company, put on their presentation of *The Conspiracy*. After the intermission, Harry Ford, 'the Inquisitive One', was closely followed by an item entitled *Yuletide Revels*. This was a 'ballet divertissement' starring Miss Topsy Sinden, 'The Celebrated Première Danseuse,' in a sequence presented in one scene with incidental music by James Sale. Ella Shields and Decima Moore individually entertained next, and Ella Retford topped the bill. As was always the case, closing the show was a speciality act, and in this very first instance it was the wonderful acrobats and hand balancers, The Dankmar Schiller Troupe. It would seem that Frank Matcham had succeeded yet again in designing a most beautiful theatre and Walter Gibbons had a mild success on his hands.

An interesting note in the very first programme stated 'Programmes offered for sale outside this Theatre are valueless as the numbers attached to each turn are altered!' The touts, it would seem, were out and about even in those days!

Strangely enough, identical programmes inside the theatre were priced for sale at one penny, two pence and three pence, so if you sat in the more expensive seats you presumably wouldn't mind paying more for the programme.

The PALLADIUM

PALLADIUM

Managing Director –
WALTER GIBBONS

PRICE

1^{D.}

The official first night programme cover depicted a motorcar, quite a rare sight on the London streets in 1910. No official figures existed prior to 1904, but it was estimated that compared with France – which had a reputed 5,000 vehicles – there may only have been 700–800 cars in London by the turn of the century, and most vehicles in Britain were concentrated in the London and home-counties area. In 1902, *The Autocar* reported a remarkable fact that 'last week a member of our staff whilst in the West End counted 23 cars within three-quarters of an hour'. Ten years later there were some 9,000 private cars and 8,000 taxis in the London area alone. Car insurance was £2 plus two per cent of the value of the car.

By February, the twice-daily performances at 2.30pm and 8.00pm were drawing big crowds, little wonder with a weekly change of programme! The Thomas Beecham Opera Company appeared one week, followed by actor Lewis Waller the next with 150 supporting extras appearing in Shakespeare's Forum Scene from *Julius Caesar*. All this and a dozen or so other variety acts as well; there was something to suit everyone's taste. With popular National Sunday League Concerts starring Fritz Kreisler, the new building was drawing the crowds seven days a week.

Programme notes respectfully asked ladies to 'remove their hats so as to afford greater comfort to those seated behind', and should you have required tea either before, during or after the performance, it was available from the Palm Court at popular prices.

Lewis Waller

THE PALLADIUM,
Argyll Street, Oxford Circus, W.
February 6th, and during the week.
Mr. LEWIS WALLER
as "MARK ANTONY"
in the FORUM SCENE from JULIUS CÆSAR.
Synopsis of the play leading up to the Forum Scene.—Scene 2, Act 3.
The Forum Scene can justly be described as the climax of Shakespeare's Great Tragedy.
The First Act has shown us Cæsar at the zenith of his career, acclaimed by the populace and envied by his peers.
The Second Act has shown us the envy taking form and substance, and culminating in a conspiracy headed by Brutus and others to assassinate Cæsar.
The First Scene of Act III. brings us to the Capitol, with the conspirators presenting a suit for the repeal of the sentence of banishment passed on Publius Cimber, and on Cæsar refusing their request, they make it, and his ambition, an excuse for brutally doing him to death. Mark Antony, the friend of Cæsar, being at the time absent, the populace, undecided as to whether they should lament or laud the act, gather in the Forum to endeavour to arrive at a decision.

The Palladium Tea - -
and Refreshment Saloons.
The Management desires to draw the attention of Patrons to the fact that a special feature is being made of Afternoon Teas, which can be obtained in the **Louis XV. Salon,** and **The Palm Court.** Single Cups of Tea can also be obtained of the Attendants in the Imperial Circle, Fauteuils, and Stalls during the Interval. **In addition to these** there are also **Refreshment Saloons** to be found on each tier of the building, where **Wines, Spirits, Liqueurs, Cigars** and **Cigarettes** of the best quality can be obtained at Popular Prices.

PROGRAMME—*continued.*

Ladies are respectfully requested to remove their hats so as to afford greater comfort to those seated behind.

By March 1911 *The Referee* newspaper had a half-page advert announcing:

A Startling Innovation on Monday Next. Gaiety Stalls for 6d. A Revolution in Variety Entertainment. The Management begs to announce on and after Monday next it is their intention to conduct performances at the above theatre on the TWICE NIGHTLY principle starting at 6.20 and 9.10, with Matinées on Wednesdays and Saturdays at 2.30. The seating is the most sumptuous and the theatre the most elegant in Europe. The prices of admission are within the reach of all.

As the lighter nights arrived, the programme times altered. On the bill then was Fred Karno presenting *Skating*; 'Introducing his troupe of comedians in the funniest skit of modern times. See the Olympia Skating Rink on the Palladium Stage.' The popularity of 'skating' in Argyll Street, it would seem, had not quite gone away.

By July, special matinées were offered to the public with Jack Johnson (then World Boxing Champion) versus George Robey (the Palladium's favourite comedian), 'In a special three-round contest for a purse of gold (teeth) and a bag of monkey nuts. The knockout blow barred unless Robey catches Johnson when he is not looking.'

In August 1911, Gibbons employed the exceptional talents of Mr Hengler who presented *Mexico: A Sensational Spectacular Adventure of the Famous Detective Nick Carter* in six scenes, the last of which was a dam, bursting forth with a roaring torrent of water. A note in the programme stated,

In submitting this entirely new production to London the management has every confidence in asserting that in point of novelty and grandeur, in scenic display, in magnitude of water effects and in the tremendous excitement in the unfolding of the story, this latest effort will SURPASS ANYTHING EVER PRESENTED TO THE PUBLIC.

This was a statement with which no one could disagree! It really was superb, but then Mr Hengler was a past master at providing aquatic spectaculars on a grand scale.

With Fred Karno presenting *Mumming Birds,* which starred Syd Chaplin, as well as regular Variety, the theatre was gaining popularity all the time and deservedly so.

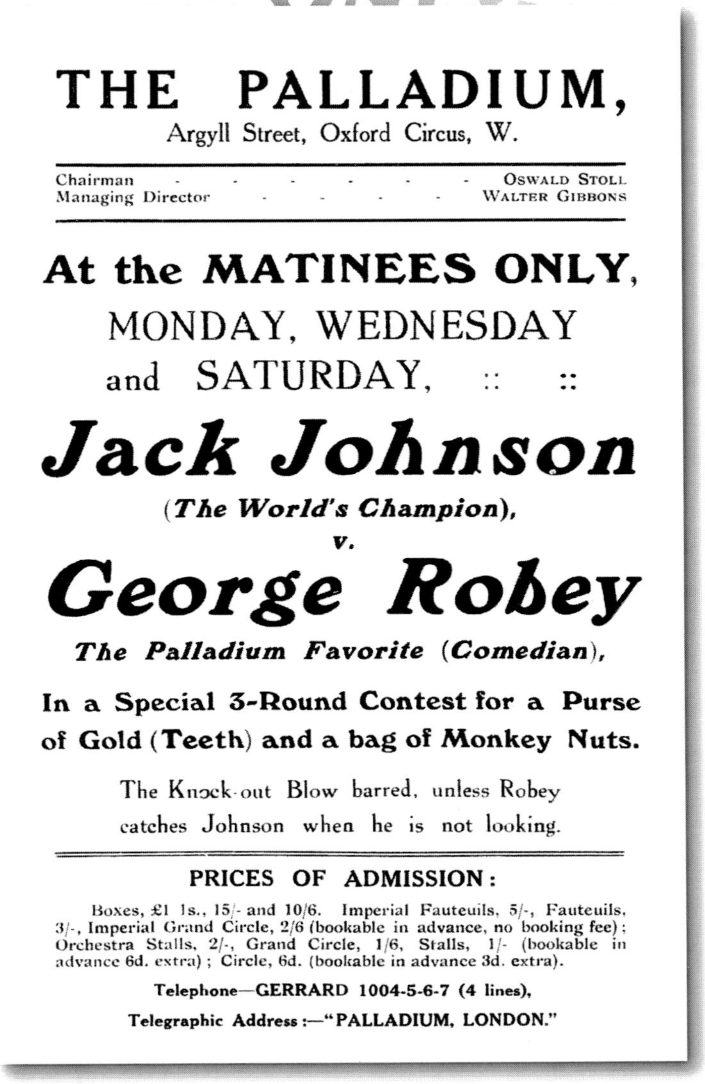

THE PALLADIUM,

Argyll Street, Oxford Circus, W.

Chairman - · · · · ·	OSWALD STOLL
Managing Director · · · · ·	WALTER GIBBONS

At the MATINEES ONLY,
MONDAY, WEDNESDAY and SATURDAY, :: ::

Jack Johnson
(The World's Champion),
v.
George Robey
The Palladium Favorite (Comedian),

In a Special 3-Round Contest for a Purse of Gold (Teeth) and a bag of Monkey Nuts.

The Knock-out Blow barred, unless Robey catches Johnson when he is not looking.

PRICES OF ADMISSION :

Boxes, £1 1s., 15/- and 10/6. Imperial Fauteuils, 5/-, Fauteuils, 3/-, Imperial Grand Circle, 2/6 (bookable in advance, no booking fee); Orchestra Stalls, 2/-, Grand Circle, 1/6, Stalls, 1/- (bookable in advance 6d. extra); Circle, 6d. (bookable in advance 3d. extra).

Telephone—GERRARD 1004-5-6-7 (4 lines),

Telegraphic Address :—"PALLADIUM, LONDON."

The elegant Palladium had been built to contrast with the more earthy type of music hall that had become part of the British way of life. By the turn of the century there were well over sixty music halls in the London area alone, so proprietor Gibbons followed the new trend and called the style of entertainment he presented 'Variety' in an attempt to attract the newly emerging middle class.

An essential part of all variety bills continued to be speciality performers with circus backgrounds: jugglers, wirewalkers, tumblers and animal acts. An important new ingredient in Variety was the inclusion of culture with a capital C, in the form of one-act plays, potted versions of opera conducted by Thomas Beecham and even ballet – all in an attempt to bring a touch of respectability and to attract family audiences. As fashions changed over the years, some of these things came and went, but the backbone of Variety was still there thanks to all the tried and tested music hall acts, with at least twelve or fourteen acts on the bill. Approaching 700 acts were needed to fill all the bills in the London area alone.

For those not familiar with the old tradition of variety shows, here is a brief résumé as to what went on. Monday morning was the busiest; at 10.00am each act, having arrived at the theatre, would attend the 'band-call.' As the acts arrived, they would put their music down at the 'footlights' and no matter whether you were the 'star' or just a supporting act, it was first come, first served and was all taken in sequence. This music rehearsal would take place with the conductor and the musicians who would play for you during the week. They would go through your music routine – hopefully to your complete satisfaction – and after you were content that the orchestra was familiar with your music cues and all special requirements, the next act would be called to go through the same format. The most important man to keep on the right side of was the Stage Manager. You then went to him to tell him all your stage requirements, what props – if any – had to be set, and where; all the various cues for the lighting etc. would be detailed at this point. After all the acts had gone through this procedure – and bear in mind that there were often a dozen acts or sometimes more to get through – it would be near lunchtime, or early afternoon. It was a busy day!

Apart from a short break for sustenance, all the stagehands would have been tying the drapes on the battens and the sometimes elaborate scenes would need to be set. They would always be set in reverse order, starting with the last act and running right through to the first act. This meant that the stage would be set, ready for the customers to come in and for the curtain to go up for the first house on the Monday evening. Each performer was engaged to present their act 'as known', without any deviation whatsoever, for timing was vital to maintain a tight show.

By 6.15pm the theatre would be full with eager anticipation. The most exciting moment was always when the conductor would enter the orchestra pit and tap his baton on his stand. At 6.20pm precisely, the number '1' sign would light up in the box at both sides of the stage. The overture would then begin, mostly with a stirring march, ready with the right tempo to get the show off to a good start.

As the curtain fell on the first house, the audience would leave by the various exits, and an army of cleaners would come in. Until the comparatively recent no smoking legislation in all theatres, every ashtray would have been emptied; discarded programmes would be picked up off the floor; every sweet wrapper and ice cream paper was removed; and fifteen minutes later when the second house entered, you would have what appeared to be a brand-spanking new theatre: spotless! The House Manager would blow his whistle, advising the staff to open the doors and allow the second house patrons to enter.

Gibbons continued to blend culture with music hall and booked everything from Imperial Russian Dancers from St Petersburg and the Milan Opera Company, to cockney singer Harry Champion. Despite this though in September 1911, less than a year after the Palladium had opened, because of the heavy losses his theatre was incurring Gibbons was forced to go into partnership with his arch-rival Oswald Stoll. In a press statement he said,

> We must play a predicament part in the amusement of the people. One thing it gives me great pleasure to say is that I shall second in every way Mr Stoll's determined attitude against stage vulgarity and indecency. No woman's ears or eyes shall ever be offended by what she sees or hears at any of our theatres, no matter where they are situated.

Over the years that policy has been maintained through successive managements. Suitability of material hasn't been the only thing a performer must watch though; timing to the second has always been essential.

Late in 1911 a special matinée was arranged in conjunction with *The Evening Times*. It was *A Grand Pierrot and Nigger Minstrel Competition,* something that would be considered inappropriate today and likely to cause offence. However, this show proved highly popular at the time, and seven acts entered from Broadstairs, Clacton, Herne Bay, Brighton, Richmond and Kingston upon Thames, with Harry Joseph's Littlehampton Troupe being the declared winners.

Ernie Lotinga was engaged to appear with Walter Bird's West End Company in *Her Husband,* a screamingly funny comedy sketch with, the programme claimed, '250 laughs in twenty-five minutes,' something which even to this day could perhaps only be equalled (or most likely bettered) by Ken Dodd!

Popular names continued to be booked: Hetty King, George Robey, Albert Chevalier, Ella Retford, Ruth Vincent, Fred Emney Senior and Eugene Stratton. One attraction who took London by storm was Joe Elvin, who appeared in what was billed as 'The Realistic Spectacular Sporting Production', entitled *A Day's Sport,* written by Wal Pink (one of the founders of the Grand Order of Water Rats) and with music by J.S. Baker and the celebrated West End company of 100. There were no less

A PERISCOPE
top of the c
submarine, a
principal of
below all th
water. Wh
nothing can

FALSE KEEL
detached fr
is used to
into the ba

THE TELEPH
float, and

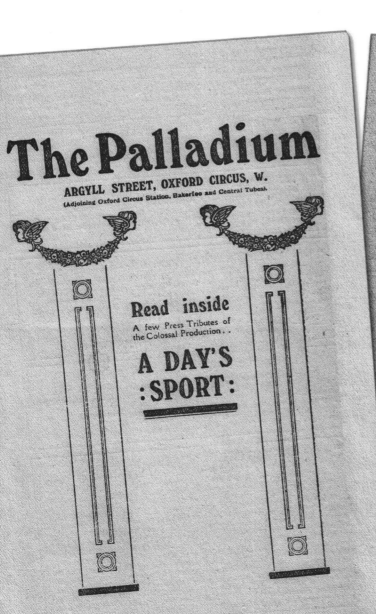

The Palladium

ARGYLL STREET, OXFORD CIRCUS, W.
(Adjoining Oxford Circus Station, Bakerloo and Central Tubes)

Read inside
A few Press Tributes of the Colossal Production..

A DAY'S
: SPORT :

"A DAY'S SPORT"
SCENARIO

SCENE I. The Club. (The Bet—5 Sports in 5 Counties in 5 Hours)

II. On the Road to Rye House by Car

III. A Field at Rye House. (The Fight)

IV. On the Road Again for the Trotting Races

V. The Trotting Track, Parsloes Park (Five Highly-trained Ponies Racing at full Speed. A Revelation of Stage Effect).

VI. Returning to London

VII. Lord's Cricket Ground

VIII. Passing through London in a Storm A Marvel of Artistic Realisation

IX. The Village Sports at Hayes Common

X. Exterior of the White Horse Tavern

XI. The Paddock at Brooklands

XII. The Brooklands Track A wonderful effect—Real Racing Cars Travelling at the Speed of an Express Engine

by an iron tube running from
wer, through the roof of the
on its top a small mirror on the
obscura, which reflects on table
g place on the surface of the
of the periscope is submerged
n the submarine.

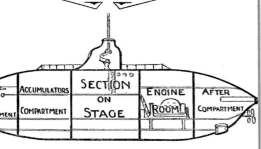

Two Performances Daily, 6.20 & 9.10.
3 Performances Wed. & Sat. 2.30, 6.20 & 9.10.

Explanation of Submarine Terms
used in
Mr. HENRI de VRIES'S
PRODUCTION OF
"SUBMARINE F 7"

A PERISCOPE is formed by an iron tube running from
top of the conning tower, through the roof of the
submarine, and having on its top a small mirror on the
principal of a camera obscura, which reflects on table
below all that is taking place on the surface of the
water. When the top of the periscope is submerged
nothing can be seen in the submarine.

FALSE KEEL is keel of lead which can be dropped and
detached from the submarine to lighten the boat, it
is used to help her to rise when too much water gets
into the ballast tank.

THE TELEPHONE BUOY is shaped like a large fishing
float, and is made of cork, it has a telephone wire
attached to it. It is fastened to the top of the
submarine, on the outside, and in case of need the
Captain casts it off, it then rises to the surface of the
water, where it is seen by the "mother ship" or one
of the battleships, which pick it up, and thus establish
communication with the interior of the submarine.

THE BALLAST TANKS are tanks, which can be filled
with, or emptied of water, at the Captain's order,
thus making the boat sink or rise.

DIVING WHEELS. The *Bow Diving Wheel* is a wheel,
which by a turn, makes the submarine dive, with her
nose downwards. The *Aft Diving Wheel* is a wheel
in the aft part, by which the boat is kept horizontal.

THE LIFE-SAVING HELMET is the newest invention
to escape from a submarine in case of accident. It
consists of a helmet and jacket, in which there is an
air flask filled with compressed air, which is breathed
through a mouthpiece, there is also an outlet valve
for the used air.

than twelve scenes, with horses travelling at full speed
through London in a storm – a marvel in artistic
realisation – and real racing cars travelling at the speed
of an express engine. Even taking into account the fact
that all forms of travel were much slower in those days,
it was a highly dramatic production. The 'bet' was that
Joe Elvin, who played the part of a Covent Garden dealer,
makes a wager that he will take part in five different
sports in five different counties in five hours – something
that perhaps one would be hard pressed to achieve even
in today's world. The press thought it superb. *The
Standard* said 'A thrilling bit of work starting with a
boxing match, and ending with a realistic representation
of a motor race at Brooklands.' *The Daily Telegraph*
reported: 'Probably the most ambitious, and surely one
of the most amusing shows that has been presented.' Even
the *Financial Times* was enthusiastic: 'the excellence of
the mechanical effects necessary to the production justifies
previous postponements ... an accomplishment seldom
equalled.'

Soon afterwards in February 1912 and due entirely to
the success of his previous production, Mr Hengler was
engaged once more to present another aquatic spectacle,
'A Wild Picturesque Sensation' entitled *The Redskin*, with
a cast of nearly a hundred. The final scene, 'The Devil's
Gorge', showed the characters shooting the rapids in
canoes with 'real water'. Another technical triumph and
marvel for Mr Hengler.

Henri de Vries presented *Submarine F7*, which showed
a sensational and realistic naval incident aboard a
submarine, or 'a representation correct in every detail of
a real submarine'. Special notes in the programme gave
specific details of a submarine and how it operated.

In June of that year Walter Gibbons resigned his
interest in the Palladium and announced his intentions to
become a MP – a true comedian at heart! His successor
was to be a man named Gulliver, who really lived up to
his name by travelling the world looking for new
attractions for the theatre. The Capital Theatre Syndicate
Limited was the name of the new company, and the man
at the helm, with his name printed firmly on the cover of
the programmes, was Charles Gulliver. Gulliver was born
in April 1882 and as a boy had worked in a solicitor's
office in Quarrendon Street, London SW6.

THE
PALLADIUM

CHARLES GULLIVER

MANAGING DIRECTOR

BRIGHTON HIPPODROME

LIVERPOOL HIPPODROME

PARIS ALHAMBRA

SHEFFIELD HIPPODROME

LEEDS HIPPODROME

WOLVERHAMPTON HIPPODROME

NEWCASTLE HIPPODROME

PORTSMOUTH HIPPODROME

SOUTHEND HIPPODROME

SOUTHAMPTON HIPPODROME

BOSCOMBE HIPPODROME

HOLBORN EMPIRE

LEWISHAM HIPPODROME

ISLINGTON EMPIRE

CAMBERWELL PALACE

ILFORD HIPPO.

GRAND CLAPHAM

WOOLWICH HIPPO.

COLLIN'S ISLINGTON

POPLAR HIPPO.

PUTNEY HIPPO.

WILLESDEN HIPPO.

SHOREDITCH OLYMPIA

CROYDON EMPIRE

HAMMERSMITH PALACE

KILBURN EMPIRE

Fred Karno continued to present his 'Laughing Creations' with Syd Chaplin in *The Hydro,* which utilised a 'real' swimming bath complete with a bevy of beautiful bathing girls. The entire production was constructed at Karno's Camberwell factory under his own supervision.

Meanwhile, Gulliver had found a new attraction to bring to the attention of the patrons. It was called the Bioscope, and it projected a silent film of the day's events or world news.

PROGRAMME—Continued.

3.—VICTOR KELLY,
Comedian.

4.—TOM HEARN,
The Laziest Juggler on Earth.

5.—CAPTAIN SCOTT'S DASH to the South Pole,
on the Bioscope, shown by the splendid pictures taken by
H. G. Ponting, F.R.G.S.

PROGRAMME—Continued

8.—"THE WAR AT A GLANCE."
Special War Correspondent at the "PALLADIUM" Epoch Making Engagements.

The Management of the "PALLADIUM" have pleasure in announcing that by arrangements with the "Daily Chronicle," they have secured the services of the FAMOUS WAR CORRESPONDENT, MR. W. B FORSTER BOVILLE, AS DEMONSTRATOR OF THE EVENTS OF BATTLE NOW PROCEEDING IN THE BALKANS. Mr. W. B. FORSTER BOVILLE is one of the Six Special War Correspondents attached to the staff of the "DAILY CHRONICLE" in connection with the present war, and has arrived in London from Sofia to watch over the despatches received from his comrades.

The Management of the "PALLADIUM" seized the opportunity of engaging him in the interests of their Patrons, who at the Special Matinees will have the unique experience of seeing the latest War News illustrated with Special Slides flashed on to the Bioscope Sheet, and of listening to the explanatory remarks of the War Expert, who has for seven years been residing in, and studying the countries involved in what threatens to become one of the greatest struggles of modern times.

In the September of 1912 the programme showed Captain Robert Scott and his valiant team in their attempt to reach the South Pole. Captain Scott and his companions had died in Antarctica on 29 March 1912; it hardly seems possible in today's world of instant communication that it took all that time for the film to arrive. Later that year, item eight in the late October variety bill – *The War at a Glance* – gave the public something to think about. The programme stated:

> The Management of the Palladium have pleasure in announcing that by arrangement with the *Daily Chronicle* they have secured the services of the Famous War Correspondent Mr W.B. Forster Bovill as demonstrator of the events in the Balkans ... The Management of the Palladium seized the opportunity of engaging him in the interest of their patrons who at the special matinée will have the unique experience of seeing the latest war news illustrated with special slides flashed onto the bioscope sheet, and of listening to the explanatory remarks of the War Expert who has for seven years been residing in and studying the countries involved in what threatens to become one of the greatest struggles of modern times.

THE PA

man .. OSWALD STOLL
ging Director .. WALTER GIB

NDAY, NOVEM

With Captain

CINEMATOGRAPHIC
pedition, from the de
present year. The Pic
are exhibited by ar
holde

SYNOP

SCENE 1.—Captain Scott on th
SCENE 2.—The Departure from
SCENE 3.—Lieutenant Rennick
Dr. Wilson is the c
SCENE 4.—On December 9th 191
the Great Ice Barri
SCENE 5.—Passing through the h
Nova was three wee
largest and heavies
SCENE 6.—The prow of the *Terra*
was taken at consid
starboard side of the
SCENE 7.—Lieutenant Rennick, R
and securing water s
of two and a half mi
but the principle incid
the water bottle, an
(it will be noticed tha
winding in the wire a
SCENE 8.—Approaching the Great
Great Ice Barrier is the
the South Pole 700 m
front is of unknown len
Victoria Land and Kin
SCENE 9.—Landing in a small boat.
SCENE 10.—Panoramic view taken f
Mount Erebus and Moun
SCENE 11.—Shipping fresh-water ice.
SCENE 12.—Unloading stores and di
The ponies are delighte
about and rub their ne
brought from the extreme
SCENE 13.—Hauling supplies by sle
carrying Cardiff coal m
stacked outside the hut.
SCENE 14.—Ski-ing on the slopes of Mo
SCENE 15.—Some fun with the penguins
SCENE 16.—Skua gulls and chicks.
SCENE 17.—Panorama of Captain Scott
SCENE 18.—The *Terra Nova.*

FIN

Variety indeed!

In the meantime, Julian Wylie's company of technicians presented *The Flickergraph*, with a performance of an exact imitation of the cinematograph played by living actors. What innovative times they lived in!

Whilst Variety continued in the evening performances in January 1913, Gulliver presented the ever popular *Palladium Minstrels* at the matinée performances, with several offerings. One of these was entitled *Minstrolographiphphoneymaticisms*. It must surely have been the

(Adjoining Oxford Circus Station, Bakerloo and Central London Tubes)

DIUM **(Adjoining Oxford Circus Station, Bakerloo and Central London Tubes)**

rgyll Street, Oxford Circus, **W.**

, 1911, and during the Week

to the South Pole"

work of the British Antarctic New Zealand, to February of r. Herbert G. Ponting, F.R.G.S., th The GAUMONT CO, LTD., ive rights.

E FILMS:

Terra Nova.

ng Dr. E. A. Wilson's hair. ntific staff on the *Terra Nova*. rg which had broken way from stant, was sighted. on December 9th. The *Terra* hrough 300 miles of ice floes, the red on a Polar Expedition. hrough ice blocks. This picture n a platform suspended over the esult is very striking. ologist Lillie, taking soundings e bottom of the sea at a depth several hours to do this work, t in this film, namely, lowering s affair, letting down the wire slowly at first, being frozen), water sample from the bottle. New Year's Day, 1911. The r in the world and flows from e sea breaks it up. The sea- ture is of the Barrier between nd.

Nova, showing the peaks of

cnies at McMurdo Sound. g their freedom, and roll ow. These animals were f Siberia. sea-ice. Sledges are also brick form. This coal is

The PALLADIUM

Please see that this Seal is unbroken

Managing Director, CHARLES GULLIVER.

PRICE 3D.

longest title of an act then and possibly remains so to this day, whereas the most *unusual* name to appear on any bill would have been the American Apache violinist, Ywaxy. If only Scrabble had been invented! Meanwhile, the Bioscope portrayed *Marvellous Pictures of the Ohio Floods*.

Even more unusual live stage presentations occurred, namely a special matinée showing the Columbia Park Boy Scouts (forty in number) in a military and vocal display. They had come all the way from California, travelling around the world, paying all their expenses out of the proceeds of their performances and returning the visit made by the Australian Boys Scouts the previous year.

On the bill was another item to catch the public's eye. It was an act entitled *The Graphophone Girl*, originated, presented and copyrighted by Adeline Francis as the 'Twentieth Century American Novelty'. The graphophone was an improved version of the phonograph, and was the forerunner of the gramophone as we know it today. Records made at the Columbia Laboratory Columbia Gramophone were used to make it play.

Towards the end of 1913, there was a strong variety bill; Perci Honri began presenting a series of matinée revues that included Lupino Lane, G.H. Chirgwin and George Robey. One of them was entitled *Tango Tea Revue*, whilst in the evening the twice-nightly paying public could enjoy *Hullo Ragtime*, starring Fanny Brice in the 'actual and original production that had played the Hippodrome to over one and half million people.'

In March 1914 a Royal Matinée took place in aid of the rebuilding of the Chelsea Hospital for Women. Flowers decorated the Royal Box, and everything was in

THE EDISON PHONOGRAPH

This Ideal Home Entertainer is the FIRST and GREATEST of all Sound Reproducing Instruments.
THE EDISON PHONOGRAPH GIVES JUST THE RIGHT VOLUME OF SOUND FOR THE HOME

The tone of the Edison is the pure, real life-like tone of the voices that sing for it. No scratching or scraping—and why? Because the Edison has a *sapphire* reproducing point—instead of a metal needle: and this point is permanent and never needs changing.

THE AMBEROLA, Price 40 guineas.

GRAND OPERA, BALLADS OR SACRED SONGS.

Operatic selections by Sarah Bernhardt, Scotti, Slezak and many other world renowned artistes, old ballads or sacred songs by the best known concert room singers whenever you want to hear them—if you own an Edison Phonograph.

VARIETY

Harry Lauder, Robey, Fragson, Vesta Tilley, Farkoa and other great "£200-a-week" funsmiths, the popular Ella Retford, George Formby and many other variety stars make Records for the Edison.

DANCING

A Strauss waltz; a Sousa march or two-step; and *every-body* dances. Amberol Records are a full minute longer than the average dance selection played by a "real orchestra."

HOME RECORDING.

The Edison is the only instrument on which Records can be made at home, which is more than half the fun.

THE FIRESIDE with Cygnet Horn. Price 5 guineas.

Edison Phonographs from £2 : 6 : 0 to 50 guineas.
Edison Grand Opera Records ... 4/- to 8/- each.
Edison Amberol Records 1/6 Standard 1/- each.

Write for Illustrated Catalogues and address of nearest agent to Dept. P,

NATIONAL PHONOGRAPH CO., Ltd.,
Edison Works, London, N.W.

WEST END AGENTS: ASHTON & MITCHELL'S ROYAL AGENCY, LTD., 33 OLD BOND ST., W.

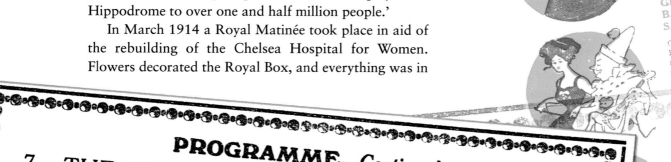

PROGRAMME—Continued.

7.—THE GRAPHOPHONE GIRL. Originated, presented and copyrighted by Adeline Francis.
The 20th Century American Novelty.
(Records made at the Columbia Laboratory.)
Columbia Graphophone used.

8.—LITTLE TICH, in new and old successes including his famous Big Boot Dance.

9.—INTERMISSION, ... "Patriotic" .... George Rosey.

pristine condition to welcome the King and Queen for the very first time. The National Anthem was duly sung by Ruth Vincent, and The Poluskis opened the show, followed by Jackson's Sixteen English Dancers. Coram the Ventriloquist was next in a *Military Scene*, followed by The Bogannys. Popular artiste Clarice Mayne was accompanied by her husband J.W. Tate, better known to regular theatregoers as 'That'. Comedy was provided by Sammy Shields, and Sir George Alexander presented *A Social Success*. Phyllis Bedells, Fred Emney and George Robey also made their mark, with the royal illusionist Rameses presenting some stunning illusions to delight Their Majesties to close the show. This was followed by the National Anthem. This matinée performance was the very first attended by royalty, and it set the seal on the future of the Palladium as a theatre.

Now that it had been seen that royalty was in approval of what was presented at the Palladium, there was no stopping the public from attending any or all of the shows. Charles Gulliver had done it again, a coup indeed! Acts like Joe Boganny and his *Fun in the Bakehouse* were only too proud to add into their billing in the programme, 'As recently performed before Their Majesties at the Palladium' – the first of many Royal Performances to come for so many talented artists.

In May, Ruffell's Imperial Bioscope was advertising 'The Official Opening of Orpington Golf Course; Braid and Vardon vs. H.H. Hilton and R. Harris.' Earlier in the programme, Henriette de Serris and the celebrated Living Art Reproductions from the Drury Lane Theatre London,

THE
HOME
al life-like
scratching
Edison has

HE AMBEROLA
Price 40 guineas

THE FIRESIDE
with Cygnet
Price 5 guineas
to 50 guineas
4/- to 8/- ea

PROGRAMME—Continued.

10. LAMBERTI, the famous Musical Impersonator.

11. RUFFELL'S IMPERIAL BIOSCOPE. — Official Opening of Orpington Golf Course. Braid and Vardon *v.* H. H. Hilton and R. Harris.

12. GOD SAVE THE KING.

35

presented *Famous Paintings, Statuary Groups, Etchings and Bas Reliefs.* These were executed by Henriette de Serris's own company of 'Fifteen Selected Professional Models' from the Academy of Sculpture in Paris. 'These art studies', the programme noted, 'have been praised by the entire press of Europe for their Fidelity and Purity.'

In July 1914, Brinn, 'The Naval Athlete', presented a new and sensational act, *The Handyman Ashore,* introducing the record feat of balancing a motorcycle mounted with a machine gun, which weighed 510 lbs. 'Brinn, the only man in the world able to accomplish this feat which is most difficult owing to recoil and vibration. The Motorcycle and Gun are Absolutely Genuine and are open to inspection', said the programme!

Just prior to the pantomime of that year, the Palladium presented a young Jack Buchanan in *A Mixed Grill,* a Bur-Revue-Lesque starring Ida Crispi and Fred Farren. The Bioscope showed the latest war pictures and the programme advertised that most charitable of organisations, the Grand Order of Water Rats and their special *Grand Matinée,* with proceeds going to *The Daily Telegraph* Belgian Fund.

The Palladium's first pantomime was the Wylie and Tate production of *Dick Whittington,* starring Clarice Mayne and Harry Weldon. It was so successful that the following year *Cinderella* took to the stage. It starred Weldon once again – this time as Buttons – with Nora Delaney as Prince Charming and Daisy Burrell in the title role. In 1917 Charles Gulliver presented his third pantomime, *The House that Jack Built,* with Nora Delaney, this time in the role as Jack, and a young Robb Wilton playing Dame Barleycorn. Each production had a cast of over a hundred and something to entertain all age groups.

Even though men were still serving at the front, and many of them losing their lives in the name of their King and country, the Palladium still managed to continue throughout the war years to give excellent value to the paying public. They presented many acts new to the stage, plus a few regulars as well: May Moore-Duprez, 'The Jolly Little Dutch Girl', Wilkie Bard, Wee Georgie Wood, Ruth Vincent, and The Tiller Troupe of Sixteen Dancers. The famous John Tiller had previously provided the routines in ballet productions as early as 1911.

May Moore-Duprez
(The Jolly Little Dutch Girl)

March 1916 saw Ernie Lotinga and Walter Bird's West End Company appearing in *Slippers,* an entirely new and sensational dramatic burlesque. This was to be followed a year later with *Jimmy Josser K.C,* for which the programme notes offered 500 laughs in twenty-five minutes: doubling up on previous claims! In May, Charles Gulliver presented Albert de Courville's new revue *Fun and Beauty,* starring Ida Crispi with a cast of sixty, and an augmented orchestra. A programme note stated 'All male members of the Fun and Beauty Company have either attested or are ineligible for service.'

In July, Gulliver engaged Jack Hulbert and Cicely Courtneidge to appear in a farcical comedy sketch entitled *A Lucky Mistake,* as well as Harry Tate in his famous piscatorial comedy *Fishing.* 'Jimmy' Glover, the well-known Drury Lane conductor, and a specially augmented band of thirty with Marie Novello, 'the famous Queens Hall Pianist' as soloist along with Ruth Vincent, all completed that particular bill. As always there was the usual array of other unknown and hoping-to-be-known acts to complete the evening's entertainment. Marie Novello was also a regular weekly attendee at the Palladium's National Sunday League concerts where Ivor Novello had made his debut in 1915, singing one of his own compositions, 'Till the Boys Come Home', and another big success, 'Laddie in Khaki'.

Charles Austin, of Parker PC fame, presented an entirely new sketch – *Parker's Wedding* – whereas titles of other more sombre offerings were *A Day in a Dugout* and *Life in the Trenches,* as well as Captain Bruce Bairnsfather presenting Harry Thurston in *The Johnson Ole.* The programme note said, 'The authors have endeavoured to truthfully depict life in the trenches in 1914', poignantly reminding those who were enjoying home comforts and the privilege of being entertained, that there were others less fortunate fighting at the front.

Gone were the colourful programme covers depicting the Palladium edifice, which were replaced by one with a more sombre, mauve-tinted appeal. Little Tich, Ella Shields, Albert Whelan, Marie Lloyd, Fred Barnes, Harry Weldon, George Mozart, George Lashwood, Perci Honri and G.H. Elliot all continued to entertain in their own inimitable way, accompanied as always by an excellent array of speciality acts.

Kind-hearted George Robey organised several charitable concerts in and around London for various well-deserving charities, two of which were on the Palladium stage. Under the auspices of the National Sunday League, he organised a concert where the beneficiary was the Union Jack Club Extension Fund, 'For those defending the flag and our homes'. It starred Shirley Kellogg and other well-known musical artists of the day. Later in the year he organised another superb concert, this time in aid of the Metropolitan and City Police Orphanage, bringing together the Metropolitan Police Minstrels, the String Band of the Royal Artillery (regulars at the National Sunday League Concerts), and Harry Dearth singing 'Duty – That's All', specially written and accompanied by

GEORGE ROBEY'S CONCERT

At the Palladium, Sunday Afternoon, March 18th, 1917, at 3 p.m.

IN AID OF

THE UNION JACK CLUB EXTENSION FUND.

GEORGE ROBEY'S CONCERT

At the Palladium, Sunday Evening, June 10th, 1917, at 7 p.m.

THAT'S ALL

IN AID OF

THE METROPOLITAN & CITY POLICE ORPHANAGE

(Under the Auspices of THE NATIONAL SUNDAY LEAGUE)

the composer Arthur E. Godfrey. Moiseiwitsch gave pianoforte solos, as well as appearing in both concerts himself. Then, in the evenings, George Robey would pop over to the Alhambra and do the same thing all over again with a totally different cast. Such stamina!

Plagiarism was not unknown even then, and to highlight this in a big way, one must look to one of the early bills. In one of the 1912 programmes there can be found the young juggler W.C. Fields, who called himself 'The Silent Humorist'. He worked most of the London halls at that time and often appeared on the same programme as Harry Tate, a Palladium regular and one of the most popular comedians of the day.

During Tate's act he noticed that Fields was often in the wings writing copious notes. Many years later, Tate went to New York to work and went to see Fields who was appearing in Variety on Broadway. He was in a sketch called *The Family Ford* which was very, *very* similar to the one that Tate had been doing when Fields was appearing on the same bill in London. Astounded that Fields could appropriate a complete act so boldly without permission, Tate went backstage to challenge him. After much discussion and little success he threw his original script at Fields and said, 'Here, read this and do the act properly!' He then promptly walked out in disgust!

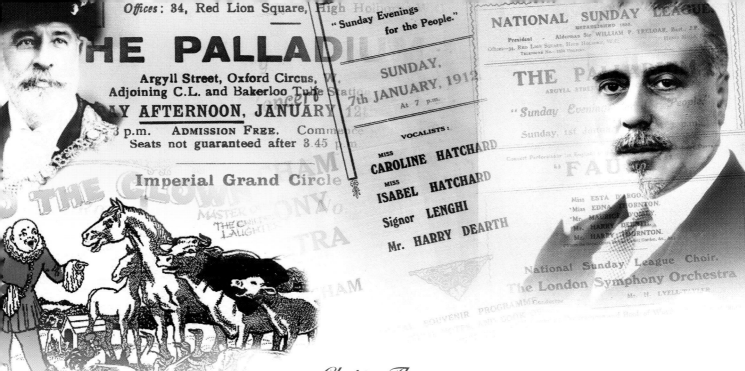

Offices: 34, Red Lion Square, High Holborn

"Sunday Evenings for the People."

THE PALLADIUM

Argyll Street, Oxford Circus, W.
Adjoining C.L. and Bakerloo Tube Station

...AY AFTERNOON, JANUARY 12th

...3 p.m.   ADMISSION FREE.   Commence...
Seats not guaranteed after 3.45 p.m.

Imperial Grand Circle

SUNDAY,
7th JANUARY, 1912
At 7 p.m.

VOCALISTS:

MISS
CAROLINE HATCHARD
MISS
ISABEL HATCHARD
Signor LENGHI
Mr. HARRY DEARTH

NATIONAL SUNDAY LEAGUE

Established 1855
President - Alderman Sir WILLIAM P. TRELOAR, Bart., J.P.

THE PALLADIUM

National Sunday League Choir.
The London Symphony Orchestra

Chapter Three

THE NATIONAL SUNDAY LEAGUE

he National Sunday League was founded in
1855 by R.M. Morrell, whose objectives were:
'To promote the opening of Museums, Art Galleries, and
Libraries on Sunday afternoons, maintaining "Sunday
Evenings for the People", Sunday Excursions, Sunday
Bands in the Park, and generally to promote Intellectual
and Elevating Recreation on that day.'

It was stated in one of the earliest programmes
that: 'The Council of the National Sunday League
conscientiously and religiously believe in brightening the
lives of the people on Sunday. They work to reform and
make the day beneficial – certainly not to abrogate it as a
day of rest. Friends in sympathy with our movement are
respectfully invited to join the League.'

With Alderman Sir William P. Treloar, (Bart, J.P.)
as its President, the League's first concert took place on
1 January 1911, just six days after the official grand

opening of the Palladium. Gounod's popular opera *Faust* was chosen and the London Symphony Orchestra provided the accompaniment. Miss Edna Thornton, Mr Maurice D'Oisly and Mr Harry Dearth all appeared by kind permission of the Royal Opera House Covent Garden especially for this important performance, together with Miss Esta D'Argo, Mr Harry Thornton, and the National Sunday League Choir.

In the weeks and years to follow at precisely 3pm and 7pm, many famous artists appeared in these much loved and well attended Sunday concerts. One of the earliest performers was John Philip Sousa, making his Grand Farewell Tour with a band of sixty performers. He is not only remembered for many notable marches such as 'The Stars and Stripes Forever', 'The Washington Post' and 'The Liberty Bell', but also for his creation of the Sousaphone.

DISTINGUISHED CORNISH

Sir William Treloar

NATIONAL SUNDAY LEAGUE.

ESTABLISHED 1855.

President - Alderman Sir WILLIAM P. TRELOAR, Bart., J.P.

Offices—34, RED LION SQUARE, HIGH HOLBORN, W.C.

TELEPHONE No.—1524 HOLBORN.

HENRY MILLS, *Secretary.*

THE PALLADIUM,

ARGYLL STREET, OXFORD CIRCUS, W.

"Sunday Evenings for the People."

Sunday, 1st January, 1911, at 7 p.m.

Concert Performance (in English) of the whole of GOUNOD'S Popular Opera—

"FAUST"

Miss ESTA D'ARGO.

*Miss EDNA THORNTON.

*Mr. MAURICE D'OISLY.

*Mr. HARRY DEARTH.

Mr. HARRY THORNTON.

(*From the Royal Opera House, Covent Garden, &c., &c.)

National Sunday League Choir.
The London Symphony Orchestra

Conductor - - - Mr. H. LYELL-TAYLER.

Special Souvenir Programme and Book of Words—Price Threepence.

VAIL & Co., Concert Printers, 170, Farringdon Road, E.C.

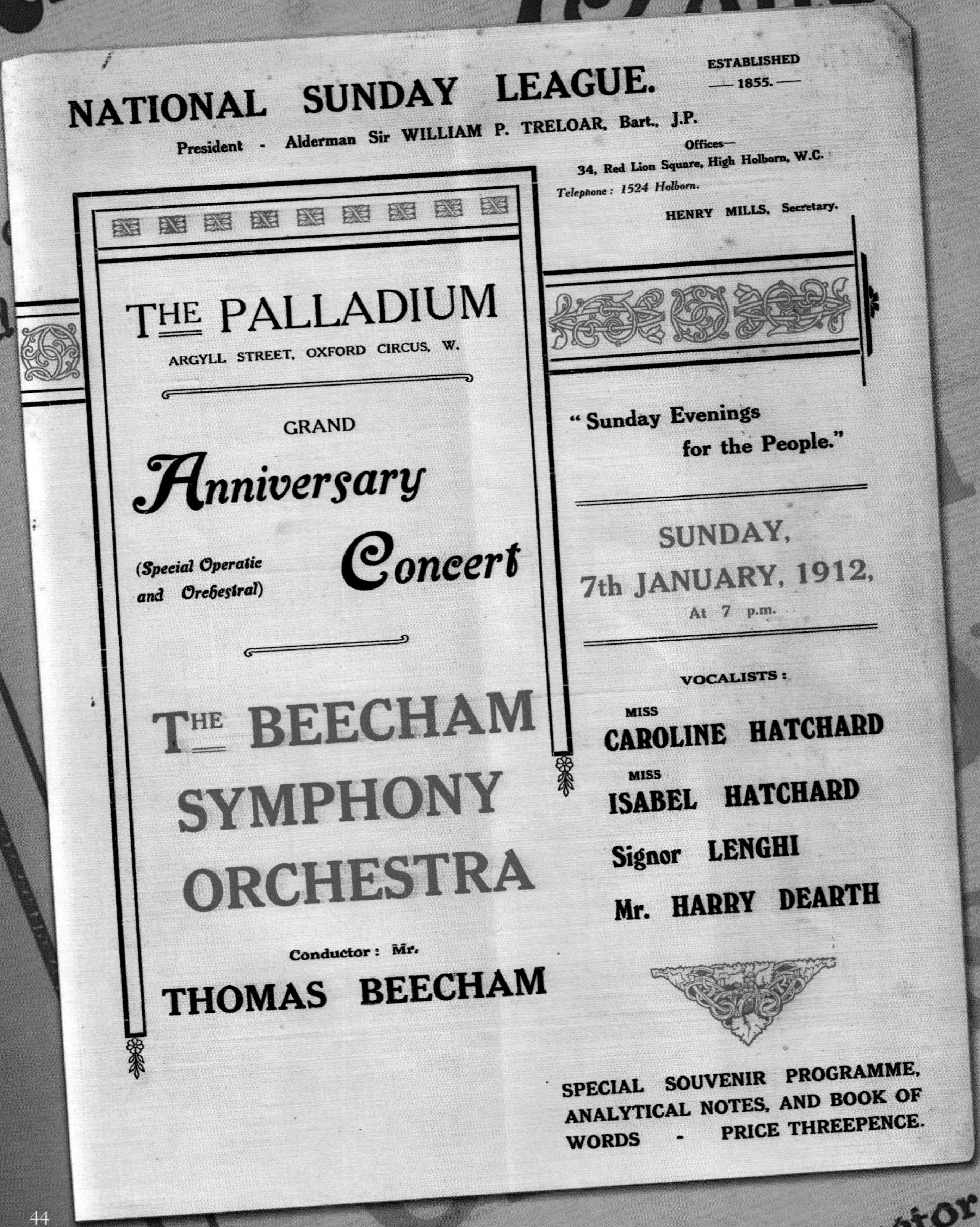

NATIONAL SUNDAY LEAGUE.

ESTABLISHED — 1855.

President - Alderman Sir WILLIAM P. TRELOAR, Bart., J.P.

Offices—
34, Red Lion Square, High Holborn, W.C.
Telephone : 1524 Holborn.

HENRY MILLS, Secretary.

THE PALLADIUM

ARGYLL STREET, OXFORD CIRCUS, W.

GRAND

Anniversary Concert

(Special Operatic and Orchestral)

"Sunday Evenings for the People."

SUNDAY, 7th JANUARY, 1912,

At 7 p.m.

THE BEECHAM SYMPHONY ORCHESTRA

Conductor : Mr.

THOMAS BEECHAM

VOCALISTS :

MISS **CAROLINE HATCHARD**

MISS **ISABEL HATCHARD**

Signor **LENGHI**

Mr. **HARRY DEARTH**

SPECIAL SOUVENIR PROGRAMME, ANALYTICAL NOTES, AND BOOK OF WORDS - PRICE THREEPENCE.

As popularity grew, additional venues were being used for similar concerts, including the Queens Hall, Langham Place, the Alhambra, and other local hippodromes, palaces and empires. Some idea as to the success of these concerts can be gauged by the fact that at the time the Palladium became the flagship of these classical concerts, there were similar concerts taking place in twenty-three other 'halls' in and around the London area on any one Sunday. This accounted for the gratifying total of over 40,000 weekly attendees, which highlighted their popularity. 'Some of the best work has been accomplished in the poorer parts of London, for there can be no doubt that the provision of good music on Sunday evenings has had a distinctly beneficial effect in some of the less favoured localities,' wrote Henry Mills, the Secretary of the NSL.

The Beecham Symphony Orchestra, conducted by Mr Thomas Beecham (later to be knighted) with his Opera Company 'direct from Covent Garden' was a frequent visitor, not only on Sundays, but also to the weekly variety programmes too. The Beecham Symphony Orchestra was in fact chosen to participate in the Grand First Anniversary Concert in 1912.

Sir Thomas Beecham

A note in the programme stated that,

The response of the public has been gratifying in the extreme, as the League's Sunday Afternoon and Evening Concerts at the Palladium have been attended by nearly 100,000 persons since the first concert in 1911. This alone is sufficient to indicate that good music and recreation are appreciated by the people of London. A feature of the Palladium concerts has been the Sunday Afternoon performances. These have been given by leading musical organisations, predominantly the London Symphony Orchestra and the String Band of the Royal Marines, not to mention the seventy-five strong Beecham Symphony Orchestra conducted by Mr Thomas Beecham providing an interesting programme in which new works find a predominant place.

Ironically, the programme note for the second overture, 'Hansel and Gretel', on that first anniversary performance went as follows: 'Among the disciples of Wagner one of the most notable is Engelbert Humperdinck, who became acquainted with the master in 1880.' Who would have thought that after that first meeting, a century later another Engelbert Humperdinck would grace the very same stage. However, that's a story for another chapter!

Fritz Kreisler made several welcome appearances, as did Ruth Vincent, Peter Dawson, George Robey and Sybil Thorndike, who were virtually unknown at the time but later became household names. Other celebrities also appeared. In 1912 a recital was given by Lady de Bathe, perhaps better known as Lily Langtry.

In 1915 a very young Ivor Novello appeared, accompanying the Royal Welsh Choir and conducted by Clara, his mother, who had made earlier appearances in her own right on the pianoforte. Bransby Williams performed selections from his repertoire and a young

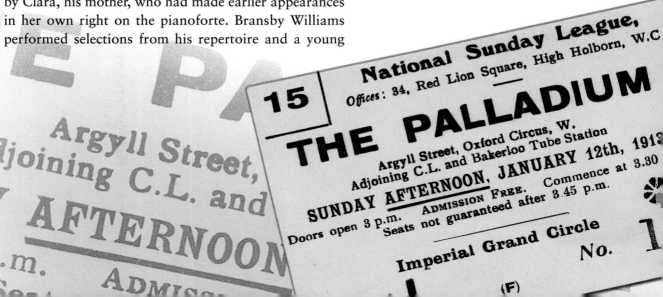

Arthur Askey, who would later make his name on 'steam' radio and television, made regular appearances. Others included Evelyn Laye, Harry Hemsley, Stanley Holloway, Norman 'Over the Garden Wall' Evans, Elsie and Doris Waters, Miss Suzette Tarri, The Western Brothers, Wee Georgie Wood, Clapham and Dwyer, Stanelli, Jack Warner and Cyril Fletcher, Leslie Sarony, Harold Berens and not forgetting 'My Brother and I' Bob and Alf Pearson. Sophie Tucker was also billed to appear on occasion, 'engagements permitting', highlighting her tremendous popularity in the 1930s.

Classical tastes, however, were also catered for admirably, with Melsa the violinist, Cortot, Thibaud, Casals, De Groot and the Piccadilly Orchestra. The handbill for this show stated 'It is predicted confidently that this concert will prove a revelation to admirers of exquisite musical performances.' Regular appearances were also made by John Barbirolli, Arthur Rubinstein, Moiseiwitsch, the Carl Rosa Opera Company, and Albert Sandler assisted by Reginald Kilbey on cello and Jack Byfield on piano, to name but a few.

National Sunday League
Founded 1855
President—Lieut.-Colonel FREDERICK LAWSON, D.S.O.
G. R. AUSTIN, Secretary

THE PALLADIUM
ARGYLL STREET :: W.1

Sunday Afternoon
March 22nd, 1931 at 3.15

MOISEIWITSCH

EINWAY PIANOFORTE

"HIS MASTER'S VOICE" REC

gement with

Programme notes often stated that 'owing to the length of the programme it will obviously be impossible for encores to be granted. It is hoped therefore that the audience will recognise the reasonable nature of this rule, the observance of which will save time!'

Later, as the years went by, standards began to relax a little and sometimes there would be a speciality act on the bill, maybe even a magician like Allan Shaw 'The Money Maker', De Biere 'The Conjurer of Princes – The Prince of Conjurers', or Van Dock the Cartoonist. One unusual act was that of Clown Argo, 'The world's greatest animal mimic and entertainer', imitator of animals, birds, instruments and machinery – most unusual to say the least!

The top bands and orchestras of the day were also a great attraction. In 1937, appearances were made by Teddy Joyce and his Band of Girl Friends (with Ivy Benson on alto clarinet), Jack Hylton, Geraldo's Gauchos Tango Orchestra (who appeared 'by kind permission of the Savoy Hotel'), Jan Ralfini, Debroy Somers and his Augmented Symphonic Orchestra, as well as Mantovani and his Tipica Orchestra, and Troise and his Mandoliers.

As the Second World War approached, these special and well-patronised Sunday concerts for the people sadly had to end. The National Sunday League Concerts had provided a much-needed outlet for those members of the public who, after their religious activities had finished, were perhaps at a loose end on a Sunday. For a membership fee of two shillings (ten pence) in 1911 this would include a copy of the *Free Sunday Advocate,* sent post free monthly, or one shilling (five pence) without the magazine. Special day excursions for members were available in order that they might visit the sea at Brighton, Worthing, Hove, Shoreham by Sea, Hastings and Eastbourne, all for as

NATIONAL SUNDAY LEAG

PALLADIU

ARGYLL STREET OXFORD CIRCUS, W.

SUNDAY at 7

AUGUST 31st 1924

A Grand Tribute Conc

TO

MR. HARRY

MASTERS

Late Booking Manager and Chief of Staff of The London Theatre of Varieties Limited.

"A NIGHT WITH THE STARS"

The following well-known Stars will positively appear by kin permission of their respective Managers :—

CHAS. AUSTIN	GEORGE ROBEY
FRED BARNES	TWO RASCALS
BURR & HOPE	LESLIE & MAY STUAR
CORAM & JERRY	LESLIE SARONY
LENA & PEGGY CHISHOLM	ELLA SHIELDS
GEORGE FRENCH	TUCKER
JACK HYLTON'S BAND	LITTLE TICH
DOROTHY LENA	HARRY TATE
JACK LANE	HARRY THURSTON
LILY LONG	VERSATILE THREE
BILLY MERSON	WISH WYNNE
NAUGHTON & GOLD	WALTER WILLIAMS
NERVO & KNOX	NELLIE WALLACE
LORNA & TOOTS POUNDS	etc., etc.

Applications for Seats should be made to the Manager.

BOOK EARLY.

Doors open at 6.30 p.m.   Commence at 7 p.m.

RESERVED SEATS (including Tax)

£1 1s. 0d., 12/-, 8/6, 5/9, 3/6, 3/-, 2/4

All seats numbered and reserved, can be booked in advance at the League Offices and at Palladium Advance Booking Office, Argyll Street. BOOKING HOURS AT PALLADIUM ADVANCE BOOKING OFFICE : Tuesdays, Wednesdays, Thursdays and Fridays from 11 a.m. to 7 p.m. ; Saturdays, 11 a.m. to 9 p.m. ; Sundays, 1 to 6.30 p.m. for Evening Concert.

N.S.L. Offices : 34, Red Lion Square, High Holborn, W.C.1.

HENRY MILLS, Secretary.

VAIL AND CO., LONDON, E.C.1.

little as *2s. 6d.* (twelve and a half pence). For *3s. 9d.* one could travel further afield to Rugby or Leicester, and for *5s. 6d.* one could go as far Sheffield! With an offer like this and the fact that in the early days admission to the Palladium was free, it paid one to be a member. How sad to think that today it costs more to post a letter than it did to travel to your favourite seaside destination!

In passing, one wonders what the NSL would have thought of twenty-four-hour shopping and Sunday trading in particular?

Chapter Four

THE GUV'NORS, MANAGERS AND NOT FORGETTING BACKSTAGE AND FRONT OF HOUSE

*A*lthough not strictly speaking one of the 'Guv'nors', **FRANK MATCHAM** was without doubt the architect in more ways than one. He was born in Newton Abbot, Devon on 22 November 1854, the second son of nine children to Charles and Elizabeth Matcham. He worked for Jethro T. Robinson, the successful theatre architect who was highly respected for his knowledge and views throughout the country, and was theatre consultant to the Lord Chamberlain. On joining the Robinson practice, Matcham was exposed to theatre design of a high order. On 9 July 1877 he married the younger daughter, Maria Robinson, but within twelve months Jethro had passed away and Frank took over the practice.

By a quirk of fate it was Jethro who had been engaged by Charles Hengler to remodel the existing building, the main feature being the Corinthian front to Argyll Street. By the age of fifty-five Matcham was semi-retired, and he died on 17 May 1920 of heart failure due to accidental blood poisoning. He shaped not only the Palladium but dozens of other beautiful theatre buildings around Britain and made everything possible for those who were to follow on in his footsteps.

The first real 'Guv'nor' without doubt was **WALTER GIBBONS**. Walter Gibbons, who was subsequently knighted, was Managing Director of the Palladium from the theatre's opening in 1910 until 1912. The first six months proved that Gibbons could not handle the business. After a shaky start to the running of the theatre and a huge injection of capital, Oswald Stoll was added to the Board of Management as Chairman. Stoll had a new name to put forward as Company Secretary – it was to be Charles Gulliver. After a highly successful career, Gulliver retired in 1927 and in the following year Sir Walter Gibbons returned to the management team. Whilst it cannot be denied that he had tremendous enthusiasm for the theatre business, he had little knowledge or experience in how to handle the temperamental artists, or how to balance figures. Once again, he flopped and sadly died almost penniless. Gibbons had left his mark however, in that along with a few fellow enthusiasts, he founded the Automobile Association, and it was at Gibbons' insistence that the programme cover featured a motorcar for the opening night in December 1910 and for all subsequent editions of the theatre programme. This was a theme that was more or less carried right through to the 1950s. Although he personally hadn't been a commercial success, but for his foresight in taking a lease on the old Hengler site in Argyll Street, there might never have been a Palladium.

Then came **CHARLES GULLIVER**. The name Gulliver immediately evokes childhood stories of travels around the world and meeting a giant. This is the reverse story of the giant who travelled the world in search of the best talent that he could find. The Charles Gulliver publicity blurb capitalised on his name, with the likes of 'North, South, East or West, Gulliver Shows are always the best', 'There's a Whirl on every Gulliver Circuit' and

PROGRAMME

6. RATOUCHEFF'S SEVEN RUSSIAN LILLI-PUTIANS.

First Appearance in England.
The Smallest Actors, Vocalists, and Dancers in Existence.
THEIR AGES RANGE FROM 19 TO 32 YEARS.
Heights from Two Feet Two Inches to Three Feet Four Inches.

MONDAY, TUESDAY, WEDNESDAY.

1, Opening Speech; 2, Ballet, "Le Conte de Nuit de Paris" (Music by Tchaikowsky, Schumann, Wieniavski, and Delibes); 3, Finale, "The Bright Brigadier."
20 MINUTES.

THURSDAY, FRIDAY, SATURDAY.

1, Opening, "Marcia des Lilliputs"; 2, Ballet, "The Red Rose"
3, Speech; 4, Finale, "The Bright Brigadier."
20 MINUTES.

'For knowledge go round the world, for amusement go round the Gulliver Circuit'.

Gulliver controlled twenty-seven venues – the Palladium naturally being the flagship theatre – with empires, palaces and hippodromes in and around London. He also provided artists for all the major cities. If nothing else, Gulliver lived up to his namesake when he booked the Ratoucheffs – Russian Lilliputians whose heights ranged from two feet to three feet, and who sang and danced to the delight of everyone!

In 1921 and for a salary of £100 per week, he brought down to the Palladium an unknown Scottish comedian who wrote his own songs. One of those was 'I Belong to Glasgow' and the song is now part of British folklore today. It was sung of course by Will Fyffe, the wonderful comic actor.

The period just after the First World War saw the introduction of two different forms of entertainment that were to establish great traditions in years to come. One was the annual pantomime and the other was revue.

Next on the scene was **GEORGE BLACK.** Black was born in 1891 in Small Heath, Birmingham and when he died at the very early age of fifty-four, he had managed to pack into that half century more than most people manage in a much longer lifetime. Some of the obituaries headed their story of his untimely passing as: 'King of Variety', 'The Man Who Kept Music Hall Alive', 'A Great Showman', 'A Maker of Stars', and 'From Cinema Lad to Variety King'. Black was all of these and more. At the time of his death it was thought that he was in control of thirty-two theatres in London and the provinces.

George Black

Britain's master showman was the son of a theatre property master and he left school at the age of eleven. He began his working life as a young boy in a travelling waxworks. The exhibition had been owned by his father, who had bought it in the early days of moving pictures and turned it into a cinema. Black had learned the job the hard way, later showing films on a Paul's Animatograph, which was an early form of cinema. Both he and his father later set up the first permanent cinemas in Britain, and young Black became the proprietor of a circuit on the north-east coast. By 1919 he had sold out at the top of the market and resolved to leave the business for good. His reason for returning was that life was dull and he was just tired of doing nothing! He came to London in 1928 and was appointed a Director and General Manager of the General Theatre Corporation. He controlled the Corporation's theatres, including the London Palladium. By 1933 he took over the management of Moss Empires Theatres and became Joint Managing Director in 1938. To watch Black conduct a rehearsal was an experience in itself. Sitting in the stalls, smoking his inevitable cigar, he could restore order out of chaos with a few quiet words, and an unassuming manner was typical of the man. He was tall, broad shouldered and bespectacled, with dark hair, a close-clipped moustache and a healthy complexion. He was a practical man and never afraid to remove his jacket on a Monday morning and help the stagehands move the scenery. As an apocryphal story goes, he was helping with the moving of some scenery and stage props, when a newly engaged stagehand got into conversation with him and said, 'I hear this George Black is a stickler to work for', only later realising who he was when Black put his coat on and went back to the stalls to conduct the rehearsals proper! He was rarely seen without a Ramon Alones cigar, but that was the only mark of the impresario. He was a quiet and shy man, with no liking for personal publicity, but his mind was constantly working on bold and startling new ideas for his shows. Always full of innovations, in the hot summer of 1928, as an inducement to get people to go to the Palladium, he offered patrons free iced water. With the influx of foreign visitors to London he even had the foresight to employ a permanent uniformed interpreter who could speak six languages. Most of George's ideas came to him whilst he was in his garden, as he was a 'hands-on' gardener and loved tending to his flowers. Great relaxation!

At the time, putting several comedians together was unheard of, and so he tried out a *Crazy Week*, which proved very successful, and then a little later a *Crazy Month*. It worked, and so The Crazy Gang was born. All hell was to be let loose on the unsuspecting public, as will be seen in a later chapter.

It was George Black who said, 'Variety is an integral part of English life, the finest expression of the English character and as necessary to our social life as food and drink'. His two sons, George and Alfred, carried on the family name admirably and were both highly respected in the business to which their father had contributed and loved so much.

The right-hand man to George Black Senior was **VAL PARNELL**. Born in 1892, Val Parnell was the son of veteran entertainer and ventriloquist Fred Russell and, following the untimely death of George Black in 1945, Parnell became the Managing Director of Moss Empires, the company that controlled the Palladium, the Hippodrome, the Prince of Wales Theatre and a very big provincial circuit. He had been the booking agent for Black for many years and with that invaluable experience, he was responsible more than any other man before or since for re-establishing the London Palladium as the top variety house in the world.

It was Parnell who persuaded his predecessor to bring Sid Field to London, but he took no credit for spotting the man who became a star. 'Anyone can pick a star', he said, 'but not everyone has the courage to start him in the West End, but George did.' Parnell's other interests included television, good cigars and golf, and one of his regular partners on the links was Bob Hope.

Parnell's contribution to British entertainment is legendary. His right-hand was his secretary Miss Woods, and his other was booking controller Cissie Williams. Nobody, *but nobody*, crossed her! Parnell's word was his bond, and woe betide anyone who crossed him. The very heavy fireproof pass door between the stage and the auditorium had a one-way traffic policy. Parnell could go up the few steps to the stage, but if any artist was caught coming the other way he would never work the theatre

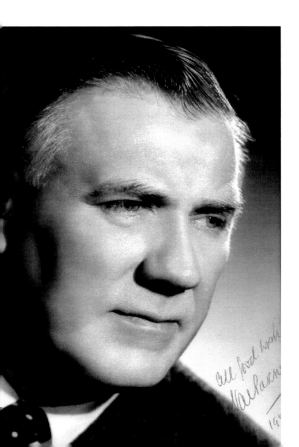

again. Such was his eye for perfection, often during a show Parnell would enter through the pass door to complain about the smallest detail.

When Val Parnell retired, the top position was then taken over by **LESLIE MACDONNELL OBE**. Leslie MacDonnell was a Wing Commander in the Royal Air Force during the Second World War and with thirty-six years' experience in show business behind him, he returned to manage artistes at the Foster Agency after the war. He was President of the Agents' Association for eight years and gave up this job to be Joint Managing Director of Moss Empires, later to become sole Managing Director in April 1960.

MacDonnell was a very neat, tidy and precise man. He wouldn't just have breakfast, he would have breakfast at 7.57am on the dot. He was a good listener and also a very generous and caring man, continually enquiring after the well-being of all the staff under his control. This was borne out by his other great love, the Variety Club of Great Britain, and in 1962 he was made Chief Barker. It was he who conceived the idea for the now-familiar Sunshine Coaches, and to date there are well over 5,000 worldwide. A fitting tribute to a man with a big heart.

MacDonnell had a natural flair for finding talent and many artists owed their stardom to his foresight and judgement. He retired from his job at the Palladium at the end of 1969, handing over to **LOUIS BENJAMIN**. Benjamin was born in 1923 and first worked for Stoll Moss when, aged fourteen, he walked into their West End offices to work as a humble office boy. With ambition in his eyes, he knew he was destined to climb to the top of the ladder. Aged sixteen, he became trainee Assistant Manager at the Finsbury Park Empire, followed by a series of jobs as Assistant Manager at other theatres within the group. Finally, after the war, he became second Assistant Manager at the Palladium. He was then promoted to first Assistant Manager at the Victoria Palace and then became Box Office Manager. In 1953 his appointment as General Manager at the Winter Gardens in Morecambe was the turning point in his short but highly successful career. In 1959 he joined Pye Records, later to become Managing Director in 1963. Then in 1970, Benjamin was appointed Managing Director of Stoll Moss Theatres. He declared: 'The greatest moment

Leslie MacDonnell

of my life was when I became Managing Director of Stoll Moss Theatre Group. It was the one appointment that I wanted when I first joined the company in 1937.'

When Variety was beginning to lose its appeal, 'Benji' as he affectionately became known, was a man not afraid to make decisions. He took the step of flying to America to approach Yul Brynner to appear in the lead role of *The King and I* at the Palladium. Brynner hummed and hawed but agreed to fly in one day to London on Concorde. He asked if he could stand on the Palladium stage on his own just for ten minutes in the dark. No one knows what really happened there, but he agreed to the show and Benji had another hit on his hands.

The apocryphal story goes that Brynner was such a taskmaster in the role of the king, which he had created, that backstage life for the cast became unbearable. So much so that they left a trail of drawing pins and tin-tacks from his Number One dressing room to the stage, showing the barefooted king how unhappy they were with his treatment of them.

Louis Benjamin

Benjamin died in 1994. At that time, three names synonymous with British entertainment over the years were from the same family – Winogradsky. They were, of course, **THE GRADE BROTHERS (LEW, BERNIE AND LESLIE)**. Born in Russia in 1906, Lew, together with Bernie, three years his junior, and his parents, arrived in the East End of London in 1912. Leslie was born in London in 1916. Between the three of them they controlled all of the top artists and venues in London as agents, managers, and producers.

One other name associated with not only the Palladium, but every top entertainment venue in the country and Las Vegas, was that of **ROBERT NESBITT**. Again, although not strictly a 'Guv'nor', such was Robert Nesbitt's phenomenal contribution to the Palladium story that his name has to be included here. One knew that if 'A Robert Nesbitt Production' appeared on the poster, one could be guaranteed a show of the highest possible calibre in terms of lighting, staging and production. His first involvement in a production at the Palladium was in 1956, in the show *Rocking The Town,* with Harry Secombe. After a successful eight-month run it was followed by Norman Wisdom in Val Parnell's eighth magnificent pantomime, *Aladdin and his Wonderful Lamp*. This success was repeated the following year, with Max Bygraves in *We're Having a Ball,* and *Robinson Crusoe* with Tommy Cooper, Arthur Askey and David Whitfield. Nesbitt produced all these shows.

Nesbitt was the Stage Director of the Royal Variety Performances for the years 1945, 1946, 1958 and 1961, and the Producer of all the Royal Variety Performances from 1962 until 1976, and also in 1978. His predecessor for many years in this particular job was **CHARLES HENRY,** who had been George Black's right-hand man. It was Henry who had helped Black to set up the *Crazy Week*s in the 1930s.

Another name who contributed to the Palladium's success for fifteen years was that of **HAROLD FIELDING**. Small in stature, but big in enthusiasm, Harold Fielding, the son of a stockbroker, was born in Woking in 1916 and had his first taste of show business at an early age as a child violinist. Realising in the 1950s that theatres were 'dark' on the Sabbath, he pioneered the Sunday Concert.

Robert Nesbitt

Harold Fielding

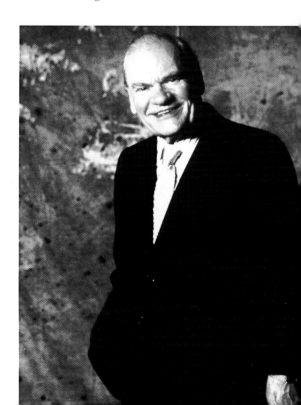

So much so that he produced as many as a thousand concerts a year all over the country, bringing entertainment to the public on a very big scale. Fielding was the first outside impresario to present musicals on the Palladium stage, and his first venture was in 1974 when he brought the fairy tale *Hans Andersen* to the Palladium. Starring multi-talented former rock 'n' roll star Tommy Steele, it was an association that was to develop and grow over the years. This was the first of many such musicals that Fielding was to present in London's West End. His big partnership was with Palladium boss of the day, Louis Benjamin. Whilst the deal was done in legal document form, it was never really considered 'finalised' until they had enjoyed a meal at their favourite restaurant, The Ivy, with their equally favourite dish, sausages and mash!

The *Hans Andersen* success was repeated four years later. Other special lavish presentations were to follow, with Michael Crawford starring as the colourful character Barnum and the ill-fated Ziegfeld, but Fielding's biggest coup after many years' negotiation with MGM was *Singin' in the Rain*. His other big triumph, which took five years to negotiate, was to bring together The Two Ronnies on stage for the very first time in 1978.

Fielding's name was also associated both with bringing over The Australian Ballet, which premiered at the Palladium with *The Merry Widow* in 1976, and with two 'special' concerts starring Julie Andrews and Petula Clark in that same year. Harold's enthusiasm for theatre on a lavish scale knew no bounds.

Next on the scene was **ROGER FILER**. An Oxford graduate, flamboyant and bow-tied, Filer also came from a cinema-based family just as George Black had done before him. With his training as an accountant, he became Financial Director, and was later appointed Manager in charge of bookings and production with Stoll Moss Theatres. Using the expertise and eloquent charm gained during his legal days at the Bar, he revitalised the Palladium stage and brought Variety back to the boards, with *How Tickled I Am,* the sell-out celebration of song and laughter with Ken Dodd being one of the many highlights.

The penultimate 'Guv'nor' was **MRS JANET HOLMES A'COURT,** who took over the reins when her husband Robert, an Australian businessman, died. He

had been at the helm of the holding company, but under his wife's expert eye, sometimes from a great distance, the Palladium continued to enjoy popularity and great success.

LORD LLOYD-WEBBER and his Really Useful Group are now the current owners of the Stoll Moss Group, whose flagship is the London Palladium. This means that it is in safe hands once more.

The backstage names which deserve a mention are almost endless. A swan gliding through the water with graceful elegance, while underneath the surface its feet paddle ferociously against the tide, is a great parallel with what goes on at the Palladium during any major production. Behind the scenes there are always many hands making the whole show seem effortless.

Stage door keeper George Cooper kept a strict, watchful eye on everyone who passed by his stage door. No one was allowed through without his say-so. He was the keeper of the privacy of all the stars he came to know over the years, who all became personal friends. He would take telephone calls and personal messages and pass them on, whether it was for a Palladium dancer or

George Cooper and Tanya

Jack Matthews
Photograph courtesy of Jennie Bisset

Princess Margaret. On one occasion, and with thirty minutes to go before curtain up on *Sunday Night at the London Palladium,* The Tiller Girls had all their knickers stolen! Who should come to the rescue but Cooper, who quickly organised a search party. They were found in the nick of time in the gents' toilet. Presumably the culprit lost his nerve once he realised that everyone was on the trail. Whilst another Sunday night show was live on air, Cooper took a telephone call from someone who had lost their cat, asking if Bruce Forsyth would alert viewers to the lost moggie! On another occasion, a young lady walked right past Cooper saying she *had* to see Val Doonican. Nothing and no one was going to stop her. Once challenged, she pulled a stiletto knife out and made a stab at Cooper. Luckily for him but unluckily for Ronnie Harris, the property master who intervened, Harris took the full force of the knife, and a nasty wound to the stomach in the process. Another time, when a lovey-dovey 'honeymoon couple' went up on stage as volunteers for *Beat the Clock*, Cooper received a telephone call from an irate wife saying 'They are certainly *not* a honeymoon couple, he is my husband!' Another volunteer for the game went up on stage, only to be spotted by a keen-eyed policeman, who realised he was on the 'wanted' list and promptly arrested him backstage. Yes, Cooper dealt with them all during his twenty-year reign.

Martinet stage manager, Jack Matthews, saw to it very effectively that his word was law, and woe betide anyone who crossed him or disagreed with any order he gave. He ran his empire backstage with a rod of iron. His place was taken over by Tommy Hayes and then Fred Pearson. The current long-time backstage resident is Linford Hudson, who started his career at the Palladium as a page boy.

Making sure everyone was seated properly and holding the post of Box Office Manager for many a year was Edwin Shaw.

Just *some* of the Musical Directors over the years have been James Sale, Horace Sheldon, Richard Crean, Woolf Phillips, Paul Fenhoulet, Cyril Ornadel, Eric Rogers, and Gordon Rose.

Front of House Manager posts have been filled by, amongst others, G. Rhodes Parry, W. 'Simmy' Simpson, John Avery, David Wilmot and Harry Claff, Neil Brooks, David Lingwood, and currently (although not related to Val) Gareth Parnell.

One lady who deserves a special mention is Lena Sophia Collins, who started working in the evenings in the early years when the theatre first opened. She died only recently aged 101, and could well have been the longest serving employee.

There has always been a vast army of devoted but unseen workers who have kept the theatre spotless and well maintained. We salute you all!

Woolf Philips

LES SYLPHIDES
(CUSSANS. arr LOTTER)
THE LONDON PALLADIUM ORCHESTRA
(Conducted by Richard Crean)
ORCHESTRA
(30-9359)

SPEED 78
Cat. No
B 4283

WHEN EVENING
SHADOWS FALL

WORDS & MUSIC BY

GORNEY,
CAESAR & MURPHY

Chapter Five

THE TWENTIES ROAR IN

Palladium

❋ CHARLES GULLIVER ❋
Managing Director

1919 ended almost as the decade had begun, with top quality entertainment from all corners of the globe. A sensation in America, and for the first time in England, Albert de Courville presented for two weeks the Great Original American Dixie-Land Jazz Band with Johnnie Dale the jazz dancer. Another week there would be The Tiller Troupe (later to become synonymous with the Palladium), Harry Tate in *Selling a Car* or *Before his flight across the Atlantic in his Tatoplane,* or another of Bruce Bairnsfather's productions, *Lucky Old Bill.* Harry Thurston had already played the role of Old Bill over five thousand times. Variety was plentiful to keep the public entertained.

Two names to make their first of hundreds if not thousands of appearances were comedic newcomers, Naughton and Gold. The managers' reports show their offerings over the next ten years to have been nothing short of hilarious: 'A laugh from start to finish', 'As popular as ever', 'The best pair of comedians we have, a rare couple, experts at fun making', and so on. The new version of Fred Karno's *Mumming Birds,* which portrayed a stage upon a stage, and was a fantasy that brought Charlie Chaplin to fame, also arrived at the Palladium. This was all part of the new calendar of entertainment. Whilst one week perhaps the illusionist Carmo would vanish a real live lion, another week there would be stalwart Ernie Lotinga presenting another new sketch, this time with 1,000 laughs in thirty minutes. Where would it all end?

The 1920s began in good style with one act that would take the Palladium by storm. True, he had been to London before, but this time it was different. Only a couple of years earlier he had been writing, producing and appearing in his own films, making all sorts of daredevil activities look so simple. His name would live on for the next eighty years and well beyond; his real name was Erich Weiss, but by then he was better known by his stage name – Harry Houdini. His bill matter was 'Houdini (Himself), The World Famous Self Liberator'. Records show from an interview in the *Melbourne Argus* that he had coined the word 'escapologist' as early as 1910, but it would be many years later before he would be known by that title.

Houdini's name was announced off stage, the curtains would part, and as moving pictures were shown on a screen of him being dropped into the sea in a heavy roped trunk from which he would escape, Houdini would then make his entrance on stage 'in person' and charm his audience. In his featured item, his legs were encased into a stock arrangement and he was then lowered head first into a glass tank filled with water. After about forty seconds he had made his escape, to the obvious relief of the audience, and he was rightly rewarded by their tumultuous applause. Commanding a salary of the equivalent of nearly 4,000 US dollars (at that time, with four dollars to the pound, it was a tidy sum), Harry Houdini was one of the highest-paid artists ever to stand in the glare of the Palladium spotlight. Houdini died in 1926, and at his funeral Broadway producers Charles Dillingham and Florenz Ziegfeld were among the pallbearers. As they carried the coffin out of the synagogue, Dillingham leaned across to Ziegfeld and whispered, 'Ziggie, I bet you a hundred bucks he ain't in there!' Typical Houdini!

Following close on Houdini's heels was another film star, Billie Reeves, who appeared in a screaming new absurdity, *The Right Key but the Wrong Flat*. Shades to come of Ray Cooney, perhaps? Owen McGiveney, the distinguished protean actor, presented the famous and often-copied but never-equalled Dickens quick-change scene, *Bill Sykes*. It was stressed in the programme that every character was played throughout by McGiveney alone. If you saw the performance you would swear that doubles or even extras were used, such was the speed with which Owen raced from one side of the stage set to the other. In the space of a split second he would appear dressed in one costume, only to reappear back again on the other side in a previously seen costume or that of a completely different character. He really was phenomenal. Many years later his son Michael appeared on the very same stage doing the same act. Incredible! It was one of the more memorable speciality acts.

Bransby Williams offered his clever character studies, Gertie Gitana performed with 'dainty songs and dances', while Gus Elen, the 'cockney character comedian', graced the stage in selections from his old popular successes. Harry Champion, Wish Wynne, The Colleano Family, The Jovers and Billy Bennett are other names to add to the list of those already mentioned.

December came and Charles Gulliver presented his *Christmas Tree Matinée* in aid of the Children of the Actors' Orphanage. Such popular names as Gladys Cooper, Gerald du Maurier, Basil Rathbone and Arthur Wontner appeared in three separate one-act playlets, which were interspersed by variety acts. Newcomers to the Palladium stage were Irish balladeer Talbot O'Farrell, along with Max Darewski, antipodean sisters Lorna and Toots Pounds, Perci Honri and Wilkie Bard with his new comedy number *Sausages*. The show was topped off with the famous American Southern Syncopated Orchestra, which played, amongst other items, 'Swannee'.

By 1921 Gulliver was presenting his third pantomime at matinées only, with Chas Austin as Widow Twankey starring alongside Lorna and Toots Pounds and Will Evans, with Jennie Benson appearing in the title role of Aladdin.

The Palladium was now well into the 1920s, and with a new decade came a new programme cover. P.T. Selbit, the famous inventor of well over five hundred different magical illusions, made his mark with *The Greatest Riddle of The Age*. He tethered a woman in a slim box with the ends of the ropes held by members of the audience, and then proceeded to saw through her! Will Fyffe also made his first appearance in London. However, if one examines the contents of the variety bills, with hindsight it is obvious, (with a few exceptions), that however good the artists were, the same old faces trotted out the same old acts week in, week out.

New material *was* being used, and with Eddie Gray, the 'novelty juggling entertainer', appearing on the same bill as Naughton and Gold, new friendships were developed. I wonder if ideas were being hatched even then for the crazier things to come? In an attempt to attract new audiences, Gulliver even presented the Northumbrian Traditional Sword Dancers, winners of the Cowan Trophy for Newcastle in 1920–21: 'Dancing which is not a mere exhibition of physical agility but an art akin to music'. Gulliver was offering the public all forms of variety with a small 'v'. This being said, it was the same supporting artists appearing, and after a while it all became a bit stale.

After the first two years or so of standard Variety, a new format was to emerge. Seeing that box office receipts were dwindling, Gulliver decided to test the market with a totally different approach. In February 1922 he collaborated with close friend Harry Day. Day had made his name with touring revues, and Charles Henry, who was the General Stage Supervisor for all of Day's revues, devised and staged a super revue called *Rockets*. Whilst gambling on its success, he did keep in the lead roles the familiar faces of Charlie Austin and the Pounds Sisters, singing 'Tell Her at Twilight', with Gus Sharland, Perci Honri and seventeen 'Rockets', each one a spectacular scene with magnificent costumes. So successful was the show that it ran for forty weeks and 500 performances!

Gulliver was pleased with Harry Day's success and, after a brief spell of Variety, a new mini revue called *Crystals* was presented to the now discerning audiences.

The Palladium

Managing Director—
CHARLES GULLIVER.

Prices of

(Exclusive of Tax)

Boxes	21 -, 15 -, 10 6	
Imperial Fauteuils	5/-	All P
Fauteuils	3/-	
Imperial Grand Circle	3 -	Bo
Grand Circle	2/-	
Stalls	1 6	B
Circle	1 -	

No allowance will be made for any ticket not used sent, nor enquiries answered, unless a stamped enclosed for reply.

Patrons expecting Telephone Calls or Messages the Numbers of their Seats at the Box Office.

THE BOX OFFICE is open daily

Seats may be booked by post, tel

'Phones: GERR

It had music by Vivian Ellis and H.J.D. Collin, and starred Kitty Collier, Jimmie Leslie and Douglas Byng, who had made an earlier appearance at the Palladium in the programme notes as the designer of gowns for Lorna and Toots Pounds. The programme noted:

> Refinement, beauty and charm stand out clear as crystal in this worthy addition to the long line of successful Harry Day revues. Wonderful scenic effects, gorgeous dresses, entrancing dances, ear haunting music, rollicking comedy and melodious song. Every detail in colour, dress, melody, word and action has been carefully considered, culminating in effect as the latest development of a Harry Day Production.

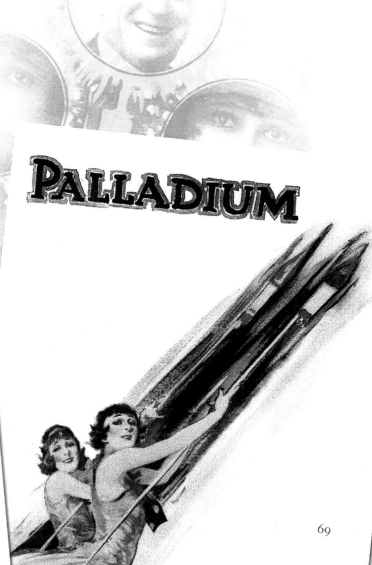

In July 1923 an American artiste by the name of Nora Bayes made an unprogrammed appearance, and she was so successful that she was immediately re-engaged to appear the following week. She had a big, powerful contralto voice to match her frame, coupled with a flamboyant personality. Her trademark was an outsize ostrich feather fan, suitably coloured to complement her many stage gowns. Such was her phenomenal success in America that there is a theatre named after her in New York. Although earlier appearances at other London theatres had not been to the liking of the other managements that had engaged her, she was to find new fame under the Palladium spotlight. Perhaps on earlier occasions the fine wine had not travelled, and her act had not registered properly with audiences, as so many future American acts would find out when it was their turn to appear on this formidable stage. However, now she was in demand, and rightly so. Not every act can feel at home in every theatre, but the 'feel' of the Palladium audience was just right for her style of work. She felt so much at home that she offered to keep her small billing in return for offering to change her programme of songs every week, a generous offer when one could tour the halls for five years or more with the same act. Such was her intractable will to capture the British audiences in the same way that she had done in the USA, she even offered to take a cut in her salary just to stay at the Palladium. Some artists since would consider offering to pay to appear on the Palladium stage, but she was, after all, a businesswoman!

By the time she had reached her third week and changed her material, there were those in the audience who had been totally captivated by her personality. They were not only cheering for more, but were actually shouting out for the earlier songs that she had deliberately discarded in favour of new material. The best advert any day is word of mouth, and many of her new-found fans were telling their friends that they had discovered, way down on the bill, an unknown artist who should have been at the top. Her thirteen-week season was a great achievement. The trick had worked for both Bayes and Gulliver, and every credit must go to Bayes for her dogged determination to succeed. On the last night of her season in October, she sang every one of the thirty-five songs that

she had made her own. And *still* they cheered for more! As Ian Bevan described in his book *Top of the Bill*, 'Singing for more than two hours, it was left to Gulliver to come on stage and plead with the audience to let her go...' *The Stage* newspaper submitted the following eulogy: 'Nora Bayes can come back and pick up her English popularity whenever she chooses to.' What more could anyone say?

As the holiday season approached, it was Nellie Wallace, Clarice Mayne, Harry Weldon and Hilda Glyder who were to star in Gulliver's 1923 Christmas offering of *Dick Whittington*. Again produced by Albert de Courville, the story was told in fourteen beautifully-costumed and spectacular scenes. It also starred Gus Sharland and Audrey Thacker, who later became a respected agent for such popular bill toppers in the 1930s and 1940s as the Amazing Fogel, Douglas Byng, George Lacy, Beryl Reid, Clarkson Rose, Randolph Sutton and Albert Whelan.

With music by George Gershwin and the book by Edgar Wallace and Noel Scott, and with producer Albert de Courville, Gulliver presented *The Rainbow* in early 1924. This was to be a vehicle for Shirley Kellogg, with Palladium regular Tubby Edlin. Item nineteen, *The Living Shadows,* direct from the Casino in Paris, had the programme notes suggesting that the audience used their special green and red glasses for this marvellous novelty. This was unquestionably the first three-dimensional showing at the Palladium.

This short season was followed quickly by Gulliver's new revue, *Whirl of the World,* starring Nellie Wallace, Billy Merson and a new name brought down specially from Liverpool , who was later to find fame and radio fortune as *That Man Again*: Tommy Handley. The world 'whirled' for over 627 performances and became the longest running show at the Palladium, holding the record until the Second World War was over. Nervo and Knox and Lorna and Toots Pounds joined the show at various stages of its run. And run it did, taking more money than any other show, with over three million people attending this production.

By now Gulliver was aiming *Sky High*, and this was the title of his next revue. Once again, tried and tested Albert de Courville produced the show that starred Nellie Wallace and George Robey. As one reviewer said,

> At present, despite the unnecessary vulgarity of certain sketches and costumes, it is a long and lavish show which should appeal to lovers of spectacular revue. De Courville has quite surpassed himself in the loveliness of some of the stage effects. On the comedy side there is George Robey, that very popular British institution, and Nellie Wallace. Both are genuinely funny comedians and in *Sky High* they are every bit as good as their material allows them to be.

THE
PALLADIUM

Managing Director MR CHARLES GULLIVER

Programme

In name only, the continental import in 1925 of the *Folies Bergère* allowed Tom Arnold to present this new revue, and Gulliver to continue his successful run. The *Folies Bergère* girls were trained by Mrs Lawrence Tiller, and whilst there was no star name to speak of in the show, except perhaps for Fred Duprez and Ernie Lotinga, it glistened and glittered its way through the run of thirteen weeks. It was the most ambitious production yet to be staged.

The ever popular pantomime *Cinderella* saw the year out with Naughton and Gold as the debt collectors, Clarice Mayne as Prince Charming, and Charles Austin as Buttons. Limited early film footage still exists, and although naturally in black and white, it shows elaborate scenes and costumes, with Clarice entering in one scene on a white charger. Ponies brought on Cinderella's coach, accompanied by two guards on horseback. The title role was taken by Lennie Deane who was under contract to another theatre, but Gulliver was so impressed by her

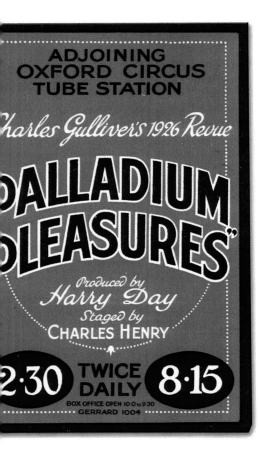

stage presence that he bought her out of that contract especially to appear in his pantomime. At the final dress rehearsal no one had told Lennie that real mice would be used and she ran offstage screaming in fright, awaiting their capture before the rehearsal could continue! The production was staged by Charles Henry and produced by Harry Day, with special music by Vivian Ellis and a strong supporting cast, including Terry's Juveniles. It proved a popular attraction for young and old.

New and delightful *Palladium Pleasures* were awaiting customers in Argyll Street in 1926, in the form of another Harry Day, Charles Henry and Vivian Ellis combination. Utilising the Billy Merson, Lorna and Toots Pounds and George Clarke formula, there was the welcome addition and return visit of Nora Bayes. Billed as 'the International Singer of Songs', she entertained delightfully for some thirty minutes, taking twenty-five curtain calls. Moreover, who could forget Lorna Pounds singing 'Soldiers of the Queen' in the finale to the accompaniment of both the Caledonian Pipe Band and the Metropolitan Brass Band?

Life in Argyll Street was very buoyant, with Clarice Mayne, G.S. Melvin and the Houston Sisters appearing in the next Maurice Cowan offering by Gulliver. Again, film evidence shows elaborate costumes and the chorus with sixteen young ladies, who in one short fast dance routine managed 434 steps. Once more Nora Bayes delighted the audience with her rendition of popular melodies, together with De Groot offering items from his more classical repertoire.

As one would imagine, no December could be contemplated without the annual pantomime, and Gulliver provided the Day and Henry production of *Aladdin*. Clarice Mayne played the title role, with Charles Austin in the role of Widow Twankey, and Bransby Williams ably taking the part of Abanazar, with Violet Essex as the Princess. The well-known deceiver Fred Culpitt provided the illusions that Mr Hymack presented in his role as the Vizier.

WYLIE - TATE

PRESENT

CARL BRISSON

IN

A NEW MUSICAL PLAY

THE

APACHE

Good-looking ex-boxing champion Carl Brisson joined Dorothy Ward, Adrienne Brune and Shaun Glenville to appear in the Wylie Tate 1927 production of the musical play *Apache*, which ran for 166 performances.

The twenties were finally drawing to a close. The paying public had had their fill of spectacle, and the Revue had run its course. Variety was brought back in three daily performances, with many new names to entertain; Jack Hylton and his Band, Ella Retford, and 'whispering' baritone Jack Smith were added to the already strong bill.

Gulliver had also acquired the Panatrope for the first time in any theatre in Europe. The printed programme stated that it was operated by a five valve set amplified by a one-and-a-half-horse-power transformer, which would play at the opening, during the interval, and at the termination of the performance.

NERMAN

THE PALLADIUM

CHRISTMAS PANTOMIME

NERVO and KNOX

CINDERELLA

80   8.0

CLARICE MAYNE

ISABELLE DILLON   DAPHNE BRAYNE

PEGGY SURTEES   RONNIE HOWARD   MDLLE. ALBION

LENA CHISHOLM

SUSIE BELMORE

TERRY'S JUVENILES with RENEE FOSTER

PICTON ROXBOROUGH QUEEN & LE BRUN ALEXANDER DANE

THE PRINCE'S FAVOURITE CHARGER

STANLEY'S QUARTETTE OF TRUMPETERS

GARDINER'S TEAM OF EIGHT FAIRY PONIES

GEORGE JACKLEY

HARRY FORD

HENGLER BROS.

SUSIE BELMORE

NERVO AND KNOX

Produced by HARRY DAY

Book by CHARLES HENRY and GILBERT LOFTHOUSE

Special Music Composed by VIVIAN ELLIS

GEORGE JACKLEY

Staged by CHARLES HENRY

Special Lyrics by JAMES HEARD

Ensembles and Ballets arranged by MDLLE. ALBION

DAPHNE BRAYNE

Ambrose and his Mayfair Orchestra, Little Tich and Nellie Wallace delighted the patrons, along with a full supporting bill. By the joint permission of the Savoy Hotel and the Café de Paris, The Savoy Havana Band and The Yacht Club Boys, 'America's most intimate entertainers', shared top billing the following week. Such was their success, the 'Boys' stayed an extra week.

Direct from the Café de Paris, Teddy Brown and his Band also enjoyed a huge success. Teddy's size matched not only his personality, but also his xylophone offering. Rob Wilton, Gillie Potter Herschel Henlère, and the Peter Pan of the music halls, Wee Georgie Wood, all had a new generation waiting to discover them.

Other performances included Ben Blue, the Cyclone Dancer of America, and his X-N-tricity Band, Will Hay in his *Schoolmaster* sketch, Nervo and Knox, and another very special item. By arrangement with the Cornwall Wrestling Association, Charles Gulliver presented 'A first appearance on any stage' of the Cornish Wrestling Champions in a thrilling display of their talents. Then in November and by arrangement with Gulliver, Laddie Cliff presented *Shake your Feet*, with music by George Gershwin, Fred Astaire and Carrol Gibbons.

With the December pantomime offering *Cinderella*, the General Manager C. Foster-Marner saw his long relationship with the Palladium managements come to an end. He had occupied this managerial post since the Palladium opened its doors in 1910. In fact, he had been associated with the Argyll Street site long before that, when the Hengler family was in charge. As irony would have it, his last event with Hengler had been a pantomime entitled *Cinderella,* and the music was specially arranged by James Sale, who had joined him as Musical Director on the opening night in 1910. Another coincidence was that Marner's last pantomime included a speciality act by the Hengler brothers. What a tale they could all tell!

This 1927 production of *Cinderella* was yet another successful Harry Day, Charles Henry and Vivian Ellis partnership. Old stalwarts Clarice Mayne and Nervo and Knox were in the lead roles, with George Jackley playing Buttons. The theatre was packed with children from the plush carpeted floor to the 'gods', and as scene followed scene with lavish profusion, the antics of the cast were greeted with shouts of joy and laughter in the highest of treble keys. One critic was happy to review it as a 'jolly good pantomime ... because it gives children three hours of heaven. The slapstick of Mr Jackley as the red coated magician and his assistants Nervo and Knox is one of the funniest absurdities I have ever seen.'

This production was to be the last time that Charles Gulliver would have his name on the programme. He had served the public well and offered them every form of entertainment possible. The Capital Syndicate would be no more. None of the entertainment provided, it was thought, could compete with the new invention of 'Talking Pictures'. Gibbons was waiting in the Palladium wings, once again ready to pounce and take over as the new Managing Director.

Chapter Six

CINE-VARIETY

It should be remembered that both Walter Gibbons and Charles Gulliver had repeatedly run variety seasons without disturbing the long-established supremacy of their rivals, the Alhambra and the Coliseum. Yet Gibbons especially appeared to be favoured with all the necessary advantages. At that time, the Palladium was at the head of a circuit that could offer at least forty weeks' work to an artist. Nevertheless, during their respective managing directorships, neither Gibbons nor Gulliver could avoid the necessity of inflicting on Palladium patrons the same old turns doing the same old acts, and refusing to alter them owing to their long period contracts. Of course, the public got to know about it and quietly stayed away. There was nothing for it but for the Palladium to go over to 'production', and as has been said earlier, there followed a long selection of revues and pantomimes, none of which exactly set the town alight.

And so it went on until 1927, when Gulliver publicised his willingness to part with the difficult property to anyone who would pay his price. American film groups had conversations with him about it, including Fox, First National and possibly United Artists. None of them could come to terms on money and so Gulliver gave way to Gibbons who, at the beginning of 1928, decided to woo the fickle goddess with a show containing Variety *and* talking pictures. The Palladium then became the finest super variety cinema in London.

In 1928, 'Talking Pictures' were all the rage: 'A new wave of entertainment!', 'The shape of the things to come in Britain!' – such were the headlines in the press. Recently knighted, Sir Walter Gibbons took over from Charles Gulliver in the knowledge that with his 'new' discovery, he would revolutionise the London scene!

The General Theatre Corporation had taken over the property, and they installed a new policy, and a new House Manager: W.J. 'Simmy' Simpson. The programme stated that the Palladium was 'The Sensation of the Cinema World'. The Stage Manager behind the scenes was a clever young Londoner, Castleton Knight. He was a man with a restless brain and an eye for publicity. So much so that whilst in charge of a previous cinema, he had dressed as a chauffeur and 'kidnapped' Charlie Chaplin to get him to make a public appearance. It worked, and Chaplin even enjoyed the joke!

The GTC spent over £20,000 on the transformation of the Palladium into a cinema, with all the latest improvements. The theatre was completely redecorated and the two back rows of the circle had to be sacrificed to accommodate the latest film projection equipment. A special glass rostrum had been created, rising from below the stage, that would contain De Groot conducting a symphony orchestra, or Teddy Brown and his Band. Even a large Wurlitzer organ had been installed to help entertain.

The cinema opened one week later than planned due to a legal injunction served by the company that supplied the cloakroom facilities, chocolates, opera glasses and programmes. They claimed none of this would be needed if the theatre changed to a cinema. Needless to say they lost their case! Having heard all the evidence, the judge

PALLADIUM

CHARLES·GULLIVER
MANAGING·DIRECTOR

noted that it was possible to consume chocolates in the dark, there would be no loss of revenue in the sale of programmes, and patrons would still need to leave their coats in the event of inclement weather.

On the opening on 19 March, a three-hour programme commenced at 8.30pm. The first film to be screened was *A Girl in Every Port* with Victor McLaglen, and the second feature was a comedy film, *The Rush Hour*, starring Marie Prevost. In-between each film, Variety was provided, with Reginald Foort at the organ and De Groot conducting a hundred musicians who played, amongst other items, the '1812 Overture', with trumpeters and choir strategically placed in the theatre boxes to obtain the maximum spectacle. It was so well received, said the *Melody Maker*, that they even received an encore! Teddy Brown and his Band, eccentric Athol Tier, and dancers Peggy Ross, Jan and Janette completed the strong bill. Ticket prices were somewhat lower than those of their competitors, costing 2*s*. 4*d*. for a tip-up seat and one shilling in the gallery. Although it received a mixed reception from the press, the near-capacity house thought it was wonderful.

The following week, 26 March, had more Cine-Variety with *The Thirteenth Juror*, starring Anna Q. Nillson and Francis X. Bushman. William Boyd starred in the second offering of *Night Flight*. Variety was provided by Teddy Brown and his Band, mimic Ann Penn, Ferry Ferrety, and sensational dancers Addison and Mitrenga.

Another complete change of programme on 2 April offered a murder mystery with a circus theme in the shape of *The Leopard Lady* with Jacqueline Logan, whilst Marie Provost starred in *The Girl in the Pullman*. On stage and with a variety show consisting of sixty performers, came Ramon Ferrata and Gladys Groom, with The Lestille Girls, comic juggler Eddie Gray, Doris Ashton and Billy Rawson and a full symphony orchestra with vocal and violin selections.

The much-publicised Herbert Wilcox film *Dawn*, about the life of Nurse Edith Cavell, made its debut on 9 April and played three performances daily. The British film industry was still in its infancy and, following a delay by the Board of Censors in issuing a certificate for public viewing, there was a great rush to secure the first London

THE SMALL B...
WITH
KENT & ANDRE BE...

THE PALLADI...

ARGYLL STREET, OXFORD CIRCUS,
TELEPHONE:
A G.T.C. THEATRE.
(THE SENSATION OF THE CINEMA W...

PRESENTS

MONDAY, 2nd APRIL, 1928,

JACQUELINE LOGAN
IN
"THE LEOPARD LADY
AND
MARIE PREVOST IN
"THE GIRL in the PULLMAN

ALSO EVERY WEEK DAY
STUPENDOUS STAGE SHOW

HOUSE MANAGER - - - - W. J. SIMPS...

The Management reserve the right to make any alteration in the Programme
be rendered necessary.

Arrangements made for the Convenience of Patrons:
Nearest Tube Stations, Central London and Bakerloo Railways, Oxford Circus.
Patrons expecting Telephone Calls or Messages are requested to leave the number
Seats at the Box Office.
Applications for Lost Property found by Staff may be made between 11 a.m. and 1
during the performance.
Fully Licensed Bars in all parts of the Theatre are under the direct contro
Management.
A special feature is made of Afternoon Tea, which is served in the salons
Auditorium at the Matinées.
Chocolates and Ices can be obtained from the Attendants until 9.30 p.m., and on S
until 10 p.m.
Cigarettes can be obtained at any time from the Automatic Machine in the Bars
floor.

THE PALLADIUM

ARGYLL STREET, OXFORD CIRCUS, W.1.
GERRARD
TELEPHONE:
A G.T.C. THEATRE.
(THE SENSATION OF THE CINEMA WORLD)

PRESENTS

MONDAY, 16th APRIL, 1928,

PREMIER PRESENTATION
OF
"CHICAGO"
WITH
PHYLLIS HAVER & VICTOR VARCO...

HOUSE MANAGER - - - - W. J. SIM...

The Management reserve the right to make any alteration in the Programm
be rendered necessary.

Arrangements made for the Convenience of Patrons:
Nearest Tube Stations, Central London and Bakerloo Railways, Oxford Cir
Patrons expecting Telephone Calls or Messages are requested to leave the nu
Seats at the Box Office.
Applications for Lost Property found by Staff may be made between 11 a.m.
during the performance.
Fully Licensed Bars in all parts of the Theatre are under the direct
Management.
A special feature is made of Afternoon Tea, which is served in the
Auditorium at the Matinées.
Chocolates and Ices can be obtained from the Attendants until 9.30 p.m., a
until 10 p.m.
be obtained at any time from the Automatic Machine in the

PALLADIUM

RGYLL STREET, OXFORD CIRCUS, W.1.

A G.T.C. THEATRE.   GERRARD 1004.

(THE SENSATION OF THE CINEMA WORLD)

PRESENTS

MONDAY, 23rd APRIL, 1928,

"SKYSCRAPER"

STARRING

WILLIAM BOYD

ALSO

"THE SMALL BACHELOR"

WITH

BARBARA KENT & ANDRE BERANGER

ON THE STAGE

JEAN MYRIO   DESHA   LEON BARTE

An International Dance Trio

"THE RHAPSODY IN BLUE."

HOUSE MANAGER - - - - W. J. SIMPSON.

Management reserve the right to make any alteration in the Programme which may be rendered necessary.

rangements made for the Convenience of Patrons:

rest Tube Stations, Central London and Bakerloo Railways, Oxford Circus. rous expecting Telephone Calls or Messages are requested to leave the number of their Seats at the Box Office.

plications for Lost Property found by Staff may be made between 11 a.m. and 1 p.m., and during the performance.

ly Licensed Bars in all parts of the Theatre are under the direct control of the Management.

special feature is made of Afternoon Tea, which is served in the salons and the Auditorium at the Matinées.

ocolates and Ices can be obtained from the Attendants until 9.30 p.m., and on Saturdays until 10 p.m.

igarettes can be obtained at any time from the Automatic Machine in the Bars on each floor.

showing of this film. It was an ambitious effort to prove that the British film producer was capable of challenging American and continental competitors, and Sybil Thorndike in the lead role was a guarantee that this was not just a casual production. Queues at three o'clock in the afternoon for the six o'clock performance most days ensured its success. A special score of Beethoven music was used to accompany this film. If no other, it was this film that put the Palladium on the cinema map. Taking into account the gravity of the storyline, appropriate low-key Variety was provided with De Groot and Zarlov's Russian Folk Singers.

Starting on 16 April and running for six days, Cecil B. De Mille's *Chicago* with Phyllis Haver and Victor Varconi was shown, along with Variety on stage which consisted of the Palladium Symphony Orchestra, once again with Reginald Foort at the organ. *A Russian Fantasy* was presented as the main attraction, described as a musical melange with eminent British and continental artistes, and featuring basso-profundo Lt. Vladimir Zaaloff. Principal dancers with the Diaghilef Company, Thadee Slavinsky and M'elle Sylvia came next, followed by the Polish tenor Jan Zalski, and Russian dramatic tenor Nicholas Schacknoff. From the production of Chu Chin Chow came the British baritone Wilfred Essex. The Russian Nightingale M'elle Cherniavsky, N. and M. Roxana Sisters, and Nat Young and his Balalaika Entertainers were also on the bill. Gordon Stamford was the Musical Director with Choirmaster G. Pronte, together with a company of twenty-seven artistes. Old-fashioned Variety was provided by Harry and Burton Lester, the 'Cowboy Comedians', assisted by Gladys Neville and The Ten Cowboy Syncopaters who completed the bill.

The week commencing 23 April had another De Mille production, this time entitled *Skyscraper* and starring William Boyd. The second film was *The Small Bachelor* with Barbara Kent and Andre Beranger. On stage in between the films was Variety, with Jean Myrio and Desha and Leon Barte, an international dance trio, whose act featured 'The Rhapsody in Blue'. Laughs were well provided by Joe Boganny and Company.

Lola with Carmel Myers and *The Samaritan* with Rudolph Schildkraut were the two offerings commencing on 30 April. Variety was offered again, and this time an attempt was made to interest the public with something different. An HMV gramophone was placed centre stage and the record 'Celesto Aidal' was played, sung by the great tenor Martinelli. This 'novelty' attraction was accompanied by De Groot and his orchestra.

At this point in his chequered leadership, Gibbons announced to the press that 'There was no truth in the rumour that the Palladium was going back to being an all variety house.' Such a robust denial is usually the opposite in today's world, because politicians tend to say one thing whilst doing something else. However, apparently life was no different then either! Within the space of six weeks, rumours increased when Cine-Variety finished at the Palladium and Gibbons had gone.

In the meantime, on 7 May, *So This is Love* was the first selected film, with Shirley Mason, Johnnie Walker, and William Collier, and the second was *The Heart of a Nation,* which starred George Sidney. Variety was well provided with Jack Hylton and his Band and Fred Sylvester and Co.

14 May saw *The Fortune Hunter* with Syd Chaplin and *The Pharisee* with Miles Mander. Variety was presented by The Eight Lancashire Lads, and Alma Barnes and Sister. On the Friday of that week *Tommy Atkins,* the British-made feature film, was released.

On 21 May the presentation was *Monkeynuts,* a film with a circus theme. The phenomenally popular Betty Balfour not only starred in the film, but also made a personal appearance on stage. *Shield of Love* with Neil Hamilton was the second film. Variety came in the shape of syncopated songster Noble Sissle, along with John Gulesco and his Hungarian orchestra.

The week beginning 28 May had *On to Reno* with Marie Prevost and also *French Leave* with Al Cooke. Billed as 'The Greatest Living Comedienne', Sophie Tucker made a most welcome return on stage. She was the only act ever to have her name outside the theatre above that of the films; this proved to be a wise move as she was a far greater attraction. The Six Rockets, an acrobatic act, also appeared and once again at the organ was Reginald Foort.

THE PALLADI

ARGYLL STREET, OXFORD CIRCUS,

TELEPHONE: A G.T.C. THEATRE.

(THE SENSATION OF THE CINEMA W

PRESENTS

MONDAY, 28th MAY, 1928,

EXCLUSIVE PRESENTATION OF

"ON TO RENO"
WITH
MARIE PREVOST
ALSO
"FRENCH LEAVE"
WITH
AL. COOKE

ON THE STAGE
SOPHIE TUCKER
The Greatest Living Comedienne
SIX ROCKETS ACROBATIC ACT

HOUSE MANAGER - - - - -
PRESS REPRESENTATIVE - - - - W. J. SIMPS
Mrs. C. '
The Management reserve the right to make any alteration in the Programme be rendered necessary.

IN ACCORDANCE WITH THE REQUIREMENTS OF THE LONDON COUNTY COUN
(1) The public may leave at the end of the performance or exhibition by all exit doors such doors must at that time be open.
(2) All gangways, passages and staircases must be kept entirely free from chairs or oth.. obstruction.
(3) Persons must not be permitted to stand or sit in any of the gangways intersect the seating or to sit in any of the other gangways. If standing be permitted in the gangw at the sides and rear of the seating, sufficient space must be left for persons to pass easily and fro and to have free access to exits.
(4) The safety curtain must be lowered and raised in the presence of each audience.

Sophie Tucker

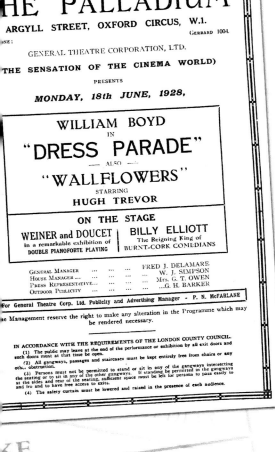

On 4 June, American college life was represented by *Hold 'em Yale* with Rod La Rocque and the second film, entitled *Jazz Mad,* starred Jean Hersholt. Variety was provided by Dick and Edith Barstow and Fred Lindsay, a stock whip and lariat expert.

By 11 June another De Mille film, *Walking Back,* was presented, with Sue Carol in the lead role. Lya de Putti appeared in *Midnight Sun.* Variety was provided by Winifred Harvard and Bruce, and The Four Harmony Kings.

On 18 June, *Dress Parade* with William Boyd was shown, along with *Wall Flowers* with Hugh Trevor. These were to be the last films to be projected in the Palladium's brief history as a cinema. On stage, Weiner and Doucet appeared in a remarkable exhibition of double pianoforte playing. Billy Elliott, the reigning 'King' of the Burnt-Cork Comedians completed the bill. Reginald Foort was once again at the Wurlitzer keyboard.

In spite of the diversity of subjects and styles, the Palladium failed to register as a home for talking pictures. During this short period there had been several changes of General Manager, and although the cinema in its new Argyll Street venue had been given a reasonably good trial, the critics and the cinema-going public alike did not feel at home in the Palladium. The lack of first class feature films didn't help, but it was felt that however wonderful this new fangled invention, the atmosphere in the Palladium was not conducive to viewing the moving pictures. It was, after all, a music hall. As a result, Sir Walter Gibbons was asked to leave the Board of Directors due to disagreements over policy, and a new Managing Director was appointed. He was to create a true variety period in September, but rather than have the theatre 'dark' till then, the new man brought in *The Yellow Mask* from Her Majesty's Theatre.

With a known storyline by Edgar Wallace, and produced by Julian Wylie with dance routines staged by Max Rivers, *The Yellow Mask* was a musical comedy drama to suit all tastes. It starred Bobby Howes and Phyllis Dare live on stage once more, and with nearly twenty musical numbers it couldn't fail. A breath of fresh air permeated once again through Argyll Street. Everyone seemed delighted that the Palladium had returned to its old roots. Even the General Manager, 'Simmy' Simpson, stated that 'it was a pleasure to see the bright lights of the Palladium all lit up again.'

The name of the man who was to make the metamorphosis possible was someone who, by the strangest of coincidences, came from a cinema background. To those he worked with, he was to be known simply by his initials, 'G.B.'

Chapter Seven

THE GANG IS HERE TO ENTERTAIN YOU – OI!

*F*ollowing the Cine-Variety episode, the theatre was dark for a short period in the autumn of 1928, but the arrival of a new Managing Director was to shed a bright new spotlight on the Palladium stage. His name was George Black.

When Black took over the running of the Palladium in 1928, the previous eighteen years had not been without their successes. Unfortunately, it was lacking in permanent results. Nearly every kind of entertainment had been tried in turn without ever really putting this magnificent theatre on the West End map. However, when George Black was appointed Managing Director, it was a turning point.

Black was a film man, and at the young age of twenty-six he had owned thirteen cinema theatres which he had disposed of for the sum of £300,000. However, he quickly came to the conclusion that in spite of the Palladium's previous failures, its real métier was Variety. So he re-opened the house on 3 September 1928 with a truly superb variety bill. Fifty-five thousand people attended the first week's show with a straight variety programme which starred Gracie Fields, Dick Henderson, the superb tumblers The Seven Hindustans, Billy Bennett, and finally Ivor Novello and Phylis Monkman in a playlet called *The Gate Crasher*. In addition to the famous stars, there were great supporting acts on the bill too, so it could hardly fail to attract big audiences.

George Black's flair for publicity was evidenced by the fact that during the evenings, Argyll Street became a congested mass of people. Extra police had to be brought in to cope with the throng, and it was often possible for 4,000 unlucky patrons to be turned away at the box office. And so, throughout the 1930s, there was a continued succession of top headlining variety shows. After one performance, Hannen Swaffer reported that, 'George Black showed us new ideas in presentation. If all music halls copied him Variety would be saved.' His words were prophetic; some years later, music halls did copy his formula, and Variety was saved, at least until television took over! Swaffer went on to say,

> The crude scenery of the old music hall has gone. There were gay curtains, bright hangings, cut out scenes worthy of revue with black curtains behind them. Everything was speeded up. One turn leaving the stage introduced the next. G.B. used every new technique in the book. Even Sophie Tucker seated in the stalls was enticed on stage as a 'surprise' item, to sing a farewell song. The next day she boarded the boat home to the United States.

By the autumn of 1928 and following the film fiasco at the Palladium, Black had taken full charge of this latent variety machine. He had picked it up by its old bootlaces and put it back on the map. The phenomenally successful formula of The Crazy Gang was yet to emerge, but Black already knew that for the Palladium, the secret of success lay in pure and simple Variety, with a capital 'V.' Black was innovative, and his ideas livened up that first opening night and the weeks that followed. It was exactly what the music halls had been wanting for years. None of the oldest hands in the business had been bright enough to see it. When they did realise what was needed, they were

too old-fashioned to be able to put their belated perceptions into practice. Their inability to do so provided Black with an additional opportunity which he seized to the full; there were more and more brainwaves to come on his part, which prompted many diverse presentations of Variety at the Palladium. More importantly still, the new directorate excelled in a booking strategy whereby they would secure the acts and then hold them until their release could do no harm.

The press were ecstatic about the revival of Variety in Argyll Street: 'All day Queues for Variety', 'Crowd of Four Thousand Turned Away', 'Variety Comes Back To Stay', 'Variety Alive and Kicking', and 'Variety Recaptures The Palladium' declared the headlines. A full-page report in the *Evening Standard* said it all: 'Vaudeville Comes Back To Its Own'. Black stated that 'the success of Variety in the future depends solely on the artists. They are the obstacles in the way. If only they would modernise themselves and play according to 1928 and not 1908 then I am certain there is a future for Variety in England.'

Big star names were promised in future offerings, including the juvenile film star, Jackie Coogan, at a reputed £750 per week. He amassed literally pages and pages of excellent press coverage which was all to the good for Black because it kept the momentum going. Coogan's appearance was so successful that he was even engaged for a second week.

Late in 1928, one item really made their mark with the press, even though they were only a support dancing act. 'Will be big one day', suggested one source. How prophetic that phrase turned out to be. These youngsters were called The Delfont Boys. One was Hal Monty, the other Barnet Winogradsky, who later changed his name to Bernard Delfont and went on not only to make his fortune, but to present some of the world's top stars upon the very same stage on which he himself had danced so successfully.

It was George Black and his assistant Charles Henry who, in the early 1930s, decided to experiment and put together a series of double acts. They gathered together comedians who were successful in their own right, and slowly built on this formula until there was a complete 'gang' of them. And so The Crazy Gang was born. They were a knockabout team, that could be satirical and yet

Bernard Delfont

sentimental, and often farcical, always improvising and ad-libbing.

The first experimental *Crazy Week* took place on 30 November 1931 with Nervo and Knox, Naughton and Gold, Caryll and Mundy, and pseudo French juggler 'Monsewer' Eddie Gray, complete with false mustachio. Not taking any chances, Black added other top variety acts as well. More often than not this would include The Ganjou Brothers and Juanita, who were in almost permanent residence too. Following this success, and after a gap of a few weeks, a *Second Crazy Week* took place on 21 December of that same year.

With the New Year came new ideas, and on 6 June 1932 came a bolder approach; 'We Go Crazy for Four Weeks with *The First Crazy Month* of 1932.'

By now Flanagan and Allen had joined the already strong team to add even more mayhem to the proceedings. To inaugurate this Crazy Season a bicycle race was organised, with The Gang racing down Oxford Street, and it garnered a lot of publicity. As one would expect, chaos ensued! Upon arrival at their destination they even took the 'House Full' notices from outside the Palladium and put them in front of the neighbouring Marlborough Street Police Station! The June run was followed by the *Second Crazy Month* in September, which prompted the headline, 'Bedlam with Scenery' in the press. During the final show of the run, The Crazy Gang was allowed to run riot, and they stole ice creams and chocolates from the attendants and proceeded to give them away to the seated patrons. They even showed Stalls ticket holders to their seats in the Circle. They stopped at nothing to gain laughs. No one was safe!

In their early days as comedians, on a visit to the Newbury Races, Naughton and Gold had no money for the fare, so they bought platform tickets only and rode the train to Newbury. When the train stopped at their destination they jumped down onto the platform and ran straight to the Station Master's Office asking, 'Where are the steps? We have come to mend the station clock.' They climbed the ladder, tinkered about with the dial and then duly left through the exit and walked to the racetrack. One must assume they won enough to buy a ticket to return home! Another time, they saw workmen digging a hole in the pavement in Southampton. They went up to the men asking to see the plans for the road scheme. When they were produced, Jimmy Gold turned the plans upside down and said, 'I thought so, you are digging the hole on the wrong side of the road. Now get busy, we are the new foremen!' They left the men quickly filling in the original hole and starting to dig another one on the other side of the road.

In September 1932 it was announced in the press that,
Nine of the highest paid British music hall comedians are to make a 'talkie'. Their salaries for the picture will amount to something in the neighbourhood of £7,000. The film is to be a screen adaptation of the Crazy Month idea which has proven successful at the Palladium and the cast will be largely provided by the comedians in the present show there. Mr George Black, the genius of the Palladium, is to

direct the Crazy talkie and it will be made soon at the Gaumont British Studios at Shepherd's Bush.

The working title was *All Crazy*, but the production was eventually called *Loose Nuts*. Black engaged Tim Whelan as a co-director, Tim being a past master of making film comedies. He was one of Harold Lloyd's chief gag-men for some years and had been associated with several British screen comedies.

Such was their villainous thinking that in the high summer of 1932, The Gang presented a Christmas pantomime, *Gingerella*. 48,000 people saw the shows most weeks, and 'House Full' signs went up as soon as their seasons were announced. The first two shows drew 6,000 people. 5,999 people laughed, so the press said, and the other one had lumbago!

In between the *Crazy Months* there was a brief spell of variety weeks with Dave Apollon, Louis Armstrong and our own 'home-grown' Jack Payne.

The incongruous high summer pantomime was followed by a *Third Crazy Month* which opened to a record advance booking in November 1932. 'Crazier Than Crazy Week', 'When The Palladium Rehearses Lunacy Everything Is Just Bedlam' and 'They're Going Crazy Again' were just some of the headlines in the press. Nellie Wallace had joined the cast, adding her own distaff comedy for which she was so well known. Those who dared to sit near the front or at the end of a gangway did so at their own peril; along with other members of The Gang, she could often be found on the wrong side of the footlights, invading the auditorium to manicure someone's nails. Or Eddie Gray would deposit a packet of hot potato chips in someone's unsuspecting hand. Then, as if the show wasn't big enough, it even had a real live elephant called Eva! Another sizeable star took part in the shape of xylophonist Teddy Brown. To get additional publicity for the show, Teddy was seen in Regent Street walking alongside Jimmy Nervo and Charlie Naughton, with both of them inside one of his suits! The show was further 'beefed up' (with carrots presumably) by Harry Champion, famous for his 'Any Old Iron.' J. Sherman Fisher provided twenty-four dancers, and Richard Crean conducted the Palladium Orchestra. These *Crazy Months* often extended to five or sometimes six weeks, and were so popular with the public that the *Fourth Crazy Month*, opening on 6 March 1933, ran for fourteen weeks! Nellie Wallace was the added attraction once again. The box office was overwhelmed with bookings; one employee sold 1,600 seats in seven hours, which was an average of four seats every minute. The police had to be called to control the crowds, and the show broke all known records. Always playing to capacity business, (including tickets for standing room only, which was two deep on most nights), the shows were not only hilariously funny but also very extravagant. In one spectacular scene, a ship called *The Atlantic* seemed to float over the footlights and right out into the audience, only to hit a mine and burst into flames.

The Gang were also known as The Knockabout Brothers, and they were often criticised in the press, even in those days, for being too vulgar. Black was always at the ready with his blue pencil in case The Gang got out of hand with their verbal quips. Their new-found patrons covered every strata of the population, with residents from Mayfair and Stepney sitting side by side, and members of royalty would even pop in for a regular seat in the stalls just to see the show, so Black had to take care not to offend anyone. Then, for the first time in its thirty-seven years' history, The Gallery First Nighters' Club gave a dinner in honour of Variety. The guests of honour were The Gang, and, not taking any chances, Black replied to the toast on their behalf.

The New Crazy Month of May was used as the basis of the programme for the 1933 Royal Variety Performance. Soon after, 'Quite Mad Again', the press hailed *The Fifth Crazy Month*, when it opened on 9 October 1933 and ran until the first week of the following January, for fifteen action packed weeks. In one scene, a shop counter was covered with various items and The Gang decided that a mock auction should take place. A roll of linoleum, a zinc bath, a deck chair, a large rug and a baby's high chair were just some of the larger items going for as little as sixpence! The joke was really on the successful

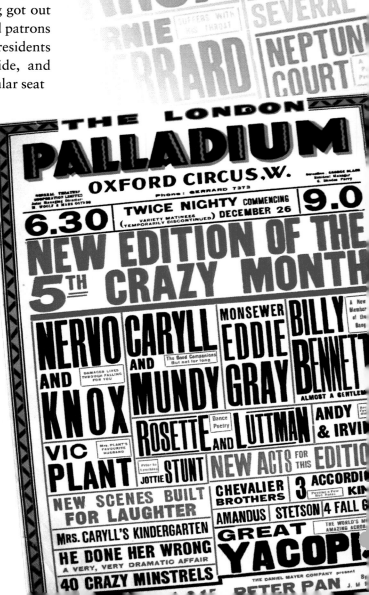

bidders, because it was only when they went up on stage to collect their prizes that they realised that they had to get them home! Negotiating crowded passages and pavements and dodging theatre traffic when carrying home a cake stand, or ten yards of garden wire fencing, created extra laughs for all the passers-by. The prize items all had publicity material attached too, telling the bewildered onlookers on the bus or under-ground what a funny show it was at the Palladium! 'Professor Grayellervitch' and his Million Volt Baby provided another of the funniest turns in that same show. The 'Professor' was none other than Eddie Gray himself, endea-vouring to wash a 'robot baby' which supposedly had a million volts of electricity running through it. Members of the audience were even invited up onto the stage to give the lively baby a bath!

The Sixth Crazy Show opened on Whit Monday, 21 May 1934, and was acclaimed by the press as a worthy successor to The Gang's previous offerings. It ran for a ten-week season which lasted until 23 July. By the end, over 130,000 people had been to see the show. Earlier that year, and sandwiched in between fun packed seasons, Flanagan and Allen appeared for two weeks along with a cast of forty in *Give me A Ring*. This musical comedy success had transferred from the Hippodrome, and delivered fifty minutes of the biggest laughs in show business. A full supporting repertoire of Variety was also provided.

The Seventh Crazy Show opened on 22 Oct 1934, and cost Black £7,000 to produce. To advertise the show, posters were deliberately pasted upside down on 260 hoardings in central London and the suburbs. Owing to the length of the show, matinées were suspended and the first house started earlier at 6.25pm, then the second began at 9.00pm. From America, the six-foot beauty Mathea Merryfield was added to the show. She gained much press coverage with her daring and effective 'Fan Dance', as did George Prentice who presented a different style of Punch and Judy Show. There was something for everyone.

George Black may have been a hard-headed business-man but that hardness did not extend to his heart, because he evidently had a soft spot for the 'old timers' who had performed at the Palladium; some were still around even from the days of Hengler's Circus. On 17 January 1935, he invited a bus load of eighty or so veteran artists living at Brinsworth House to be his guests at the matinée performance of *The Crazy Show*. Prior to seeing the show, these theatrical senior citizens were treated to a sumptuous meal, and they were waited on by Mrs Black and members of The Crazy Gang.

By now the shows were getting even more spectacular; indeed, they were more like revues. They were tried out in Brighton, with Black tightening up the production where necessary. After a successful series of *Crazy Weeks* and *Months*, Black called his new venture *Life Begins at Oxford Circus: A Roundabout of Life and Laughter*. It starred Jack Hylton and his Band, with vocalist Ken Tucker. Ken later changed his name to Len Lowe, the other half of comedy duo Lowe and Ladd. In addition to these stars, the show could boast of a return visit of Flanagan and Allen, along with The Western Brothers and J. Sherman Fisher's Sixteen Girls, plus a host of performers who had made their name on the wireless in Britain and America. The new show opened in a scene representing the Oxford Street Tube Station from which the principals emerged, and then they eventually passed through the stage door of the Palladium. In one scene, a total of nine pianos were played simultaneously, and in 'London on a Rainy Night' a real rainstorm was introduced, with the water falling from special pipes in the 'flies' and running away in troughs which were specially fixed around the set at stage level. Shades of *Singin' in the Rain* were in evidence here!

One big innovation in the show was to bring new acts from the provinces to the discerning West End public, an idea which would be used in later Royal Variety Performances. Jack Hylton was driving from a rehearsal at the Finsbury Park Empire to the Palladium when the traffic lights changed from green to red. He switched on the radio in his car (remember, this was 1935) and he heard two brothers broadcasting from Scotland. Hylton had both an eye and an ear for talent-spotting, and he was so impressed with their musicality that he stopped at

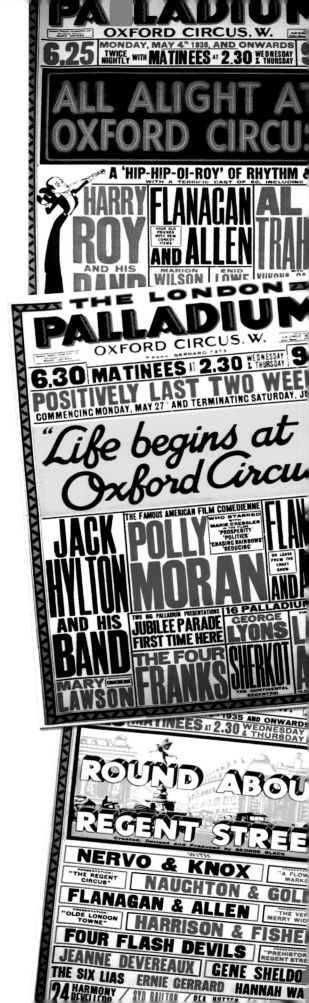

the next Post Office and put through a long distance call to the Aberdeen BBC Radio Studios. He spoke to the two Miller Boys and promptly booked them for the new show. Mr Hylton said in a press interview with the *Daily Mirror*, 'I consider this to be the quickest booking in the history of Vaudeville. I don't know what they look like, whether they are mechanics, engineers or bookmakers, but they can sing. I could recognise harmony as soon as I heard them, despite the honkings and hootings of indignant taxi drivers as I sat at the traffic lights!'

The second edition of *Life Begins at Oxford Circus* ran from 20 May until 8 June 1935, with Stanley Holloway and Florence Desmond added to the already strong cast. Also in June, the classic thriller, *The 39 Steps* by John Buchan (who later became Lord Tweedsmuir), was released at cinemas, directed by Alfred Hitchcock. One of the main features of the film was the scene that had been shot on the Palladium stage during an earlier Crazy Gang run.

This being 1935, it was the Silver Jubilee of the London Palladium, and it was now time to sit back and enjoy another helping of that George Black magic. This time the production was entitled *Round about Regent Street*, and it ran from 26 August until 7 March 1936. This show featured Nervo and Knox, Naughton and Gold, and of course Bud and Ches.

The following year another superb show, *All Alight at Oxford Circus*, ran from 11 March 1936 until 30 May 1936, with average takings of £5,000 per week. During the run of this show it was found that there was a break of fifty minutes when Bud and Ches were not needed on stage, and such was their tremendous popularity that this break enabled them to appear twice nightly at the Holborn Empire as well! A cab would stand by at the Palladium stage door, ready to whisk them there and back in time. The volume of traffic which now packs the London streets would certainly make that impossible today!

To mark the 1000th consecutive performance of Flanagan and Allen, George Black threw a cocktail party on 29 April 1936 in the Tudor Room at the Palladium. Unbeknown to The Gang, Black had invited the Arsenal Manager and his team, who had earlier had their own success in the Wembley Cup final. When called upon for a speech, Bud said that during the five years that he and Ches had been starring together in Variety, three and half of those years had been at the Palladium, and they had

been very happy times. A huge 'prop' cake was wheeled in with a '1000 candle power' lamp. Inside the cake were found enough small presentation bottles of whiskey for all the company and the guests. At the first evening performance following the party, Black invited the whole of the Arsenal team up onto the stage for the finale. Manager George Allison made a short speech and showed off the Wembley Cup to the audience!

O Kay for Sound was the next production and this ran from 2 Sept 1936 until 27 March the following year. Heaven knows where The Gang got their energy from, for in the daytime they could often be found at the studios making a film.

Swing is in the Air began on 29 March 1937 and ran until 26 June. This new 'musical frolic' was not strictly a *Crazy Show*; although it did contain Flanagan and Allen, it was more of a vehicle for the ever popular Jack Hylton and his Band. It was also the Coronation show and had Vic Oliver, Afrique, and the ubiquitous, lovely Sherman Fisher Dancers.

After the run of *Swing is in the Air* ended, in order to give The Gang a much needed rest, a short variety season took place, which featured The Cotton Club. This brief but fascinating story will be told in a later chapter.

The spectacular show *London Rhapsody*, featuring The Gang again with support from 'Britain's Foremost Conjurer', Cardini, opened on 1 September 1937 and ran until 30 April 1938. The *Sunday Graphic* commented, 'This is George Black's finest production; an ideal blend of beauty and humour.' 'I have never seen anything as good at the Palladium in all my life', proclaimed the *Sunday Dispatch*. 'Without a doubt it is the best show of its kind we have ever seen', said the *Empire News*. It seems that they were all thrilled with Black's latest offering. Some of the beautiful and elaborate costumes used in *London Rhapsody* were so heavy that they had to be lowered onto the dancers. Then, with the aid of a pulley, the dancers were suitably released of their heavyweight garments at the end of the routine. Lavish is not the word!

In the November of 1937, The Royal Variety Performance took place in the presence of Their Majesties the King and Queen. It was billed as 'A variety programme in aid of the Variety Artists' Entertainment Benevolent Fund and Institution'. In the *Radio Times*, it was noted that, 'Listeners are to hear the longest variety broadcast that has ever been given, for the whole of the Royal Command Performance, except the Intermission and two acts which appeal to the eye rather than the ear, is to be broadcast.' (Although not stated, the two exceptions were the Man on the Flying Trapeze, Jack LaVier, and the wonderful Ganjou Brothers.) The performance starred amongst others The Crazy Gang, Gracie Fields, George Formby, and Max Miller, who stopped the show, according to the press! The big highlights were Ralph Reader and *The Gang Show*. The first half overran by eight minutes, and it was thought that the BBC would fade out the end of the show. There was relief all round as the BBC jettisoned their schedule. At the close of the show, Will Fyffe turned to the Royal Box to say thank you and he began singing 'A Hundred Pipers'. The stage lights dimmed, the stage revolved to show Edinburgh Castle as a backdrop, and in the distance out in Argyll Street the sound of 100 pipers could be heard. The full blast was heard as they entered the theatre, marching down the centre aisle and onto the stage. Stirring stuff, but what a finale!

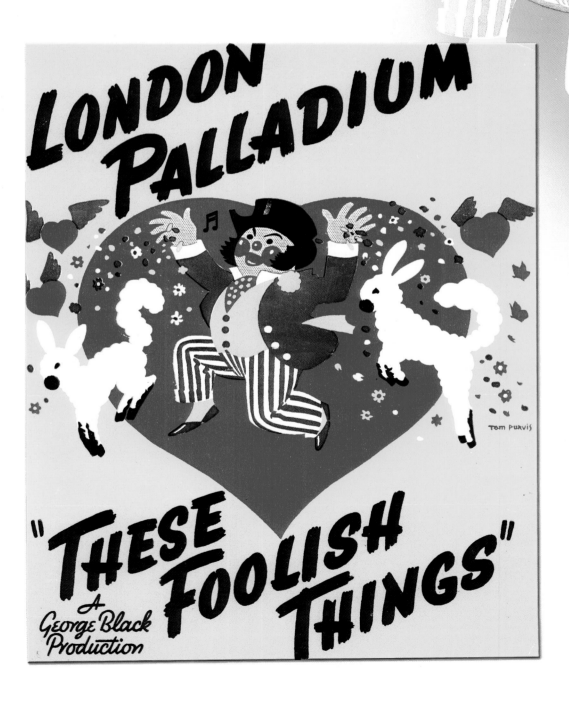

All day, every day and a good deal of the night too, George Black was busy editing, cutting and dovetailing his new, mammoth scale production, *These Foolish Things*. This production opened on 28 September 1938 and ran successfully until 3 June the following year. Whereas the previous Crazy offerings had centred in and around London, this new spectacular would transport the audience on a world tour, taking in such idyllic places as Hawaii and Greece. The 'tour' commenced on a railway station terminus. Jimmy Nervo had been at Kings Cross Station for a week, learning how to drive one of their electric trucks so that he and the rest of The Gang could make their entrance on stage with aplomb! Complete with a cast of eighty, this new musical was produced by Black, who was once again assisted by Charles Henry, with the book written by Black, Bert Lee and Harris Weston. The 'original' Crazy Gang, (Nervo and Knox, Flanagan and Allen, and Naughton and Gold), aided and abetted by Syd Railton, were to appear, with no less than twenty-seven of J. Sherman Fisher's Girls. The second half opened with a sports theme, with The Fisher Girls in a bicycling routine, The De Tuscans showing their fencing prowess, and then a badminton exhibition by Hugh Forgie and Ken Davidson, which was played at such a pace that it had the whole house in uproar! One of the hits of the bill!

'In dipping his brush into a palette of exquisite colours George Black has painted on the plain canvas of music hall scenes of enchanting beauty', wrote one reviewer of the show. 'Do six men dressed as bedraggled charwomen amuse? They do. But not as much as when they undress to ancient stays, long cloth 'drawers', torn chemises with Union Jack insertions and multicoloured waistcoats flip-flapping among the chimney pots. If the Craziness is not as sustained as in previous shows it is sufficient for those who like humour broader than it is long', said another report. The *Performer* said in their revue, 'When we witnessed the opening performance of the last Crazy production at this house, we admitted that we had seen the finest staging possible for the Palladium. We have to admit that we were wrong, for the latest G.B. opus transcends anything yet seen at the Argyll house.'

Bearing in mind that as early as 1937, George Black had signed The Crazy Gang up for a film and stage contract worth £100,000, the momentous date of 3 September 1939 was about to change the daily habits of everyone in Britain, which could easily have prevented them from filming. With a potential loss of 77,000 customers each month suddenly seeming a likely prospect, Black nevertheless soon decided that the Palladium without a show was unthinkable, and so at the first opportunity the show would go on. So, not all lorries seen on the roads at that time were carrying the sinews of war. Thirty tons of scenery and props and 547 costumes were carried in thirty oversized lorries down the London to Brighton Road. By now, George Black had thirty-six theatres under his control and he was a constant transatlantic traveller, always in search of new acts. He had found new faces to appear in his next production, but come the opening of *The Little Dog Laughed* on 11 October 1939, the political scene had changed dramatically, and the blackout was being enforced. Although the show was doing very good business, it was still ensconced at the Brighton Hippodrome when the show was set to open in London, and the move to the West End regrettably had to be delayed.

Whilst there was a 6.00pm curfew on cinemas in the West End, the Home Secretary granted permission for the Palladium and a few other selected theatres and cinemas to open their doors. No one knew at that time how long this would last, but a month later the show opened, with matinées three times a week and twice-nightly performances at 5.40 and 7.55pm. Whilst the show was in Brighton, there were several American scenes with American acts, but these had to be edited out owing to the war as the acts had to return home.

This latest show, *The Little Dog Laughed,* was devised and produced by Black, and he was assisted by a newcomer, Robert Nesbitt, who had learned his craft with André Charlot some years before. With new dance routines by Wendy Toye, they had another winner. Once more The Gang entertained like never before. Within five weeks 175,000 people had been to see the show that boasted a cast of 100. As well as men from the ships *Exeter* and *Ajax*, George Black invited 1500 servicemen to previews of the show and the critics once again

acclaimed it as one of the best Palladium presentations. 'Last night's audience devoured every moment, including the flagrant patriotism, raucous horse play and mass attack.' The first half ended with a military spectacle, with drums, bearskins, tanks and Union Jacks on the stage, and even Bud Flanagan in uniform, looking very patriotic. Then came the Palladium touch: to the sounds of planes flying overhead, the curtain fell and so did special propaganda leaflets with a German influence, as though they were dropping down from the sky. With typical Crazy Gang humour, they informed patrons about wartime recipes such as 'Reich Pudding', 'Peace Soup', 'Vienna Steak' and 'Gestapo Jelly', etc. They also included apologies to Rudyard Kipling and, complete with war undertones, a specially composed poem, 'If'. As one would expect it was all obviously tongue in cheek, guying Hitler and the Gestapo, as the illustrations showed only too well. Before the year was out, over a quarter of a million leaflets were dropped over the course of the run of the show.

It was in this show that Bud Flanagan got to popularise the Noel Gay tune, 'Run Rabbit Run'. It was predicted by the reporter on the *Daily Sketch* as being, 'an up and coming best seller.' Little did the 'Stupid Boy' realise! Bud actually produced the very rabbit that German bombers had killed in the Shetland Islands, which prompted the writing of this number. The owner of the estate on which the rabbit had met its fate when the bomb landed had arranged for the animal to be stuffed and sent down to Bud. Such was the popularity of the show that an excerpt was broadcast on radio, with Bud also singing 'Franklin D. Roosevelt Jones'. Also, The Gang announced during the show, 'Don't forget your gas masks on your way out!' In a press report, would you believe, as many as eighty-six assorted gas masks were on the shelves of the theatre's lost property, all awaiting a claimant! A programme note also made mention that the 1939 copyright for the title of the show *The Little Dog Laughed* was held by the General Theatre Corporation for the world and the USA!

Living in Brighton was considered possibly safer than living in the West End, and on one occasion the matinée had to be abandoned because The Gang were held up as their train just never made it to London on time. A packed house waited for the curtain to go up. At the scheduled time the orchestra played the overture, but it kept on playing for an hour... The show could not proceed, because the four essential members of the cast had not yet arrived! The Gang had been stranded in their railway carriage. They usually caught the 2.15 train from Brighton that normally arrived into Victoria at 3.30pm, giving them time to have a long game of cards before making up for their contribution in the first house. However, the train didn't arrive until 7.15pm. It had been unheard of for twenty years or more, but the severe wintry spell of that year brought public transport to a standstill. Even in those days it seems that there were problems with snow on the line!

One of the speciality acts of this show was Edna Squire Brown. She had been trained by the Grecian Ballet and had represented England as a dancer at the Empire Exhibition in South Africa in 1937. With her well-trained doves (of peace?) and diaphanous gowns, she proved to be the most popular act with both the servicemen audiences who were specially invited to the dress rehearsals and the real show audiences. As Edna danced on stage, seven Basra Doves were released from the back of the theatre to fly across the heads of the audience and land on various parts of her anatomy. By the time of her 250th performance, someone had worked out that the doves had flown a total of fifty miles without one misdemeanour! Another act was provided by 'A Billion Building Blunders', the programme billing of Lancastrian comedians Willie, West and McGinty, and they brought the house down with their bungling builders routine. This was a typical knockabout act that The Gang was always at home with.

Seats for this show were specially reserved for members of the armed forces and were always made available to those showing their overseas leave-pass. With packed houses taking nearly £7,000 per week, it was a generous gesture. There were also occasional Sunday charity concerts for the war effort. At this time it was laid down in the Sunday regulations that no props, stage

Edna Squire Brown

costumes or any form of Variety should be included in performances given on the Sabbath. Only musical entertainment and the human voice were permitted. These rules were usually strictly adhered to by the artists, but during wartime these restrictions were overlooked more often than not.

19 December 1939 was a date to celebrate, for at least two of The Gang, Naughton and Gold, had been together for twenty-one years. They had made their first public appearance together as a duo in 1918. 'We have acted together 7,119 times, covered 30,000 miles on stage and thrown something like 30,000 eggs at each other! We started at the end of one war and now we have come of age at the beginning of another!'

After thirty-one weeks and 461 performances, a record-breaking 77,000 people a month had seen this latest George Black production, and the show sadly closed on 11 May 1940. A programme note stated: 'Photographing in the theatre Forbidden. Productions and Variety Acts being the copyright of the theatre's proprietors or variety artists, the unauthorised photo-graphing of scenes and acts is illegal.' Was this a sign of relative affluence, one wonders, if there were sufficient cameras available to the general public to try and prevent them from using them in the theatre?

Maybe it was to break the boredom in between performances, or maybe they were just a mischievous group of schoolboys who had never really grown up, but The Gang played some great pranks, both on those inside the theatre and those outside who had no connection with show business whatsoever.

Once, armed with specially faked plans and dressed as Post Office officials, they went into Great Marlborough Street to witness the final cementing in of a red pillar box. In spite of the protestations of the workmen, they were able to convince them that the box had been placed on the wrong side of the street and promptly made them dig it up and move it to the other side of the street, where it stands to this very day outside The Dog and Trumpet public house. On another occasion, suitably dressed as road workers and armed with traffic bollards, shovels, barrows and other road mending paraphernalia, The Gang went into Regent Street, redirected the traffic, and proceeded to dig a big hole and remove the (then) cobble stones that surfaced the road. After this had been accomplished, they just walked away and left it, which caused disruption to the flow of traffic and a few headaches at the roadworks head office as they puzzled over exactly *who* had authorised this fiasco.

No one was safe inside the theatre either. During a long run of one show, the members of a trapeze act would remove their light overshoes before ascending the rope ladder to their high perch. On one occasion, whilst they were working the lofty heights of the Palladium stage, The Gang proceeded to nail these overshoes to the floor, so that when the trapeze artists had completed their successful turn and descended to the stage to take their final bow, they found themselves rooted to the spot! Another time, 'Monsewer' Eddie Gray went on stage to do his cod juggling act, only to find that his clubs had been plastered with Vaseline, rendering them useless. In retaliation and at a suitable opportunity, he stealthily made his way into The Gang's dressing rooms and promptly sewed up the bottoms of the trouser legs of the suits which they needed for a quick change!

Eddie himself was not unknown for his own diabolical antics. Once, in a busy London street, he peered into a red pillar box and exclaimed, 'However did you get in there? Don't worry, I will find someone who can get you out!' He used his ventriloquial skills to carry on the conversation with this imaginary person, trying to establish how it had all happened. A crowd gathered,

equally puzzled as to how someone could actually get themselves into such a bizarre situation. Once the crowd had grown to a respectable size, Eddie disappeared quietly, leaving a very concerned gathering worrying about when help would come.

Perhaps *London Rhapsody* was The Gang's worst behaved show of all. Anarchic humour abounded, with a soda siphon squirted at not only members of the cast but also the stage crew, which left them soaked. In one scene a manhole cover on stage was lifted up and a man partly climbed out, (whilst remaining standing on a ladder below), placed his elbows on stage and proceeded to sing a song. What he didn't realise until it was too late was that The Gang had made their way under the stage and climbed part of the way up the ladder after him. They undid the braces holding up the man's trousers and then proceeded to daub his legs with white paint. True professional that he was, he carried on singing throughout this escapade, with the audience knowing exactly nothing as to what had been going on 'underground'. George Black was informed however, and whilst heads didn't exactly roll, The Gang's knuckles were rapped.

The average season attendance at one of the Crazy Shows was anywhere between 500,000 and 600,000 people. Big business indeed! Bud and Ches were even able to form their own limited company, 'Flanagan and Allen Limited'. One press writer speculated, 'If "Simmy" Simpson, the Box Office Manager, who for a quarter of a century could have retained all of the £11,000,000 he has taken during his term of twenty-five years' service, I wonder how he would have spent it!' Other than the Palladium, I wonder if any other theatre has ever been able to say: 'Every seat is booked for the night of the Cup Final.' That's how it was at the Palladium in the 1930s. And did it not also show huge faith in the management on the part of patrons that such bookings could be made so far in advance, without the bookers having any idea what the performance would be?

During the nine-year 'reign' of The Crazy Gang, there had never been another single attraction which had brought people to one theatre in such large numbers over such a long period. They dominated comedy at the Palladium throughout the 1930s. Were The Gang crazy? Maybe, but loved by one and all.

Chapter Eight

I CAN FLY,
I CAN FLY!

*W*hen J.M. Barrie was born, his parents little thought that their son's name would live for all time, and that so many children and parents would be forever grateful for his bequests to the Great Ormond Street Hospital in London. Countless children have been cared for at this wonderful medical centre due to the generosity of this much-loved man, whose fantasy *Peter Pan* occupied the Palladium stage every Christmas for nearly ten years in the 1930s with special matinée performances.

James Matthew Barrie, who was born at Kirriemuir, Tayside in Scotland in 1860, and was later to be knighted in 1913, was an author of some merit. Although perhaps best known for *Peter Pan*, which he wrote in 1904, he should also be remembered for other familiar works; namely *Quality Street* (1901), *The Admirable Crichton* (1902), and *Dear Brutus* (1917). After he divorced, he

ANNA NEAGLE
as "PETER PAN"

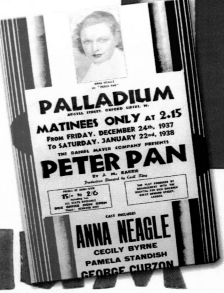

PALLADIUM

ARGYLL STREET, OXFORD CIRCUS, W.

MATINEES ONLY at 2.15

FROM FRIDAY, DECEMBER 24th, 1937
To SATURDAY, JANUARY 22nd, 1938

THE DANIEL MAYER COMPANY PRESENTS

PETER PAN

By J. M. BARRIE

Production Directed by Cecil King

PRICES OF ADMISSION
15/- to 2/6
Including Tax
ALL SEATS BOOKABLE
BOX OFFICE NOW OPEN
'Phone: GERRARD 2055

THE PLAY PRODUCED BY
ARRANGEMENT WITH THE
HOSPITAL FOR SICK CHILDREN
GREAT ORMOND STREET,
LONDON.

CAST INCLUDES

ANNA NEAGLE

CECILY BYRNE

PAMELA STANDISH

found great consolation in his somewhat obsessive affection for four young children whom he virtually adopted after their mother was widowed. It is thought that these children inspired him to write his immortal children's classic.

Barrie's first encounter with the Palladium was in 1912, when Miss Irene Vanbrugh and Mr Arthur Playfair appeared in his play, *The Twelve Pound Look*. This one act play was repeated in 1934, this time with Miss Ethel Barrymore playing the lead role of Kate, and Sir Nigel Playfair as Sir Harry Sims. However, it was to be the story of Peter and his friends that would immortalise Barrie's name and captivate the British public some years later.

Barrie donated the copyright of *Peter Pan* to the Great Ormond Street Hospital in 1929, and it was a year later that Peter and his friends were to fly for the first time at the Palladium. It was for matinées only, and the title role was played by Jean Forbes Robertson. She was to hold this title role for almost all of the time that the play was to be seen at the Palladium. However, other famous names included the sixteen-year-old British film star Nova Pilbeam in 1935–36 and Anna Neagle in 1937–38.

In the 1936–37 season Elsa Lanchester took over the role and partnered her husband, Charles Laughton, who played the double role of Mr Darling and Captain Hook with great distinction. Bud Flanagan recounts in his life story that when The Crazy Gang were out filming *O Kay for Sound* each day, by the time they had finished filming they had just about enough time to get back to their dressing room to change into their Palladium clothes, and they often exchanged pleasantries with Charles. In his autobiography, Bud says 'I must say he was the most considerate of actors; he kindly left us all his gin bottles!' Whether it was true or not, it was a typical Bud Flanagan remark. Other famous Captain Hooks have been played by no less than Seymour Hicks, George Curzon and Ralph Richardson.

One name that has been associated with *Peter Pan* for many years is that of Kirby, whose technology made it possible for Peter to fly. In 1934 *The Evening News* carried an interview which stated:

> Mr W. and Mr Joseph Kirby have, like their father before them, been engineering flight in ballet sequences and various plays and pantomimes for the past fifty years. The

first Peter flew in 1904. Such was the doubt of the London County Council inspectors that it took six of them to hang on one wire all at once before they were satisfied that it was strong enough to take the weight of Peter in the performance!

The breaking strain of the wire was 1200 pounds, and the twenty-two stone xylophonist Teddy Brown was allowed to fly for just a few moments to test the system. In 1906, when he was only sixteen, Mr Joseph Kirby went to tour the American and Canadian theatres with *Peter Pan* and the flying equipment.

Mr Kirby stated in an interview,

Before every performance the wires and ropes are thoroughly tested – that is why one never sees any hitch in the flying arrangements on the stage. [There would be specially trained backstage flying staff in attendance at each performance.] Each actor or actress has their own personal 'flyer' to manage their own individual ropes and wires. They are each responsible for the initial fixing of the apparatus and for the making of the flight during the performance. Much responsibility is attached to the job as, not only can the flying men make the show absurd, should the actor fly backwards or swing helplessly suspended above the set, but there can even be accidents where bones may be broken. A specially designed harness is fitted to the body of the performer in question and there is a little slit in the back of the costume for the hook to be attached when the performer is in the wings ready to make an entrance in any particular scene. The lights are suitably dimmed so that the carrying wires will not show. It is a surprisingly thin, but strong wire designed not to show, but at the back the ropes that pull the wire are a thick as your wrist, and the muscles of the men who pull them are equally reassuring. To take off on the 'flight' the actor must stoop very slightly and unnoticeably. Kirbys have brought the take off and landing to a fine art as though there is no connection. When, for example, the children take off to fly through the window, they must stand in specially predetermined marks on the stage. If this is not done precisely then they will hit against the window frame with possible damage to themselves and the scenery!

LONDON PALLADIUM
Argyll Street, London W1. 'Phone: 01-437 7373. Box Office open daily 10am to 9pm (except Sunday)
Commencing Weds. Dec. 17th at 7.0. subs. 2·45 twice daily 7·30 until Jan. 17th, thereafter Evenings at 7·30 Matinees: Wed., Thurs. & Sats. at 2·45
By arrangement with LOUIS BENJAMIN
TOM ARNOLD PRESENTATIONS LTD.
in association with HOWARD & WYNDHAM LTD.
present
LULU
RON MOODY
RACHEL GURNEY
in
PETER PAN
J.M. BARRIE'S Immortal Play
with
TESSA WYATT
TONY SYMPSON
PETER BLAND
THE ROBERT HELPMAN PRODUCTION
Directed by ALAN PINNIGER
Choreography by AUBREY BUDD
Musical Director DEREK TAVERNER
Music by GRANT FOSTER & JOHN CROOK
Fight Director MALCOLM RANSON
Flying Effects by HI-FB

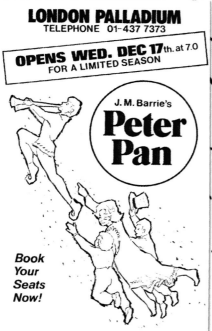

The Daily Sketch often donated the whole house so that poor and deserving children could witness the magic of *Peter Pan.* Sir James Barrie often sat in the box at the side of the auditorium to witness the thrill on the faces of the children. He always picked the actress who would play Peter.

After the 1938–39 production, it took the 'tick, tock, tick, tock' of villainous Captain Hook's clock some thirty-seven more years to pass before Peter Pan flew again at the London Palladium. This time in the role of Peter, primarily through the success of her TV appearances and in the pop music field, was Marie MacDonald McLaughlin Lawrie, better known and loved by us all as Lulu. The rest of the cast was made up of names from TV and films. The versatile and very talented Ron Moody played a very dramatic Hook, and clearly loved every minute of the hisses and boos and consequential audience participation. Classical theatre actress Rachel Gurney was Mrs Darling, with Wendy being played by TV actress Tessa Wyatt. This being a Robert Helpman Production, precision and meticulous detail were exacted from all the cast and a wonderful production yet again benefited the Great Ormond Street Hospital in London.

Just as Peter Pan lived forever, so will J.M. Barrie's wonderful story, with his kindness and generosity benefiting thousands of children along the way.

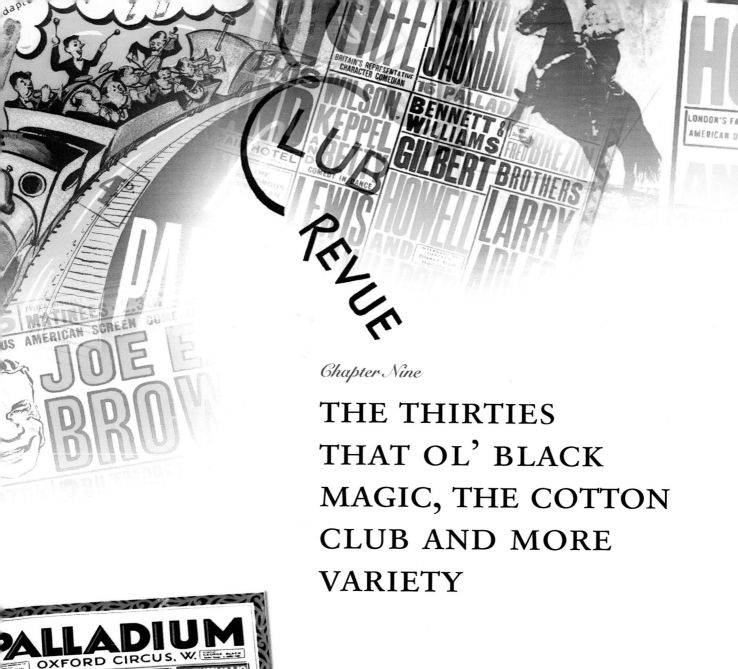

Chapter Nine

THE THIRTIES THAT OL' BLACK MAGIC, THE COTTON CLUB AND MORE VARIETY

*W*ith television very much in its embryonic stage and with only the radio and moving pictures for regular entertainment, to have an evening out, perhaps with a meal first, and then a trip to the theatre, was a real 'event' for members of the general public. The ladies would dress in all their finery and the gentlemen would wear black tie to sit in the stalls and view their favourite stars; famous names, who up until then could only be seen on the big screen or heard over the air waves.

It would take a complete book all on its own to list *all* the celebrities who appeared on the Palladium stage. The home-grown stars included individuals like Nellie Wallace, Charlie Austin, Will Hay, Nat Mills and Bobbie,

119

Will Fyffe, Wee Georgie Wood, Robb Wilton, and Hutch, whose popularity ensured that they all made many appearances. George Clarke bought and sold his car many times in his trademark routine. Whole orchestras and popular bands topped the bill on many an occasion, with big names of the day like Billy Cotton, Jack Payne, Jack Hylton, Geraldo, Harry Roy and Debroy Somers. Ambrose appeared in 1938, together with the up-and-coming trombone player Edward Heath, and the talented young vocalist Vera Lynn. Christopher Stone was 'steam'

radio's first disc jockey, whose stage act consisted of sitting in an armchair and playing a few selected 78s of the day. I doubt if today's public would stand for that!

In 1932 Jack Hylton brought to London 'the Continent's Greatest Symphonic Jazz Orchestra', Ray Ventura et Ses Collegiens. It would be Ray's nephew, Sacha Distel, who would make his own mark at the Palladium some forty years later. Lew Stone and his Monseigneur Band, with Al Bowley on vocals and guitar, made several appearances because they were so successful with the public. The best bands from overseas came too, with Dave Apollon, Louis Armstrong, Cab Calloway singing 'Hi de hi', super jazz from Hollywood with Abe Lyman, Glen Miller's arranger bandleader Ray Noble, and Ted Lewis and his Musical Clowns. And, of course, not forgetting Duke Ellington. Duke once recounted to the press how he started as a young boy of thirteen by playing at a private party for four hours non-stop. At the end his fingers bled from the ordeal, but he managed to rush home with his fee of seventy-five cents to show his proud mother. This was notably different from his current fee at The Cotton Club of £1,400 a week. The press report went on to say that as Ellington was olive skinned, he had to use make-up to darken his skin for some of his appearances in the southern States. His UK tour was an immediate sell-out.

Talented individual musicians came too, like Joe Venuti, The Hot Club de France with Stephane Grappelli and Django Reinhardt, and xylophonist Teddy Brown. Layton and Johnston also graced the stage. They all said that the real star was the theatre itself.

In between the various Crazy Gang offerings, George Black produced some really exceptional shows with some of the world's top variety stars. Although the Johnny Mercer lyrics of 'That Old Black Magic' would become popular a decade later, Black himself certainly had a touch of 'magic' with all his productions. He had flair and a talent for spotting which was the perfect act to complement each variety bill. One such double act was George Burns and Gracie Allen, who made several later appearances. The press stated that at that time they were the highest paid radio stars in the world, which really was some achievement, bearing in mind that five years earlier they were just a small-priced music hall act. As a result of their Palladium appearance they gained literally pages and pages of press coverage. Their close friend, Jack Benny, also made an appearance, not to mention Arthur Tracy, 'The Street Singer'.

The best known nose in the shape of Jimmy Durante appeared for two weeks, as did Bebe Daniels and Ben Lyon. They both came over to Britain specially and loved it so much that they stayed to make a considerable impact on radio. Metro-Goldwyn-Mayer (MGM) matinée idol Ramon Novarro made a rare stage appearance and the fans had to be cleared from the stage door area with a fire

hose! Other American imports included Joe E. Brown, Tallulah Bankhead, and Will Mahoney, whose act was to tap dance on a xylophone, tapping out the tune. Everyone's 'Yiddisher Momma', Sophie Tucker, must not be forgotten either. The Boswell Sisters were another act, and it is interesting to note that it was these visitors from the USA who were the first act to appear at the Palladium with their own amplification system. The Stage Management were so impressed with this equipment that they asked them to leave it behind after they had finished their week's stay. To this they happily agreed, and in doing so they made their niche in Palladium theatre history. Columbia Picture stars, Curley, Larry and Moe, (better known as The Three Stooges), topped the bill for two weeks. Musical comedy star Carl Brisson, Molly Picon, The Mills Brothers, Fats Waller, and Tom Mix, complete with his wonder horse 'Tony', also featured. Billy Costello, known to millions as the voice of 'Popeye', and America's foremost entertainer, Harry Richman, came to Argyll Street too. They all made their own individual mark of distinction, not only with the public but also with the press. It really was a 'Who's Who' in the showbiz world all of its own.

Sandwiched in between the acts from America were Max Miller, always making a welcome return, Henry Hall and his Orchestra, and Gracie Fields. The Western Brothers, George Robey, Stanley Holloway, Billy Bennett, George Formby, Lucan and McShane, Evelyn Laye, Dick Henderson, Jessie Matthews, and Florence Desmond; they were all topping or joint-topping their respective highly successful bills. Equally competent supporting acts like Wilson Keppel and Betty in *Cleopatra's Nightmare* were there alongside them. Their act became a classic in a very short space of time. None of these shows could have been presented without a plethora of supporting acts, and their highly important role is detailed in another chapter.

Whilst it can be verified that the metal palladium was discovered in 1803, according to the press radium was discovered in July 1933... at the Palladium. Those who have studied medicine or science will know that this is not strictly accurate. However, it appears that a Dr Bertram Shires of Welbeck Street, who was honorary radiologist to the Infants' Hospital in Vincent Square,

London, had been lending radium to another hospital every Friday on a regular basis. By Saturday, Dr Shires had not received back the lead-lined attaché case. He rang the hospital immediately and was told that it had been sent off in the care of a taxi driver in the normal way. The case was valued at £1000, and the mystery deepened when Scotland Yard was brought in. Luckily, as a precaution, the number of the cab had been taken on this occasion. The cabbie was traced very quickly and it turned out that the hospital had said 'radium' as the driver pulled away. Thinking they had said 'Palladium', he had delivered it to the Manager of the theatre who had signed for it, not really knowing what was going on. Like every good fairy story it all ended happily!

In July 1937 and for the first time outside New York, the authentic *Cotton Club Revue* in its entirety came to the Palladium. The Cotton Club was to New York what the Folies Bergère is to Paris. It was the Mecca of entertainment seekers. Ever since 1924, The Cotton Club had reigned supreme over the nightlife of Harlem. Every world celebrity had made the journey to Lennox Avenue

to visit the sanctuary of the black population. Since its inception, The Cotton Club had been the cradle of every black entertainer of note in the world. Such famous personalities as Florence Mills, Cab Calloway, Duke Ellington, The Mills Brothers, Ethel Walters and The Nicholas Brothers all made their first appearance there. Songs and dances created by The Cotton Club were sensational. Every year it introduced a new dance, each one more popular than the last, 'The Black Bottom' and 'The Lindy Hopper' perhaps being the most internationally famous.

Now it was London's turn to judge The Cotton Club, and highly successful it was too. Sixty of Harlem's famous entertainers in the fastest entertainment show in the world took London by storm on 26 July for a short season. Running twice daily for five highly successful weeks, the first half of the show was highlighted with top English acts such as the inimitable Ted Ray, Wences the famous ventriloquist, Norman Evans, Lucan and McShane, Gene Sheldon and Tex McLeod. The second half had the complete *Cotton Club Revue* with Teddy Hill conducting The Cotton Orchestra. The show comprised such acts as Bill Bailey the Rhythm Tap Dancer, The Three Berry Brothers, Whyte's Hopping Maniacs, and The Twenty-Five Copper Coloured Gals. The press said it all: 'Supercharged jazz served at breathtaking speed by sixty boys and gals from New York. It is chock full of irresistibly accurate and varied rhythm.' It was a highly profitable short season that London's West End will not forget.

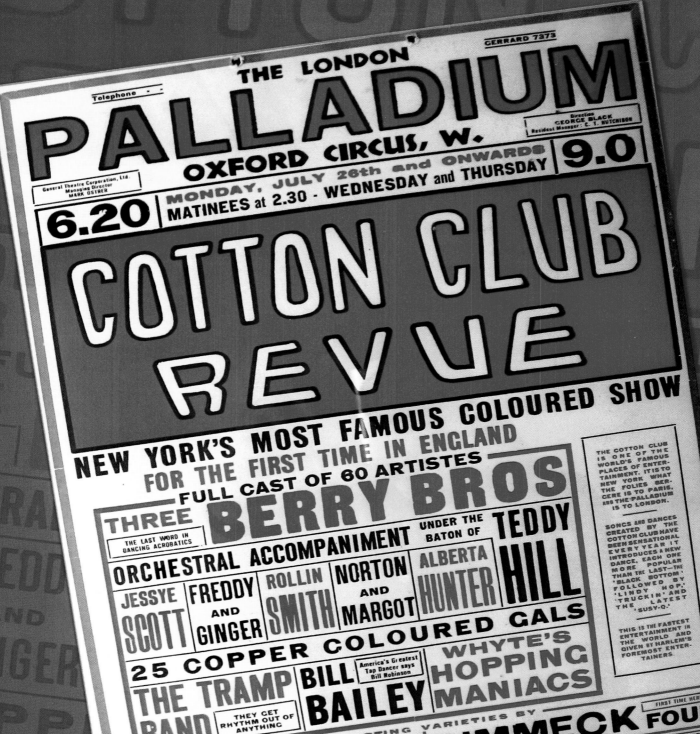

Lookalikes are nothing new today, for in 1938 The Hollywood Star Doubles made an appearance for their first time in Europe. Their act featured doubles and stand-ins of famous names on the silver screen, such as Loretta Young, Greta Garbo, Mae West, Joan Crawford, Marlene Dietrich, Zasu Pitts, Hugh Herbert, W.C. Fields, Victor McLaglen and Bing Crosby.

In 1939, *Bandwaggon* was another show to transfer to the stage from its successful radio platform. It starred Arthur Askey, Tommy Trinder, Richard 'Stinker' Murdoch and Florence Desmond, and just like a stick of rock, it had laughter all the way through. Richard Murdoch said that during one of the sketches they were all dressed up in brightly coloured, floral plus four costumes and white trilby hats. One afternoon, Max Miller heard about the item and came along to see the show. He came to the front and engaged in some light-hearted banter with Tommy Trinder, who got the better of Max only because he had access to a microphone! One of the items in the show introduced the British public to the dance sensation of 1939, the 'Boomps-a-Daisy', onstage for the first time. Richard Murdoch and others in the cast would venture into the audience to pick a partner for the 'Boomps-a-Daisy' routine. One of the girls in the show told Richard, 'my sister is coming in this afternoon, do you think you could Boomp her Daisy?' Murdoch, ever the gentleman, said he would be happy to. The girl in the show was Kim Kendall, and the twelve-year-old in the audience was Kay Kendall, who later went onto bigger things. On another occasion, American comedian Jack Durante told the cast, 'Bob Hope is coming round this afternoon', to which everyone replied, 'Who is Bob Hope?' Remember this was 1939!

Within this successful *Bandwaggon* show was an item entitled *Youth Takes a Bow*. Several youngsters appeared for the very first time in public, with some making their first of many appearances to come on this prestigious stage. Lucille, the talented teenage conjurer, for example, or Maureen Potter, the lovely Irish colleen, who later became an institution in her native land with co-star Jimmy O'Dea. Arthur Tolcher, the wizard of the mouth organ, who would find later fame on the *Morecambe and Wise* TV show. Another teenager was Mary Naylor from Nottingham, who enchanted the audience with her lovely voice and charming personality. Perhaps the name to last the longest though was that of Ernest Wiseman. He later teamed up with Eric Bartholomew, and they became the much loved duo, Morecambe and Wise. Ernie started his career as a very young singer with Jack Hylton's band, and on this occasion sang 'Lets Have a Tiddly at the Milk Bar.'

Ironically, *Bandwaggon* closed on 2 September 1939, as it had come to the end of its run. The following day was one that the whole of Britain would never, ever forget.

Chapter Ten

WWII IN W1

W hile the West End (W1) was generally suffering after the war had started, Jack Hylton had meanwhile acquired the stage rights to the popular BBC radio programme *Garrison Theatre*, featuring Jack Warner and his 'little gel' Joan Winters. After a week's try-out in Brighton, home to many a West End trial run, the new show finally took to the stage at the Palladium on 13 May 1940, and it proved to be very popular with West End audiences. And just like *Bandwaggon*, here was another occasion where the public were able to actually see their idols from 'steam radio' in the flesh. A novelty indeed! With few exceptions, the press and public alike enjoyed the radio stars in their new, albeit temporary home.

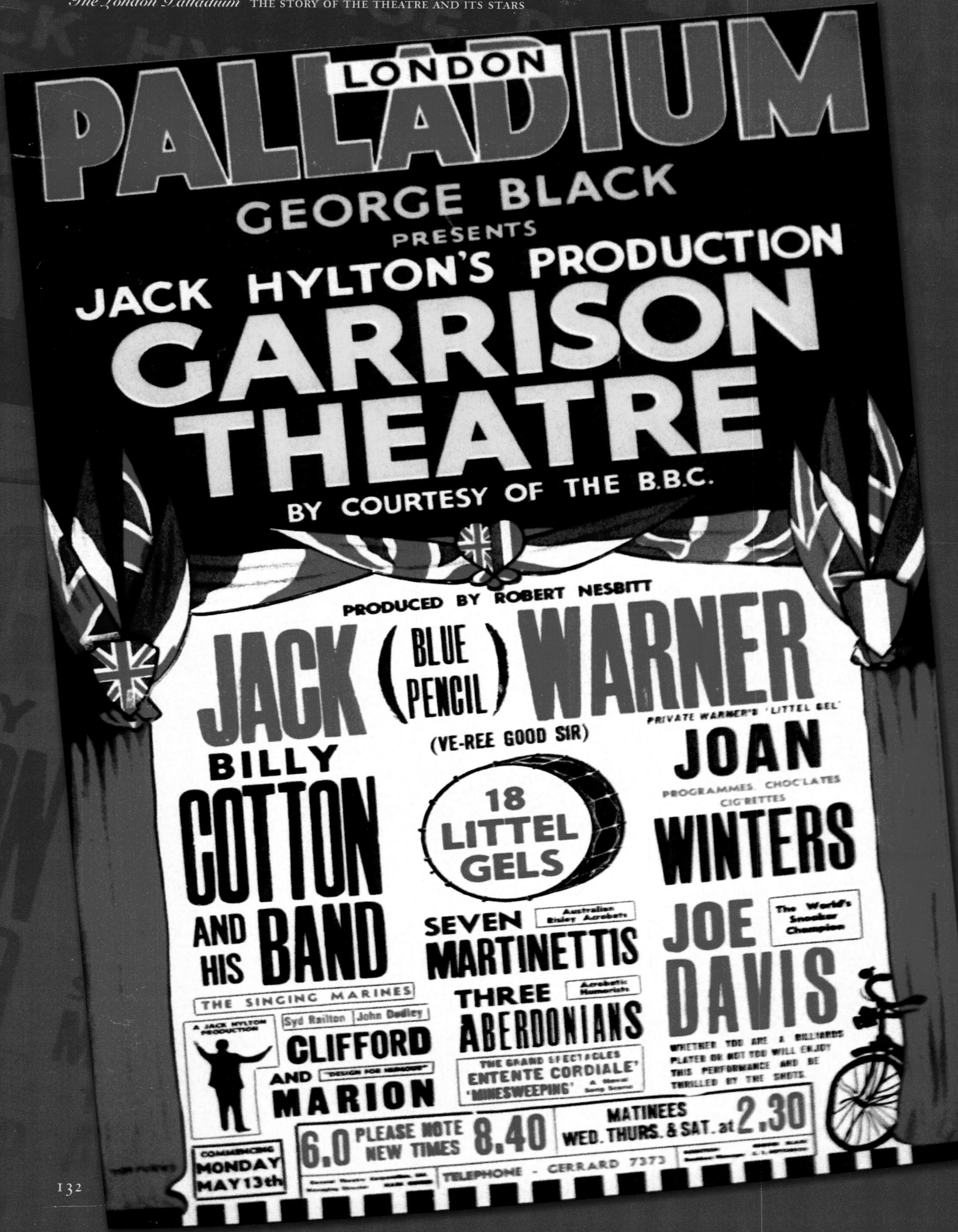

LONDON
PALLADIUM
GEORGE BLACK
PRESENTS
JACK HYLTON'S PRODUCTION
GARRISON THEATRE
BY COURTESY OF THE B.B.C.
PRODUCED BY ROBERT NESBITT
JACK (BLUE PENCIL) WARNER
(VE-REE GOOD SIR)
PRIVATE WARNER'S 'LITTEL GEL'
JOAN
PROGRAMMES, CHOC'LATES CIG'RETTES
WINTERS
BILLY COTTON AND HIS BAND
18 LITTEL GELS
SEVEN MARTINETTIS
Australian Risley Acrobats
JOE DAVIS
The World's Snooker Champion
WHETHER YOU ARE A BILLIARDS PLAYER OR NOT YOU WILL ENJOY THIS PERFORMANCE AND BE THRILLED BY THE SHOTS.
THE SINGING MARINES
A JACK HYLTON PRODUCTION
Syd Railton
John Dudley
CLIFFORD AND MARION
THREE ABERDONIANS
Acrobatic Humorists
THE GRAND SPECTACLES
'ENTENTE CORDIALE'
'MINESWEEPING'
COMMENCING MONDAY MAY 13th
6.0 PLEASE NOTE NEW TIMES 8.40
MATINEES WED. THURS. & SAT. at 2.30
TELEPHONE - GERRARD 7373

As well as Tessie O'Shea and Billy Cotton and his Band beefing up the show, The Three Aberdonians and Joe Davis, 'The Wizard of the Cue', completed the cast. Joe, who had been the World Snooker Champion for fourteen successive years and the UK Billiards Champion for ten years really entertained the audience with his skill. For them to be able to see his trick shots more clearly, a huge angled mirror was erected at the back of the stage to show the snooker table and demonstrate the undoubted skill of this unlikely addition to this show. Another item in the show which was more on the lines of traditional Variety was provided by Harry Tate Junior carrying on the family tradition with his father's immortal *Motoring* sketch.

Jack Warner was of course in uniform, as one would expect, not to mention the members of the orchestra. There were men who sat 'guard' on each side of the proscenium, and to keep the mood the commissionaires and other attendants were all similarly dressed; even the ladies who dispensed the drinks in the bars were wearing military attire, which all added to the atmosphere. The press announced 'Servicemen on leave in London may see the show free of charge. They will be admitted showing their leave passes or they may apply to the Management at the theatre.' All they had to do in return was join in the fun and help with the choruses. A fair exchange! It was very appropriate that the 200th anniversary of the song 'Rule Britannia' should be commemorated in a special tableau at the Palladium in August 1940, when it was introduced into part of the *Garrison Theatre* production.

After a seemingly continuous run of record-breaking productions at the Palladium, the next show which followed *Garrison Theatre* would also eventually end up in this theatre's record books, but this time for the shortest run ever. Only four performances! *Top of the World* was the name of the show, and once again George Black had invested a tremendous amount of money and effort into this Robert Nesbitt production, with Harry Parr Davies writing the music. With relative newcomer Tommy Trinder and a somewhat diminished Crazy Gang in the shape of Flanagan and Allen together with Nervo and Knox, the show was backed up by Pat Kirkwood, Helen Breen and Nancy Evans. A chorus of sixty and sixteen spectacular settings completed the show. The cast was as good as anything that had gone before, and the cost of the production was £36,000, a lot of money to invest in a show that would eventually close down after such a short run of so few performances.

Unfortunately, everything was rationed, from food to fuel. Paper shortages dictated that all printed matter had to be reduced and so the programmes appeared in a very limited edition. What had previously been colourful items with copious notes and detail were now reduced to slimline editions with very limited information.

Thoughtful programme notes informed theatre patrons that, 'those expecting Telephone Calls or Messages are requested to leave the number of their seats at The Box Office.' Other sombre notices were already beginning to appear in the programmes:

> If an air raid warning is received during the performance the audience will be informed from the stage. The warning will not necessarily mean that a raid will take place and in any case it is not likely to occur for at least five minutes. Those desiring to leave the theatre may do so, but the performance will continue and members are advised in their own interests to remain the building.

These were grim warnings indeed. The Great Marlborough Street police station was immediately next door, so there was never any doubt about hearing the warning that the siren was about to go off; everyone in the theatre would be able to hear it.

On the first night of *Top of the World*, the theatre was crowded. The Manager, having received the siren warning, waited for a pause in The Crazy Gang's dialogue, and then going onto the stage, made the announcement. Not one person left the theatre. The show

went on uninterrupted! Later, when Tommy Trinder was doing his front cloth act and telling the audience how 'lucky' they were that he was on the stage, the Manager signalled to him from the wings. 'What you have been waiting for has happened', he said. 'It's the all clear.'

Astute businessman Tommy then instituted a novel idea of a sweepstake amongst the cast. The eight principals in the cast contributed half a crown (2s. 6d., or twelve pence in new money) at each of the performances, and the pool was taken by whoever was speaking when the siren sounded. Tommy won the second round and all subsequent rounds, for he had worked out that the air raid siren went off at a specific time, and he happened to be on stage at that time! 'You Lucky People'!

George Black had invested a considerable fortune in the three shows he was presenting in the West End at this point. An estimated total of just over 100 tons of scenery was in use at the Palladium, the Hippodrome, and the Holborn Empire. To have sent the shows out of town and then brought them back again would have entailed a horrendous logistics problem. He would have needed at least 320 railway trucks to transport the scenery and effects needed. With petrol rationing, road transport was out of the question. These shows therefore had no tryouts in Brighton; they opened 'cold' in the West End.

Peter Yorke hardly had time to lift his baton on the fourth night when, due to a very serious air raid on London, the siren went off. A bomb had landed on the Holborn Empire theatre, destroying not only part of the theatre itself but also most of the scenery in the show *Applesauce*. As a result, *Top of the World* at the Palladium came to an end, and by order of the government all theatres in the West End had to close due to concerns for public safety. A massive blow indeed, not only to the producers who had invested large sums of money, but also to the profession, whose members would either be out of work or end up entertaining the troops at the front. The war was getting decidedly worse.

Salvaging what he could from the Holborn Empire theatre, George Black added extra scenery and new cloths and re-edited the old Holborn show. On 5 March 1941 *Applesauce*, subtitled 'A Laughter Blitz Showered with Stars', re-opened at the Palladium. The 'New Recipe', as the press hailed it, starred Max Miller and Florence Desmond, Kenneth and George, and The Western Brothers (who were really cousins). Bud Flanagan and Chesney Allen sent a telegram to George Black wishing him luck with the show and the message ended: 'Tell Max Miller to keep our dressing room clean'!

Also in the show was a relative newcomer to the Palladium stage, the 'Singer of Sweet Songs', Vera Lynn. Vera had appeared earlier in 1938 as a singer with Ambrose and his Octet and alongside 'The Continent's most glamorous personality', Josephine Baker. However, in a very short space of time Vera had become one of the biggest money-makers in the entertainment world. Her records were selling as many as Bing Crosby's. Although her signature tune was 'Yours', another song,

'We'll Meet Again', was already becoming her most popular tune. All these years later it is still the piece of music that has become synonymous with Dame Vera Lynn. On one occasion when she was taken ill in the wings with appendicitis, Fred Emney deputised for Vera, but he couldn't match her charm and box office draw.

Before the Blitz and the theatre closures, the number of Palladium staff, excluding artists, was 190. One by one, almost to a man, they returned to keep the theatre wheels turning. Because of the blackout and its strict regulations, shows had to finish early in order to allow patrons to return home in reasonable time. In order to help this situation Double Summer Time was considered by the Government. If an extra hour was to be added to the existing summertime, shows of all types could continue until 9.00 or 10.00pm in the evening and still leave enough light for the theatregoers to get home in time. Sunday theatre was even considered and finally approved along with that extra hour, giving box office receipts a much-needed boost. As it was, the box office receipts were in the region of £5,000 per week.

With the two daily performances of *Applesauce* beginning at 2.00pm and 4.30pm, the times would be put forward an hour each month. Advance bookings for the show were almost as they would have been pre-war. One paper declared:

> Max Miller, the enfant terrible of the theatre, walks as near to the censorial precipice as he dares and, grinning disarmingly, threatens less than usual to topple over. The man is a natural born comic anyway and is quite capable of amusing the crowd even away from the edge of things. He said that he had to pay eight shillings and sixpence a yard for the lovely crêpe de chine material for his stage outfits that were always made by a company called Binns of Morecambe. [I hate to think how many clothing coupons he needed for his ten suits a year.] "I've got to have new ones, you know, because the ladies are always catching up with my colours!" It was reported in the press that he had ten new suits made a year.

Due to the generosity of an anonymous benefactor, the cost of the hire of the theatre was paid for, which enabled a tribute show to take place in recognition of the tremendous efforts all the London Air Raid Wardens had put in during the Blitz. George Black arranged a special morning matinée where the audience was composed entirely of London ARP Wardens. Mr Herbert Morrison, the Home Secretary, addressed this special audience and declared that they occupied a unique position amongst all the branches of the Civil Defence Services. Among those also present were the King of Norway and Crown Prince Olaf.

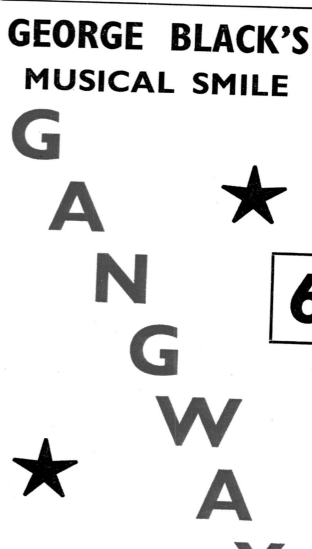

THE PALLADIUM
OXFORD CIRCUS, W.I
TELEPHONE : GERRARD 7373

2-30 — TWICE DAILY — 5-15

GEORGE BLACK'S
MUSICAL SMILE

GANGWAY

6d

Produced by ROBERT NESBITT
DANCES ARRANGED BY WENDY TOYE
THE WHOLE PRODUCTION UNDER THE PERSONAL SUPERVISION OF
GEORGE BLACK

On 29 November the theatre closed to allow George Black to prepare for his new 'musical smile', *Gangway*, which opened on 17 December 1941. Just like a number of earlier shows it had been derived from the popular BBC radio series. It starred Bebe Daniels and Ben Lyon bringing their own 'Hi Gang!' radio personalities to life. Ben had become a film star just by asking a director, 'How do I get into films?' The director said, 'Report here tomorrow' and he did just that. There was a box in the theatre that had been bought by Ben and Bebe purely for the benefit and use of US servicemen who wanted to see the show. Anne Ziegler and Webster Booth also starred, and the ubiquitous Tommy Trinder. Once again Robert Nesbitt produced the show and the choreography was by Wendy Toye.

Few comedians of the day or perhaps even since could equal Tommy's flair and ability to get to know the audience in the shortest space of time. He had the quick-witted resource to secure laughs without a script. He was without doubt the master ad-libber. He once said: 'You work all your life to get your name in lights and then comes the blackout!' Stardom had previously eluded him on two occasions. (Remember that *Top of the World* had closed after four days due to the war.) The press now hailed him as 'a One Man Crazy Gang'. At the same time he embarked upon his own original public relations campaign, whereby he had his name emblazoned on a selected number of hoardings in Piccadilly Circus, Leicester Square and other major sites with the slogan, 'If it's Laughter You're After, Trinder's the Name. You Lucky People!' With no mention of the Palladium at all, it was a remarkable piece of outdoor advertising.

Even in Aldgate, there were a dozen or so shop windows embellished with posters in Yiddish extolling the talents of Trinder. What lucky people! He had engaged the services of a Hebrew scribe to translate his famous slogan into Hebrew script. When asked how much he required for the exercise, the scribe said 10s. 6d. (fifty-five pence). Tommy was so thrilled with the work that he proceeded to pull out a big white fiver from his wallet and happily handed it over to him for the work. Remember that Trinder was not only earning big money, (£3,000 a week), such was the demand for his services, but he was also paying 19s. 6d. in the pound in income tax, so this was all legitimately 'tax deductible'.

It was rumoured that a question was about to be asked in the Houses of Parliament as to how, in these times of war with paper rationing, could enough paper be found and used for such trivial advertising? 'Let them ask,' Tommy said, 'and I'll get more publicity by telling them it is painted on tin, and that isn't rationed!!' The whole concept of the slogan 'If It's Laughter You're After' was dreamed up by a Mr G.L. McLellan, the General Manager of the Borough Bill Posting Company.

On the opening night of *Gangway*, Tommy received a telegram from Vic Oliver saying, 'Please use all my best gags, I've got to maintain my reputation!' Along with others, Tommy did fire duty after the curtain had come down until 9.00am the following day. 'It pays me to look after my own interests,' he said. 'If the theatre burned down I would lose my job!' Kim Kendall, sister to Kay Kendall and daughter of Marie Kendall, introduced Teddy Brown the xylophonist. Added to the already strong cast were Rona Ricardo, Lamar and Rosita, and the gowns were by Hartnell. (Rationing was in place; surely you remember clothing coupons?) Choreography by Wendy Toye coupled with Debroy Somers and the Palladium Orchestra ensured another success for George Black. An experiment of offering afternoon tea at 4.00pm in the Palm Court prior to the matinées at 5.15pm proved a great success. After 535 performances, a run of forty-five weeks and a record of £250,000 in takings, the show ended on 24 October 1942.

Best Bib and Tucker was the next George Black wartime production and it opened on 7 November 1942. 'An opulent show', said one reviewer. 'For colourfulness, variety and humour, *Best Bib and Tucker* ranks high in the long list of Palladium shows', 'as lavish a production as any in town', 'a sumptuous show' and 'gay, witty and amusing', said others. The critics loved it and it would seem that George Black had another hit on his hands. It ran for twenty-one weeks. Whether as a song and dance man, or as a witty conjurer, Tommy Trinder starred once more. In one of his famous sketches he dressed as Carmen Miranda, complete with long green eyelashes and scarlet fingernails, and appeared with Edmundo Ros and his Band (the popular 'name' at the Astor Club and the Bagatelle Room) in a new number: 'No, No, No, No Columbus', specially written by Val Guest. Edmundo went on to become one of Britain's best loved and

most sought after latin music artists, appearing again in the 1950s in *The Peep Show* and culminating in an appearance at The Royal Variety Performance in 1962. He was still entertaining well into the 1990s. Crazy comic dancer Nat 'rubberneck' Jackley, songstress Mary Naylor, celebrated clowns The Cairoli Brothers, and Baker, Dove and Allen, the international jugglers, all complemented the bill, with Debroy Somers in charge of the pit band. Perhaps not one of George Black's strongest bills, but successful nevertheless at the box office. It took between £5,000 and £6,000 per week, and ended on 21 August 1943.

Mary Naylor

With tours to North Africa for ENSA and two films, *Fiddlers Three* and *Champagne Charlie* to make, Trinder's gruelling schedule was too hectic to contemplate another season at the Palladium, even though he had been 'doubling' at the Hammersmith Palace at the time that *Best Bib and Tucker* was ending. After an absence of five years a welcome change was needed, and George Black decided it was time to revert to that which the Palladium had earlier become synonymous with. Variety! English Music Hall at its best!

Variety Comes Back opened on 24 August with five acts which were new to the Palladium: Anne Shelton, Syd and Max Harrison, The O'Doyle Brothers and Jean, The Four Kenways and The Australian Air Aces. 'A High Speed show with an entire absence of stage waits, elaborate full sets and appropriate "drops" for front cloth acts which is a tribute to George Black and Harry Brack and his backstage crew', noted the *Performer* in its write-up. When 'Cheeky Chappie' Max Miller, Billy Cotton and his Band and Issy Bonn were added to this list, you had a very strong bill indeed.

The opening night's two houses were sold out long before the show opened. Business remained at capacity with 'House Full' signs at both daily performances. With shows at 2.30 and 5.15pm, local patrons still had enough time to return home before the blackout. Although originally booked for four weeks it ran for eleven, and nearly 320,000 people saw the show. Just before the short season closed, a special Sunday Concert was laid on in October for all the Forces with all the artists giving their services for free. At the end of the season Max Miller was to embark on a completely different aspect to his career. The young impresario producer, Bernard Delfont, had acquired the rights to *Sailor Beware* and had booked Max to play the lead.

The next production to grace the Palladium was to be one that would be remembered for many, many years to come, primarily because of its star performer, Irving Berlin. The show, *This is the Army*, consisted entirely of 150 US Soldiers; privates, corporals, and sergeants (and no officers!). Ninety per cent of them were amateurs, and they had played all over America to packed houses and made millions of dollars for the American Army Emergency Relief Fund. After the first night on Broadway

Irving Berlin

in early July 1942 the American critics all agreed that this was one of the grandest musicals to hit 'The Great White Way'. It opened in London on 10 November 1943 and was sponsored by the British Services Charities Committee, Lady Mountbatten being one of the joint Chairmen. The entire production was staged under the personal supervision of Irving Berlin. 'This is the Army Mr. Jones', 'I Left my Heart at the Stage Door Canteen', 'With my Head in the Clouds' and 'This Time' were just some of the hit songs.

The highlight naturally was Irving Berlin himself, dressed as a serviceman from the First World War and singing 'Oh How I Hate to Get Up in the Morning'. This was a song that he wrote and introduced in his World War One show 'Yip Yip Yaphank' when he was a sergeant stationed at Camp Upton, Yaphank, New York. This was not Berlin's first time to be singing in Britain, however. He had appeared in *Hullo Ragtime* for a week in 1913 with Ethel Levy and George Graves and he had sung later with Ambrose and his Orchestra on his honeymoon in 1926. He was to sing again much, much later in 1948 when, as an ordinary paying guest in the theatre, he had come to see The Andrews Sisters and was persuaded to come up on the stage by Patti and sing 'Alexander's Ragtime Band'.

A front page programme note for *This is the Army* stated:

TO OUR ALLIES: In initiating an overseas tour of Irving Berlin's *This Is The Army*, General George C. Marshall, Chief of Staff of the United States Army, personally imposed two stipulations: First, that the soldiers of our Allies, as well as American enlisted men, should see this Army show free of cost; and, second, that all monies realised from the tour of the United Kingdom should go to British service charities. Several performances will be given exclusively for Allied troops, and one-third of the house for each public performance will be reserved for soldiers; while all funds from the purchase of tickets by officers and civilians will be handled by the British Service Charities Committee. Also, it should be made clear that the one hundred and fifty men who make up the cast are soldiers. Following their tour of Great Britain, they will be sent to Africa to play before Allied soldiers, then will join America's fighting forces. If you find *This Is The Army* entertaining, it will have served an important purpose. Entertainment is an essential to high morale, a fact which is understood, surely, throughout the British Empire, where astonishing esprit stood alone, for a time, against the barbaric effort to conquer the civilized world. Also, I hope *This Is The Army* will play a part in cementing international friendships along the grim road to eventual victory.

signed Jacob L. Devers,

Lieut. General US Army, Commanding

During this run, some 30,000 soldiers saw the show for free, programmes were gratis too, and after the all too short season it toured to other major cities in Britain and Northern Ireland and then went to North Africa. In all it was thought that the show raised somewhere between three and ten million dollars for charities.

At the young age of fifty-four Berlin, born Israel Baline, the son of a Russian rabbi, was reputed to earn £100,000 from his song-writing successes. In thirty-five years he had already written over 800 songs, with 'I'm Dreaming of a White Christmas' and 'God Bless America' being the most popular. His works also included 'Blue Skies', 'Easter Parade', 'Top Hat, White Tie and Tails', 'Lets Face the Music and Dance', 'A Pretty Girl is like a Melody' and, perhaps the most famous, 'There's No

THE PALLADIUM

TO OUR ALLIES :

In initiating an overseas tour of Irving Berlin's "This Is The Army," General George C. Marshall, Chief of Staff of the United States Army, personally imposed two stipulations : First, that the soldiers of our Allies, as well as American enlisted men, should see this Army show free of cost ; and, second, that all monies realised from the tour of the United Kingdom should go to British service charities.

Several performances will be given exclusively for Allied troops, and one-third of the house for each public performance will be reserved for soldiers ; while all funds from the purchase of tickets by officers and civilians will be handled by the British Service Charities Committee.

Also, it should be made clear that the one hundred and fifty men who make up the cast are soldiers. Following their tour of Great Britain, they will be sent to Africa to play before Allied soldiers, then will join America's fighting forces.

If you find "This Is The Army" entertaining, it will have served an important purpose. Entertainment is an essential to high morale, a fact which is understood, surely, throughout the British Empire, where astonishing esprit stood alone, for a time, against the barbaric effort to conquer the civilized world.

Also, I hope "This Is The Army" will play a part in cementing international friendships along the grim road to eventual victory.

JACOB L. DEVERS
Lieut. General, U. S. Army, Commanding.

g an overseas tour of
n's "This Is The Army,"
orge C. Marshall, Chief
the United States Army,
mposed two stipulations :
e soldiers of our Allies,
American enlisted men,
this Army show free of
second, that all monies
m the tour of the United
ould go to British service

erformances will be given
for Allied troops, and one-
e house for each public
ce will be reserved for
while all funds from the
f tickets by officers and
ill be handled by the British
arities Committee.

should be made clear that
undred and fifty men who
he cast are soldiers. Fol-
eir tour of Great Britain,
be sent to Africa to play
lied soldiers, then will join
fighting forces.

find "This Is The Army"
ng, it will have served
tant purpose. Entertainment
ential to high morale, a
ch is understood, surely,
ut the British Empire, where
ng esprit stood alone, for a
inst the barbaric effort to
the civilized world.

hope "This Is The Army"
a part in cementing inter-
friendships along the grim
eventual victory.

JACOB L. DEVERS
ieut/ General, U. S. Army,
Commanding.

Business like Showbusiness'. This latter song would really come to epitomise the London Palladium and all the stars that had and would grace its stage in well over ninety-five years' history. After the last night of the run, the whole cast went to Teddington Studios to film 'My British Buddy' in Technicolour for inclusion in the forthcoming movie of the same name.

When the box office opened for *This is the Army*, the theatre had to engage five extra staff to cope with the demand for tickets. There were 2000 postal applications alone on that first day. There was a hiccup just before the opening, and the show almost failed to open on time. None of the shoes or stockings or even the props had arrived by air when they were supposed to. With only three days to rehearse the show, the props finally turned up. Everyone breathed a sigh of relief, especially Berlin. The first night was a tremendous success; it knocked London sideways. 'Seldom have I heard such applause', 'A lively light theatre show', 'A smashing show without a weak spot', 'If you can get a seat during its brief run you will be lucky', 'It has zip, zest and zing that's all too rare in British shows today', and 'No other show has registered so instantaneously with the public', shouted the headlines in London and national papers, and these were just some of the comments from the press.

So successful was this show that the King and Queen and their two daughters, the Princesses Elizabeth and Margaret, attended a matinée performance. Gone were the days when a previous Queen had hidden her face so as not to see Vesta Tilley dressed as a man. Here were beefy US soldiers, dressed as women and performing songs and sketches that pleased everyone. There was even a real live magician in the shape of Sergeant John Prince Mendes, and a very fine juggler, Corporal Larry Weeks, not to mention a twenty-six piece pit orchestra.

The Royal party insisted on visiting backstage to meet Berlin. They congratulated him on a fine show and shared a cup of tea and cakes baked in an 'American Canteen'. Before the Royal party left, the King congratulated Berlin on his song 'My British Buddy', a song for which Berlin had donated the copyright ownership and royalties to the British Fund. The show played to over 250,000 people on its nationwide tour of eleven weeks, comprising 127 performances. British War Charities benefited tremendously from the sum of £80,525 which was raised.

LOOK
who's here!
AT THE
LONDON
PALLADIUM

6ᴰ

PROGRAMME

THE LONDON PALLADIUM
OXFORD CIRCUS, W.

The English Music Hall at its Best

2-30	TWICE DAILY	5-20
Termination Approx. 5.0	COMMENCING BOXING DAY, DEC. 27th, 1943 FOR A LIMITED SEASON	Terminating Approx. 7.50

MAX MILLER
THE CHEEKY CHAPPIE

WEBSTER **BOOTH** AND ANNE **ZIEGLER**
Stars of Musical Comedy and Radio

JIMMY JAMES
THE INEBRIATED ONE

IVY BENSON
AND HER LADIES BAND

CHAS **WARREN** AND **JEAN**

LAMAR AND **ROSITA**

CHARACTER COMEDIAN **SCOTT SANDERS**

MARIORA
GIRL JUGGLER WITH ASSISTANT

MAVIS RAY

LUCILLE GAYE

RECO MAY

CAIROLI BROS.
World's Greatest Clowns

PALLADIUM GIRLS

AND **RAWICZ LANDAUER**
A THRILL ON TWO PIANOS

GENERAL THEATRES CORPORATION LTD.
Joint Managing Directors
MARK OSTRER & L. W. FARROW

BOX OFFICE OPEN 10 to 8   'Phone: GER. 7373
ALL SEATS BOOKABLE   2/6 to 13/- INC. TAX
ADJOINING OXFORD CIRCUS TUBE STATION

DIRECTION
GEORGE BLACK
Business Manager
C. T. HUTCHISON

Old Mother Riley

With no time to catch their breath, the West End public were soon to be entertained by a totally different show, *Look Who's Here*. Again preceded by two special shows for soldiers, the opening night was on 1 December 1943, and the show ran for two weeks. It starred joint tops of the bill, Lucan and McShane, better known as Old Mother Riley and 'her' daughter Kitty (they were really husband and wife), together with Cyril Fletcher and some of his famously odd odes, including the most well-known which was 'Dreaming of Thee'. Talented virtuosi pianists Rawicz and Landauer, some superb impressions of the famous from Binnie Hale, those much-loved circus multi-instrumentalists The Cairoli Brothers, Richard Haydn, vocalist Bob Arden, Mavis Ray and The Palladium Girls filled out the bill. Lamar and Rosita also appeared in a delightful ballet sequence, again choreographed by Wendy Toye. The popular show had the comedian Michael Howard as its compère. Afternoon teas were served in the Palm Court or auditorium, as noted in the programme.

Some people considered that this was a 'filler' whilst the Palladium was preparing for the return of more Variety on Boxing Day. Max Miller was back again, as cheeky as ever, along with 'Radio Favourites' Ivy Benson and her twenty piece All Ladies Band, Anne Ziegler and Webster Booth, Jimmy James and Company, and Scott Sanders. The Cairoli Brothers and Rawicz and Landauer were retained, as were the Lamar and Rosita ballet sequences from the previous production.

On 15 May after some twenty weeks, the variety bill changed again. It featured 'Two Ton' Tessie O'Shea, newcomers Freddie Bamberger and Pam, Hal Monty with 'Monsewer' Eddie Gray, The Ganjou Brothers and Juanita with their graceful and perfectly timed adagio act, and Maurice Colleano with Rubye, Joyce, Bonar and George, the acrobatic dancing funsters. Top of this bill was Geraldo and his Orchestra, with a young Ted Heath on trombone. (Ted was later to fill the stage himself with 110 performances, complete with his own orchestra!) During one of these appearances, Geraldo was proud to announce that sitting in the audience was none other than Glenn Miller. This was Glenn's first appearance in the UK.

One of the strangest additions to this variety bill was that of sixteen times World Champion at table tennis, Victor Barna, and the British International Champion, Alec Brook. Add to this the superb rope, whip and bicycle act of El Granadas and aerialist Marie Louise, and you had one of the best bills for many a day. It ran until 3 July 1944.

For security reasons it only came to light after the war ended, but way back in 1941 a parachute bomb landed on top of the Palladium building. Two brave young naval men, armed only with a flashlight, safely extracted the fuse and the detonator and saved the Palladium from total destruction. For brave gallantry Sub-Lieutenant Graham Wright, who later died on an Atlantic convoy mission, was awarded the George Medal and Able-Seaman W.H. Bevan was awarded the Bar to add to his already well-earned George Medal. It appears that the two men first saw the mine through broken slates during a routine rooftop hunt. They climbed inside the roof onto a girder eight feet below the mine, which they could see was jammed into the roof timbers. The fuse was masked by a broken rafter that had cracked under the weight of the mine. Wright lashed himself to a rafter and, aided only by the light of a torch held by Bevan, he sawed through the wood and exposed the fuse at the same time as fitting a safety gag. Whilst Wright was working on the screwed ring that held the fuse, the clockwork began to run. He wrenched himself free, jumped for one of the ropes that held the scenery and both men dropped to the floor, but the safety gag held. They quickly returned to their task and Wright lay on top of the mine while Bevan held his feet until the dangerous task was completed. Their courage saved the Palladium theatre from annihilation.

Owing to the severity of the bombing in London, the theatre was 'dark' for fourteen weeks during July, August and September of 1944. George Black was then to present what was to become his last production. It was to have been called *If It's Laughter You're After*, but was ultimately renamed *Happy and Glorious*. Owing to problems in the West End with the V2 Flying Bombs, the production had a try-out first in Birmingham and then Nottingham to iron out all the problems. Billed as 'the New Musical Funfare', *Happy and Glorious* eventually opened on 3 October 1944 and ran until 6 April 1946,

THE PALLADIUM

OXFORD CIRCUS, W.I

TELEPHONE: GERRARD 7373

2-30	TWICE DAILY	6-20
Terminating rox. at 4-50		Terminating Approx. at 8-40

GEORGE BLACK

Presents

HIS NEW MUSICAL FUNFARE

HAPPY *and* GLORIOUS

PROGRAMME PRICE **6**D.

Nearest Tube Station
Oxford Circus
Box Office Open 10 a.m. to 8 p.m.

with a record-breaking 938 performances. It smashed the twenty-year-old record that had been held by *Whirl of the World* which had played for fifty-four weeks. By the time of its first anniversary, the show had played to one and a half million people! It starred Tommy Trinder and Elisabeth Welch, who had to withdraw due to illness, so her place was taken by her understudy, Paddie O'Neil. The Cairoli Brothers and The Dagenham Girl Pipers completed the bill. *The Stage* newspaper commented in its review that,

> It is at once stirring, thrilling, colourful and artistic. Full of humour and be it noted, humour of the best type, and contains as well, music which embraces classic and jazz put over extremely well. There are many ingenious touches both in the comedy and stagecraft and it is safe to assert that *Happy and Glorious* will run well into the piping days of peace ... Robert Nesbitt's production is of course amazingly good and so are the dances arranged by Joan Davis, but overall it is a triumph for George Black.

The show, which opened with a fanfare and Zoe Gail singing 'Happy and Glorious Day', was full of vitality. Tommy Trinder made his entrance and was seemingly never off the stage for the whole show; he was either performing himself, or he was introducing The Cairoli Brothers, Elisabeth Welch, and Jack Billings and the girl dancers. Trinder was at his best like never before. The whole cast wanted to show the world that in spite of all their troubles, laughter was the best antidote.

One of the hits of the evening was the appearance on stage of Debroy Somers and his fifty piece orchestra. This was stirring stuff when in one scene, The Dagenham Girl Pipers also made their entrance to complete the patriotic picture. During the run, on one Sunday afternoon over fifteen hundred wounded servicemen were entertained to a special concert laid on by George Black. The whole cast, including the theatre staff, gave their services for free, and afterwards the whole audience was treated to afternoon tea.

After fifty-four weeks the Management gave Tommy a silver tray to mark the record-breaking achievements of the show thus far. On completion of the run, several members of the company, including some that Tommy would describe as his stooges, were proudly displaying silver cigarette cases. They bore the inscription, 'Thanks. London Palladium Record-Breaking Run 1944–1946... Tommy Trinder'. Many of the ladies in the show received powder compacts.

It should be mentioned here that it was during this run that Tommy Trinder 'created' the brass name plate on the door of the dressing room, and he called it an 'Oscar'. It would be removed by the artistes at the end of a week or a season to take home and treasure!

In typical Trinder style, Tommy commented at the end-of-run party about the new incoming show. 'It will be called *High Time* for the first week and *High Time Trinder Was Back* for the second!' He was then off for a delayed world tour, taking in Cairo, India, Ceylon and Burma, Australia, New Zealand, Hawaii and finally ending up in Hollywood to take advantage of his MGM contract deal.

With the long, hard war finally over, Britain was happy and glorious once more. The only sad thing at the Palladium was that the man who had made it all possible for the past seventeen years or so never lived to see his last show break all box office receipts *and* hold the record for the longest running show. George Black died on 4 March 1945. His booking assistant of many years, Valentine Parnell, was to take over the running of this entertainment machine, and under his new leadership it would achieve even greater things.

Chapter Eleven

THE POST-WAR
US INVASION

*A*fter many, many months of difficult days, not to mention dark nights too, with the blackout being de rigeur during the terrible war, it was high time for a new show. Indeed, the show itself was called *High Time*. Opening on 20 April 1946, it starred 'Two Ton' Tessie O'Shea, along with up-and-coming popular radio comedians and cousins Jewell and Warriss, who were accompanied by 'rubberneck' Nat Jackley.

Following closely on their heels was pre-war favourite George Formby, who made a subsequent short variety season appearance. The stars of the next all too brief two-week season were those 'Film Fun' favourites and monarchs of merriment, Laurel and Hardy. Although the 1947 temperatures outside the theatre were well below freezing and blizzards were bringing the traffic to a halt, inside the packed audiences immediately warmed to the cinematic duo. The press loved them and so did the paying public, who packed out the theatre night after night. Presented by Bernard Delfont and initially contracted for two weeks, they were so successful that they stayed an extra week! As soon as the first few notes of 'The Cuckoo Song' sounded, the audience was agog at seeing their own very special 'silver screen' heroes live on stage. They were a tremendous success to say the least, and their kindness backstage to the rest of the cast was unheard of. It wasn't unknown for them to walk up two or three flights of stairs to the top of the building to ask for the autograph of all the other acts on the bill!

Returning from his world travels, Tommy Trinder followed for thirty-nine weeks in the aptly titled *Here There and Everywhere*. Another radio favourite, *Just William*, came to the stage, appearing for matinées only in December 1947.

Laurel and Hardy

However, the American invasion was about to begin. As we have seen in another chapter, Val Parnell had been the booking manager for George Black and was now in charge. In his new capacity of providing all that was best in terms of Variety, he proceeded to travel to the USA to secure every top name that he could lay his hands on and his chequebook could afford. Mickey Rooney was his first choice, but unfortunately, even though Rooney was already a popular and successful film star, his transition to the variety stage proved to be a bit of a disaster, according to the press at the time. His four-week contract ended in dispute, with Rooney leaving British shores on the grounds of illness. Sid Field deputised for him for the last few performances.

Apart from wanting to witness the great comedian Sid at work, sitting in the box all that week was Daniel Kaminsky, who was then unknown as a theatre star, but popular as a film personality. He is better known to us all as Danny Kaye. After trying to glean what made an English audience tick, as well as soaking up the atmosphere of this wonderful theatre, Danny Kaye's appearance on his first night on 2 February 1948 took Britain by storm. All the sadness of his predecessor was quickly forgotten, not only by Parnell but also by the public.

First night nerves come to most artists, but with an experienced star like Danny one would hardly believe that it was necessary for the Stage Manager, Jack Matthews, to literally push him onto the stage. Kaye had some good reason to be nervous. Not only had Rooney flopped, but he had also returned to the USA saying that the British were anti-American. However, after the first few seconds Kaye had the audience in the palm of his hand. He could do no wrong. He 'Balled his Jack', he 'Minnied his Moocher', and already Argyll Street was buzzing with the word that Variety was back home once again. Not only back but back with a vengeance! Once he had found his English 'feet', his kindness to his new found audience knew no bounds. He once invited a small child of three onto the stage to sing with him. After the show, along with her parents, she was invited backstage to his dressing room and given her first taste of Coke. Kaye's love for children was highlighted by his UNESCO involvement later on. Such was his phenomenal success that his future

PALLADIUM

OXFORD CIRCUS. W.
TELEPHONE GERRARD 7373

CHAIRMAN:
PRINCE LITTLER
MANAGING DIRECTOR
VAL PARNELL

PROPRIETORS:
MOSS' EMPIRES, LTD.
MANAGER
HARRY WOODS

★ ACE VARIETY HOUSE OF THE WORLD ★

6.0 MATINEES AT 2.40 WEDNESDAYS AND THURSDAYS 8.30

THOUSANDS MORE WANT TO SEE

DANNY KAYE

OWING TO PRIOR COMMITMENTS HIS ENGAGEMENT DEFINITELY TERMINATES MARCH 13th

SO HE IS STAYING TWO EXTRA WEEKS

THE MERRY MACS
FIRST TIME IN ENGLAND

HOLLYWOOD'S DISTINCTIVE CLOSE HARMONY TEAM

SKYROCKETS ORCHESTRA

DOWNEY AND DAYE
America's Skating Aristocrats

YVONNE WATTS

SCOTT SANDERS
THE OLD PHILOSOPHER

COOKE'S PONY REVUE

The Sophisticated Funny Man
FREDDY
Assisted by
PAUL KING

TED RAY
FIDDLING AND FOOLING

MARCH 15th 2 WEEKS ONLY JEAN SABLON
THE WORLD-FAMOUS FRENCH CABARET & RECORDING STAR

Palladium bookings were literally sold out before the opening night.

With such a very hard act to follow, Jean Sablon, Martha Raye, Carmen Miranda (the real one this time, not Trinder dressed up!), Tony Martin and an unforgettable reappearance of the 'Duke' himself, (Ellington, that is), followed in fortnightly succession. Edgar Bergen and Jack Benny, who was dubbed by the press as 'The Quiet Riot', came next. They were followed by The Andrews Sisters, Dinah Shore, Betty Hutton and Gracie Fields. One supporting act on Gracie's show was the then virtually unknown Ella Fitzgerald. In an interview I conducted with Ella many years later, where her failing eyesight was very much in evidence, her mind immediately switched from that warm summer's evening on which we spoke right back to 1948, and she recalled how kind Gracie had been, offering her own 'Oscar' nameplate as a memento of Ella's appearance there.

Duke Ellington

The 1948 panto offering was the ever popular *Cinderella*, with Tommy Trinder as Buttons and co-starring Evelyn Laye, Zoe Gail and George and Bert Bernard.

Jimmy 'Schnozzle' Durante had already made his Palladium debut in 1936, and George Burns and Gracie Allen had also made a similar impact in the early 1930s. Now it was their chance to return and captivate the London audiences once again in 1949. Parnell went on to reprise Danny Kaye for a second successful season. He then presented 'donkey serenader' Allan Jones, singing star Kathryn Grayson, The Marx Brothers Chico and Harpo, Benny Goodman with his new vocalist Buddy Greco, and The Ink Spots. They all enjoyed two weeks of happy memories.

The British public had been hearing a lot about the mindreading radio stars, The Piddingtons. Val Parnell wanted to book the antipodean act, and such was his determination that he made a four hundred mile round trip from London (with no motorways in those days) especially to see their much talked about mental telepathy. He was very impressed. Back in his office the very next morning he booked them for a two-week season in September 1949 at £600 per week. It was their act which broke the chain of US imported acts that had headlined the Palladium posters. Gracie Fields appeared next for

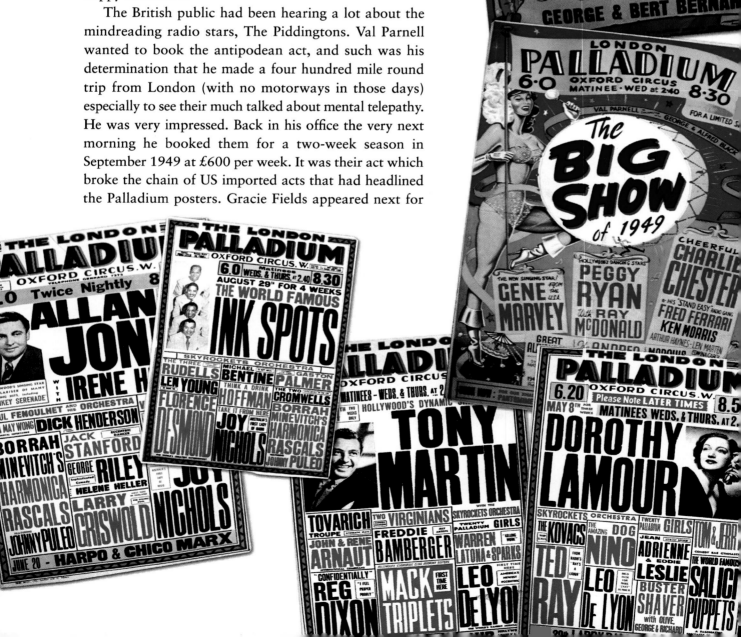

two successful weeks and then, following on in their father's footsteps, the two sons of the late George Black, George and Alfred, presented *The Big Show of 1949* with Cheerful Charlie Chester and his Gang. *Puss in Boots* was the traditional pantomime offering that year, with the ubiquitous Trinder, Zoe Gail and The Bernard Brothers.

To commence the 1950 variety season, Parnell booked Danny Thomas to open, before following on with Tony Martin, Dorothy Lamour, Larry Parks, Jack Benny and Frank Sinatra, who were just some of the names that Parnell brought over from the US. Abbott and Costello, and Britain's own Donald Peers and Gracie Fields were always popular returning artists. Lena Horne and Nat King Cole completed the 1950 list of star names. When the festive time came around again, *Babes in the Wood* with Eunice Gayson, Carole Lynne, and Jewell and Warris was enjoyed by all ages.

Nat King Cole

On reflection, 1951 will be remembered as the year that Frances Gumm made the first of her several appearances on the Palladium stage. Loved by us all and better known as Judy Garland, she was a very nervous performer who would sit down on the stage and take off her shoes in order to relax. To this day, this picture of Judy sitting shoeless, with her legs dangling over the edge of the stage, will long remain in the hearts of all her devoted fans. This was thanks to Woolf Phillips, The Skyrockets' conductor, who suggested the idea to her. Prior to her season at the Palladium she had had a run of bad luck in the movie business, and she seized the chance to get back on top with both hands. On her Argyll Street opening night, the sympathy for her strained the atmosphere. After her first number, she curtsied to

acknowledge the applause, caught her heel in the hem of her long evening dress, and down she went. She just sat on the stage and burst out laughing! The audience broke out laughing too and the ice was broken. Immediately the reserve they felt for this talented artiste vanished and in its place a great warmth flowed across the footlights as they really took her to their hearts. No wonder that Judy's eyes were streaming with tears when she quietly sang the closing notes of 'Over the Rainbow'. Her triumph was complete and it was as a direct result of this appearance that the Palace Theatre in New York decided to reintroduce a policy of Vaudeville with Judy Garland as its first headliner.

After his untimely passing, in memory of the late Sid Field, a special charity show was arranged in late June of that year. Sid had made such an impact in his West End shows *Strike a New Note*, *Strike it Again*, and *Piccadilly Hayride*, and he had even appeared in the 1946 Royal Variety Performance. Following the making of his second film, *Cardboard Cavalier*, he appeared in *Harvey*, and during the run of this play he suffered a heart attack and died on 3 February 1950. His deserved success and its consequent financial rewards had come a little late in his life and his family were as not as well cared for as Sid's friends would have liked. Laurence Olivier and Danny Kaye set about arranging a very special show, *The Sid Field Tribute*.

With the kind co-operation of the Palladium Management and Staff, the show included Jack Hylton who conducted the Overture, with The Skyrockets Orchestra directed by Woolf Phillips. Tommy Trinder was 'at home' with the Palladium, Victoria Palace, and Prince of Wales Girl Dancers, and Ted Ray, Patricia Morrison, Ciceley Courtneidge, Arthur Askey, and The Flora Dora Octette specially routined by George Carden all made an appearance. Judy Garland also performed. 'Les Boys' were Florence Desmond, Pat Kirkwood, Carole Lynne, Moira Lister, Margaret Lockwood, Patricia Morrison, Joy Nicholls and Julie Wilson, and 'Les Girls' included Richard Attenborough, Jack Buchanan, Douglas Fairbanks junior, Danny Kaye (whose initial idea it was and who, along with a few others, organised the show), Teddy Knox, Charlie Naughton, Tommy Trinder and Bud Flanagan. This concluded the first half. There were more stars yet to come. Those already mentioned, plus Jerry Desmonde, Chesney Allen, Harry Green, Bill Johnson, Ben Lyon, Jimmy Nervo, Laurence Olivier, George Robey, Lou Spencer, Billy Russell and Peter Ustinov all appeared. Orson Welles, a great conjuring aficionado, presented a special magic act with his assistant Elizabeth Taylor. They all sat around informally at tables and made their own individual contributions. They were *real* stars, with even bigger hearts. The Duchess of Kent and Noel Coward were amongst the guests who enjoyed what amounted to a midnight feast of the best in entertainment. The show concluded at 3.15 in the morning!

What a line-up and 'What a Performance!' Sid would have been proud.

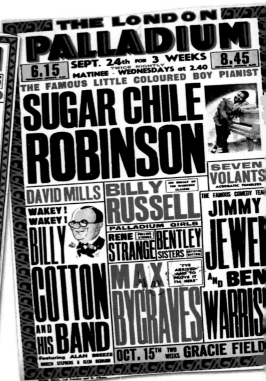

Also in 1951, Donald O'Connor and Hoagy Carmichael made a tremendous impact in their own right, as did Red Skelton. Patty, Laverne and Maxene, better known as The Andrews Sisters, made a successful return visit too, and as one would expect, so did Danny Kaye. When he appeared in 1951, he was earning a reputed $20,000 (£7,140) per week, the largest payment that had ever been made to a single performer. Other memorable performances came from Tony Martin, Jack Carson, Hazel Scott, and the young black star Sugar 'Chile' Robinson playing the piano for all he was worth. 'Our' Gracie then closed the variety season.

Ending the year with a brief run up to the pantomime season was *The Palladium Peep Show*, starring Vera Lynn, Edmundo Ros and Jack Jackson. Amongst the other supporting acts was a young dancer by the name of Gillian Lynne. It would be Gillian who would be responsible in the years to come for the choreography of most of the major West End musicals. Talent in the making on the Palladium stage once again!

The pantomime *Humpty Dumpty* was based on the original Robert Nesbitt production and the book was by Barbara Gordon and Basil Thomas. The ballet was by

Pauline Grant and everything was staged by Charles Henry. It starred Peggy Mount, Gillian Lynne, Herbert Hare, Terry Thomas, The Three Jokers, Jean Bayless, Noele Gordon, Betty Jumel, Norman Evans, Bunny Westney, William Clothier, David Dale, John and Rene Arnaut, and Bob Hammond and his feathered friends. This line-up was augmented by The Aida Foster Babes, The Three Bentley Sisters and Kirby's Flying Ballet. It was quite a cast! Overseeing the musical requirements was Woolf Phillips with The Skyrockets.

The variety season in 1952 saw much the same variety format as in previous years. The first star to headline was someone who had made an earlier impact when he acted as an understudy for Ted Ray in the 1950 Dorothy Lamour season. His name was Max Bygraves. Max was to prove so successful and achieve such great heights that by the 1990s he had appeared in no less than *nineteen* Royal Variety Performances, not to mention countless other regular variety shows and other charitable performances. This meant that one of Britain's top stars was in every branch of the entertainment industry for over five decades! He was rightly honoured by Her Majesty when she awarded him the OBE for his services to the entertainment industry.

Billy Daniels, Jo Stafford, Sophie Tucker, Jimmy Durante, Lena Horne and Jack Benny all starred in their own individual two-week 'seasons'. The next headliner, Peter Lind Hayes and Mary Healey, were to have a support act that would soon become a legend in British comedy. A six-foot plus giant of a comedy genius who bumbled his way through magic. He just never got it quite right. He would enter the stage and without saying a word would have the whole audience in uproar. His trademark was a fez and need I say more? His name was Tommy Cooper. Guy Mitchell and Dolores Gray soon followed these acts with their own two-week seasons, along with Frankie Laine. It was Frankie who broke all known box office records, which had previously been set by Judy Garland and Danny Kaye. He couldn't see how he could break any records, for their seasons had both been sell-outs too. The answer was that he had sold his 'house' the quickest! Bob Hope made another popular return visit, and guitar virtuoso Les Paul and Mary Ford

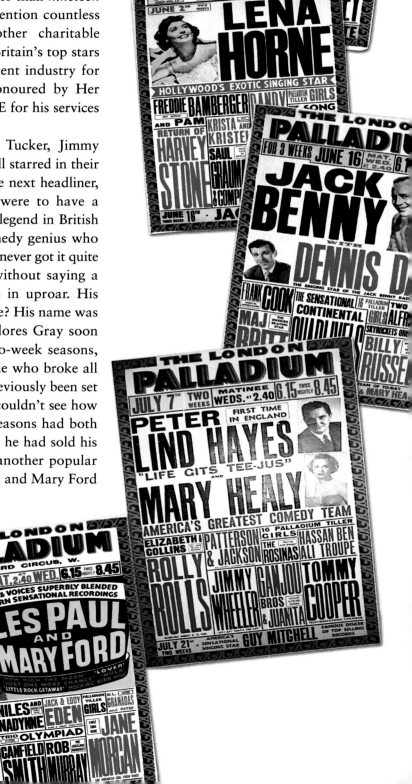

also headlined, quickly followed by the powerhouse voice of Betty Hutton. By then it was time for the big autumn show and *Wonderful Time* took to the stage, starring Max Bygraves, Joy Nicholls and Billy Cotton, who were aided and abetted by those wonderful mime artists George and Bert Bernard. In December *Dick Whittington* starred Frankie Howerd, Warren Mitchell and Mr Pastry.

1953 saw Max Miller opening the season, closely followed by Johnnie Ray. Tennessee Ernie Ford was next to top the bill. In the smaller print further down the bill was a double act that the British television public would eventually take to their hearts. No TV Christmas in the 1970s would have been complete without *The Morecambe and Wise Spectacular*. As mentioned earlier, Ernie had made his debut in the 1939 show *Bandwaggon* in a Jack Hylton talent spot. Eric was another Hylton protégé and together they teamed up to make arguably the greatest double act that spanned the stage and television in British history. Gracie Fields, Eddie Fisher, Danny Thomas, Al Martino, Dean Martin and Jerry Lewis, Billy Daniels, Guy Mitchell, Abbott and Costello, Kay Starr, Frankie Laine, and Bob Hope all topped their own successful variety bills. It was in one of these Bob Hope appearances that, as the gag, Lew Grade got to dance with Hope and then proceeded to do the Charleston, something for which he was well known and would often do only for charity. Prior to the seasonal offering of *Cinderella*, starring Julie Andrews, Max Bygraves and Jon Pertwee, the autumn slot was *Fun of the Fair*, which starred Billy Cotton and his Band, Terry Thomas, The Deep River Boys, and that female bundle of fun, Audrey Jeans.

In 1954, having proven his popularity with over 100 Sunday *Swing Sessions*, bandleader Ted Heath topped his own variety bill with his own splendid singers Lita Roza, Dennis Lotis, and Dickie Valentine. Nat King Cole, Johnnie Ray, Billy Eckstine, and Jean Carroll with her wonderful mink coat routine all appeared in the lead up to the highlight of *The 1954 Big Palladium Show*, which starred Norman Wisdom. Produced by Dick Hurran, this was to be Norman's first of many seasons at the Palladium. His foil on many an occasion was to be the debonair Jerry Desmonde, who had starred alongside Sid Field in his later film years. One of the highlights was Bob Williams and his talented dog assistant, who did everything but obey his master! The Three Monarchs and Teddy Peiro and his brother provided the speciality as they all did collectively and individually on so many occasions.

In June 1954, the first of many *Night of a Hundred Stars* took place in aid of The Actors' Orphanage. There were literally one hundred well known names on stage at the end. There were real stars in those days. With Noël Coward as President, Dame Edith Evans, Sir Laurence Olivier, and Richard (later to become Lord) Attenborough on the Executive Committee, the pulling power to obtain all the best artists from around the world was enormous. The rightful top of the bill for this very first occasion was none other than Marlene Dietrich who was appearing by kind permission of the Café de Paris night club. Douglas Fairbanks was compère for the whole show, which also included Errol Flynn amongst other top names. Over the following years many stars would appear; the names included Roger Moore, Tony Curtis, Josephine Baker, David Niven, Lauren Bacall, John Gielgud, Humphrey Bogart, Tony Martin, Paul Robeson, Eddie Fisher, Elizabeth Taylor, Bob Hope, Jack Benny, Tyrone Power, Esther Williams, The Beatles, Richard Burton, John Mills, Peter Ustinov, Jack Buchanan, Paul Scofield, Ralph Richardson, Danny Kaye, and Judy Garland. This list was almost endless, and all of them appeared not only for charity but mostly out of their normal environment, either singing, dancing, or appearing in a playlet. Staged annually for almost a decade the shows were highly successful, never to be repeated nights of nights, raising endless amounts of money for the much needed charities.

In midsummer of 1954, Parnell took the London Palladium to Las Vegas with acts that were totally new to this Mecca of Variety. Pat Kirkwood topped the bill along with Mr Pastry, alias Richard Hearne. He had made a big hit on *The Ed Sullivan Show* and had them laughing in Nevada too. They were supported by a full variety bill. One of the acts, Wilson Keppel and Betty, presented their act 'as known', the highlight being their sand dance. Wherever they went, they took their own sand, and Las Vegas was no exception! Either no one had told them that the venue was in a desert or they weren't taking any chances that it would be the right kind of sand for their routine. Eventually, it turned out that they were asked to leave out the sand dance, as they were kicking the sand onto the tables of those dining and seated near the front!

Commencing on 22 December 1954, Parnell presented his seventh magnificent pantomime, *Mother Goose*, with the book by Phil Park and Eric Sykes. It starred Aileen Cochrane, the Mathurins, Peter Sellers, Shirley Eaton, Max Bygraves, Richard Hearne, and Margaret Burton. Sid Millward, The Nitwits and The Aida Foster Babes completed the strong cast. The Skyrockets were conducted by Eric Rogers on this occasion.

After the successful pantomime season, Eddie Fisher made a welcome return, and the one-time Palladium call boy and singer with The Ted Heath Orchestra, Dickie Valentine, topped his own variety bill in 1955. Adored by all his record buying fans, he proved a worthy headliner. 'The Mighty Mannequin' Joan Rhodes proved that ladies could not only look pretty, but also tear telephone directories in half. American import and top speciality act Jay Marshall introduced the Palladium to his hand puppet, 'Lefty', who along with talented Jay held the audience in the palm of his other hand. 'If I Had My Way' was his signature tune and if I had my way he would be on my top variety show every week! Twice nightly Johnnie Ray and The Four Aces came up trumps on separate occasions and then they made way for the 'standing room only' Danny Kaye fourth season when he made a most welcome return. Rosemary Clooney followed and was supported by Leslie Randall, Authors and Swinson and The Salici Puppets. Her special guest was the legendary, suave sorcerer Channing Pollock.

Norman Wisdom starred in a second spectacular, *Painting the Town*. It was once again presented by Val Parnell and Bernard Delfont and produced by debonair Dick Hurran. It was in this show that Nanci Crompton left her little village for the big time and 'went to town' to the music of the re-named 'Startime'. A few weeks into the run, one very special and memorable Sunday was written into the Palladium history books as being the very first *Sunday Night at The Palladium*. The date was 25 September 1955, and the memorable signature tune, 'Startime', would haunt everyone who had access to a television set for many years to come. As will be seen in another chapter, almost everyone from all corners of the theatrical globe appeared on this highly popular TV show.

Many new names would emerge for the remaining variety seasons of the decade, including Slim Whitman, Dave King, Howard Keel, Billy Daniels, Frankie Lymon and his Teenager Friends, Johnny Ray, the Platters, and Liberace. There was a changing pattern in the Palladium format. It was harder to get top new American artists, so longer seasons of more spectacular shows would take over from the variety week or fortnight. Home-grown stars like Harry Secombe had their own shows such as *Rocking The Town*, which sometimes ran for six months or more. With a unique vocal distinctiveness all of her own, songstress Alma Cogan strengthened the show, as did Winifred Atwell, comedienne Beryl Reid, and the delightful songstress Joan Regan.

Norman Wisdom as Aladdin held the *The Wonderful Lamp* in December 1956, much to everyone's delight. This was followed by two-week seasons of Variety that included Frankie Lymon and The Teenagers, Johnnie Ray, Frankie Laine, Howard Keel and Eddie Fisher. The long-running summer spectacular was *We're Having a Ball*, which commenced in June. This starred Max Bygraves, Joan Regan, The Clark Brothers Page and Bray, The Carsony Twins, The Kaye Sisters with Janet Mahoney and Angela Bracewell, and The Goofers. Choreography was once again by George Carden.

Frankie Vaughan then had his own special spectacular, *Startime*, with new comedians Joe Church and Roy Castle creating plenty of laughs. Pinky and Perky, those popular piglet puppets, also made an appearance thanks to the deft hands of Jan and Vlasta Dalibor.

Frankie Vaughan

In 1958, there was another short early fortnight season of Variety with a welcome return of Liberace, accompanied by Dick Shawn, followed by Jerry Lewis and then Johnnie Ray. Next, Harry Secombe was back again in *Large as Life*. Also on the bill supporting him were Terry Thomas, Eric Sykes and Hattie Jacques, Adele Leigh, Lynette Rae, and Harry Worth. Over the long season of this show, The Three Monarchs, Charlie Cairoli and Paul, and Johnny Puleo and his own Harmonica Rascals were all added at different times to the speciality spot. It was a very strong bill, and it was made even better with a further addition of the re-appearance of G.H. Elliott, Hetty King and Dick Henderson in a music hall segment. What a show!

Max Bygraves closed a decade packed with colour and comedy when he went *Swinging down the Lane* with funny men Hope and Keen, The Peters Sisters and the much missed, lugubrious antipodean juggler, Rob Murray. Bob Williams and his dog also made a welcome return. Also, no show in this period would have been complete without the artistic eye of designer Charles Reading, and his name appeared on most programmes and posters.

The pantomimes for '57, '58 and '59 were *Robinson Crusoe*, *Sleeping Beauty* and *Humpty Dumpty* respectively. The stars of *Robinson Crusoe*, Arthur Askey and David Whitfield, together with newcomer Tommy Cooper, all enjoyed the desert island romp. Parnell's tenth pantomime included a 'beauty' of a cast with Charlie Drake, Bernard Breslaw, Edmund Hockridge, and another newcomer to pantoland, Bruce Forsyth. The decade ended with Harry Secombe back again in the title role of Humpty Dumpty, aided and abetted, (not that he needed it), by Alfred Marks, Paddie O'Neil, Roy Castle and Gary Miller.

It was perhaps the busiest decade yet, especially at the box office.

PRESENTS
NG SESSION
NO. 2.
LONDON PALLADIUM
DECEMBER 23rd, 1945
4D.
HEATH RECORDS EXCLUSIVE
FOR DECCA RECORDS

TED HE
AND HIS M
BOBBIE BRITTON
JOHNNY HAWKSWORT
DON LUSHER · DU

Chapter Twelve

THE TED HEATH
SWING SESSIONS

W ithout doubt, the name of bandleader Ted Heath will long remain in the musical memory of the British public. He provided a quality that has seldom been equalled, if at all, and his dedication to perfection rightly perpetuates his name. His early formative years with the bands of Maurice Winnick, Sidney Lipton, Ambrose and Geraldo enabled him to gain the necessary experience so that when he formed his own band, it would stand him in good stead in the years to come. His constant quest for precision and perfection, which up until then he had heard only in his favourite Glenn Miller Orchestra, set him on the road to form his own British band in search of a similar quality.

His early days with his father's brass band set the seal on his future, and after he had struggled for a long time, as is so often the case a chance in a million occurred of him being in the right place at the right time. He had formed a 'busking' band and happened to be outside the Queens Hall Roof Gardens just as Jack Hylton was desperately looking for a trombonist.

In October 1931, Ted occupied the prestigious brass position in The Ambrose Band that was so popular at that time at the Mayfair Hotel and which made several appearances at the Palladium in the early 1930s, before later appearing with Geraldo for a season in 1944. In 1956, Ted was the first to break the American Musicians' Union ban on incoming English bands. He took his band to the United Sates in exchange for The Stan Kenton Band, which visited England in reciprocation. This was to be the first of many such visits abroad, and with international world tours as well, The Heath Band was now well established.

Ted Heath

TED HEATH

PRESENTS HIS

WING SESSION"

NO. 2.

THE LONDON PALLADIUM

DECEMBER 23rd, 1945

4 D.

ED HEATH RECORDS EXCLUSIVELY

FOR DECCA RECORDS

A Christmas Message

This being our last Palladium "Swing Session" before Christmas I am sending a seasonal greeting from the boys and myself to you in this audience to-day. I want to thank you sincerely for the inspiration and encouragement you have given us. We are all deeply appreciative of your support and our sincerest hope for ourselves in the year ahead is that we shall continue to merit it.

hope we shall have your company at some of our agagements during the Festive Season. On these asions, and in all your other pursuits, we wish you ry happiness.

Ted Heath

RACTS FROM TED HEATH'S DIARY

Ted Heath was a dignified and dedicated man who organised his beautifully rehearsed and often high swinging outfit near the close of the big band era. It created a furore with its London Palladium concerts, regular broadcasts and a succession of quality recordings. Although he was perhaps not the easiest of men to work with, such was his quest for excellence, he was always receptive and open to new ideas. He would often be very tense, tetchy, and irritable, but always as a result of the obsessive search for that elusive perfection. The band contained a number of virtuoso musicians, men with fine technical artistry who were equipped with the gift to improvise. Ted was deaf in one ear due to the many years of standing in front of a double forte brass section, and his other ear was showing signs of deafness too. On stage he always wore a smart grey suit and dark tie. Being one of the 'old school' he was never, *ever* seen without a jacket, even on the hottest of Palladium nights.

Ted was essentially a quiet man, gentle, kind, and in the beginning very shy and retiring. The loud exciting aggressive sounds of his music were his alter ego. The soft deep quality sounds would sometimes almost reduce him to tears. He loved his work beyond anything else in his life. What a wonderful joy to have been able to work at what he loved best, with the people he knew and cared for, and to achieve the heights of success in his profession, and to be remembered with love and affection by so many. He dreamed a dream and the dream became a reality.

So said Mrs Moira Heath on the sleeve of one of his many recordings.

His signature tune was 'Listen to my Music', and to those dedicated followers who religiously attended his *Swing Sessions* at the Palladium, (some dedicated aficionados attended all 110), it was a thrill to hear that tune every fortnight or so, for then they knew that at least two hours of solid music lay ahead for them. The first *Swing Session* was in December 1945. With the war still remaining in the memories of so many, it was a wonderful way of quickly regaining their long-lost happiness by listening to their hero. Many names which appeared in the programme later became famous in their own right, such as

Ella Fitzgerald

Kenny Baker, Tito Burns, Petula Clark, Johnny Dankworth, Ray Ellington, Jack Jackson, Benny Lee, Dennis Lotis, Don Lusher, Jack Parnell, Sid Phillips, Lita Roza, Ronnie Scott, George Shearing, Dickie Valentine, Johnny Wiltshire and many, many more.

When he engaged America's Queen of Swing, Ella Fitzgerald, such was the demand for tickets that Ted arranged for there to be an extra performance in the afternoon on Sunday, 17 October to accommodate the vast number of followers who just could not miss this 'once in a lifetime' appearance. The *Swing Session* was the launch pad for so many names with stardom just around the corner, and Ted was always happy to lend a helping hand on the way up the ladder.

The last *Swing Session*, No. 110, was on 2 September 1956. This ended a unique record at the Palladium. No other musician before or since provided the British public with such a fond memory of music loved by all. The line-up for that momentous last night was as follows:

Saxophones:
Les Gilbert, Ronnie Chamberlain, Henry Mackenzie, Red Price, Ken Kiddier
Trumpets:
Bobby Pratt, Bert Izzard, Duncan Campbell, Eddie Blair
Trombones:
Don Lusher, Wally Smith, Jimmy Coombs, Ric Kennedy
Drums:
Ronnie Verrell
Bass:
Johnnie Hawksworth
Piano:
Frank Horrox
Vocalists:
Bobby Britton, Peter Lowe

Not to be outdone by fashion, Ted Heath appeared regularly in Variety and on two very special occasions he was invited to appear in the Royal Variety Performance. In 1948 he appeared with such legendary names as Randolph Sutton, Nellie Wallace, Billy Danvers, Ella Shields, Talbot O'Farrell, Gertie Gitana and G.H. Elliott,

TED HEATH presents his "SWING SESSION"

No. 110 SEPTEMBER 2nd, 1956

at

THE LONDON PALLADIUM

TED HEATH records exclusively for "DECCA"

MOSS' EMPIRES Ltd.
CHAIRMAN:
PRINCE LITTLER

VAL PARNELL
Manager: GEORGE MARGRAVE

THE LONDON
PALLADIUM
OXFORD CIRCUS, W.

'Phone: GERRARD 7373 & GROSVENOR 6944-5

SUNDAY, SEPT. 2ND 1956 AT 7.45 P.M.

TED HEATH presents

SWING SESSION

WITH

TED HEATH
AND HIS MUSIC

WITH

BOBBIE BRITTON · PETER LOWE
JOHNNY HAWKSWORTH · RONNIE VERRELL
DON LUSHER · DUNCAN CAMPBELL

GUEST ARTISTE
DYNAMIC

DENNIS LOTIS

Prices of Admission (including Tax) 3/- to 8/-

SEATS BOOKABLE IN ADVANCE AT THE LONDON PALLADIUM ADVANCE BOOKING OFF

not to mention the thirteen-year-old Julie Andrews, Danny Kaye, those mime experts George and Bert Bernard, Ted Ray, Cheerful Charlie Chester and his Gang, The Nicholas Brothers, The Twenty-Four John Tiller Girls, Derek Roy, The Radio Revellers, George Melachrino and his Strings, and the fifty-six members of The Luton Girls' Choir. Then, (as if that were not enough to please the patrons), after the interval came Arthur Askey, The Crazy Gang, Danny Kaye, and Henry Hall and his Orchestra. The Skyrockets Orchestra was also there under the direction of Woolf Phillips. What a wonderful night, and then to be presented to Their Majesties the King and Queen!

In 1954, a similar honour was bestowed on Ted Heath and his music when he was invited to appear on the Royal Variety Performance once more, alongside such top artists as Jimmy Wheeler, Eric Robinson and his Orchestra, Eddie Calvert, Joan Turner, Richard (Mr Pastry) Hearne, MGM singing star Howard Keel, Chesney Allen, Arthur Askey, Max Bygraves, Bud Flanagan, Jack Hylton, Billy Russell, Donald B. Stuart, Harry Green, Catherine Boyle, Al Read, Norman Wisdom, Gillian Moran, Pat Cutts, David Whitfield, Guy Mitchell, Dickie Valentine (not just a singer with The Ted Heath Band any more, but a star in his own right), Frankie Laine, Jack Parnell and his Orchestra, and Dawn White and her Glamazons. And that was only the first half!

Ted's line-up on this occasion was as follows:
Saxophones:
Les Gilbert, Roy Willcox, Henry Mackenzie,
Danny Moss, George Hunter
Trumpets:
Bobby Pratt, Duncan Campbell, Bert Ezard, Eddie Blair
Trombones:
Wally Smith, Don Lusher, Ric Kennedy
Rhythm:
Ronnie Verrell on Drums, Johnny Hawksworth on Bass,
and Frank Horrox on Piano

After the intermission Her Majesty the Queen and her party, along with the London Palladium audience, were entertained by The John Tiller Girls, juggler Rudy Horne, and Noël Coward. This was followed by *The Shop Girl Princess*, a 1918 musical comedy with Diana Churchill,

Jack Buchanan, Joan Sims, Frankie Howerd, Gladys Cooper, Binnie Hale, Peter Sellers, Donald Wolfitt, Elsie Randolph, Thora Hird, Leslie Henson, Dick Bentley, Michael Denison, Nigel Patrick, Thorley Walters, Anthony Steele, Brian Reece, Walter Crisham, Bruce Trent, Peggy Cummins, and Dulcie Gray. What a cast!

As if this was not enough, top of the bill was Bob Hope, with Moira Lister and Jerry Desmond assisting, in *The Hope Repertory Company*. Eric Rogers was conducting The Skyrockets Orchestra this time, as well as playing for the supporting speciality acts and numerous dancers.

Throughout the 1950s and early 1960s, Ted's Band was rated among the top four in the world. He loved his work, and it was only ill health that forced him to retire. He died at home in Surrey on 18 November 1969 at the age of sixty-seven.

Since the death of a much missed Ted Heath, the name of the Band lives on by kind permission of the family. In 1974, Stan Reynolds fronted The Ted Heath Band at the Palladium and the line-up was as follows:

Reeds:

Dennis Walton, Danny Moss, Henry Mackenzie, Dave Shand, Ronnie Chamberlain

Trombones:

Don Lusher, Wally Smith, Bill Geldard, Keith Christie, Ken Goldie

Trumpets:

Kenny Baker, Eddie Blair, Duncan Campbell, Derek Watkins, Ronnie Hughes, Greg Bowden

Rhythm:

Derek Warne

Piano Vibes and Percussion:

Bobby Orr

Drums:

Johnny Hawksworth (Bass)

Vocals:

Denis Lotis, Lita Roza and Monty Babson

Special Guest:

Jerry Allen

A message appeared inside the programme for those two Palladium appearances and it speaks for itself:

Ted was a very gentle man. Surprising, when you listen to his music, which was strong and vital and came hurtling at you, sometimes assaulting your ears and emotions with exciting thrilling sounds – then contrasting with tenderness which could bring you close to tears. I and my family are happy to see Ted's loved musicians together again, recapturing the wonderful sounds and spirit he generated and making true the dream that nothing ever dies.

Music perpetuates the man, man perpetuates the music.

signed Moira Heath

There could not be a better epitaph to a man who loved and was loved by his family, the members of his band, and all those who listened to his music.

Today it is down to others to keep the Ted Heath flag flying, and when they can all be assembled the remaining members of The Heath Band go on tour, and the following doesn't get any smaller either. Their performances are always a sell-out wherever they go, with fans sometimes travelling for many miles, such is their devotion to the memory.

Ted Heath's name and his music will live forever.

Amen!

The London Palladium appearances for Ted Heath and his Orchestra were as follows:

(With Ambrose)	12 October 1931
(With Ambrose)	19 October 1931
(With Ambrose)	29 July 1935
(With Ambrose)	5 August 1935
(Season with Geraldo)	15 May 1944
Swing Session No. 1	9 December 1945
Royal Variety Performance	1 November 1948
Variety	8 March 1954
Royal Variety Performance	1 November 1954
Swing Session No. 110	2 September 1956
Ted Heath and his Phase4 Music	20 April 1962
Accompanying Tom Jones, The Ted Heath Orchestra (Musical Director Ralph Dollimore)	13 November 1967
Stan Reynolds and The Ted Heath Orchestra	14 July 1974
Stan Reynolds and The Ted Heath Orchestra	21 July 1974
Sunday Tribute	2 November 1980

Chapter Thirteen

HI DE HI!

$\mathcal{S}$ ir Billy Butlin, the holiday camp king, was always astute in knowing how to make people happy. Obviously realising the importance of audience participation, and apart from the usual obligatory seaside 'Knobbly Knees' and 'Glamorous Grandmother' competitions, he chose to have a 'Star Trail' talent contest at his holiday establishments. In short, this was a search to find the best amateur artists. For all those hopefuls who would eventually end up in the final, the prize attraction was a chance to appear on that famous Palladium stage. For everyone taking part, even their families and supporters in the audience, it was a thrill of a lifetime. Each artist had already taken part in a series of nerve-racking preliminary heats around the country at the various holiday camp locations.

Sir Billy Butlin

In association with *The People* newspaper, the first Butlin's Palladium Final commenced in 1971 and a panel of celebrity judges from all walks of showbiz life watched a dozen or so 'amateur' acts. Whilst the judges deliberated, the followers and supporters were entertained in the second half by top professional acts. The shows were invariably produced and directed by Cyril Fletcher and Betty Astell, and often compèred by their daughter Jill. Some of the names, whilst perhaps not making the grade on the night in the competition, are still entertaining us today. A one-time lorry driver and ultimately a popular comedy entertainer and TV actor, the late Mike Reid eventually ended up being one of the judges a few years later, such was his meteoric rise to fame. Another example was talented musician, songwriter and pianist, Bobby Crush. By the third year Beryl Calvert, a ventriloquist, landed a part in the Palladium pantomime as one of their speciality acts. Quite a prize in itself!

To enhance this already successful competition, by the mid 1970s a junior section had been introduced. In the senior section, comedian Stan Boardman not only took away the Challenge Trophy but also £1000 in prize money. Happily, but perhaps ironically, he recalls that this cheque went straight to the Bank Manager to clear his overdraft, and the beer that was bought to toast his success in the cup went missing, so for Stan it really was a night to remember! He is still going strong today and making us laugh.

Sunday People

NATIONAL TALENT CONTEST 1973

organised exclusively with

Butlin's

GRAND FINALS

The London Palladium
Sunday December 2
Souvenir programme 15p

THE GRAND FINALS OF THE 1977

BUTLIN'S STAR TRAIL

TALENT CONTEST

London Palladium
Sunday November 27th 1977

SOUVENIR PROGRAMME
30p

GRAND FINALS

The People
NATIONAL TALENT CONTEST 1971

organised exclusively with

Butlin's

The London Palladium
Sunday October 31

Souvenir Programme 15p

One particular name to emerge from this successful talent showcase was a highly talented and brilliant juggler, Mark Robertson. With a special gift far beyond his young years, he made many successful appearances at the Palladium as well as other prestigious venues around the world, before he was tragically robbed of international stardom due to his untimely death of a heart attack at the age of twenty-four.

Billy Butlin was knighted in 1964, and many artists today owe a great debt of gratitude to him. Sir Billy's Entertainments Director was Basil Brown, and between them they founded the Redcoats, a band of entertainers who learned their trade at his holiday camps around Great Britain. Many will remember with great fondness the time spent in hard work under all sorts of conditions, learning their craft. There have been many, but Des O'Connor, Charlie Drake, Jimmy Tarbuck OBE, and Jimmy Perry OBE are just a few of the star names who were once proud to wear their red coats.

In 1996, to celebrate the Diamond Jubilee, *The Butlin's Story* was presented in a specially written musical at the Palladium. This was a fitting tribute to a man with a giant heart, who not only gave so much to charity but also so much happiness to many families whilst on holiday.

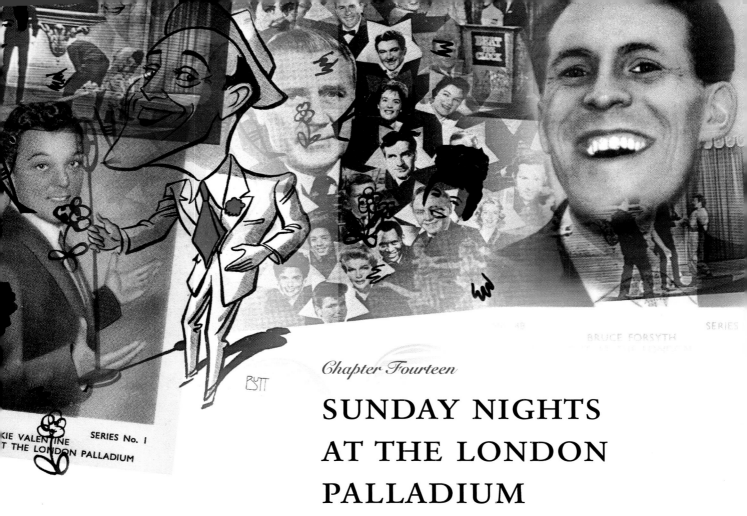

Chapter Fourteen

SUNDAY NIGHTS AT THE LONDON PALLADIUM

In September 1955, commercial television finally arrived in Britain and overnight the BBC lost its monopoly. It was also a bad time for Variety generally, with theatres beginning to close up and down the country. Those that managed to stay open had a tough fight on their hands to stay alive. Had Val Parnell been a cautious man, he might have closed the Palladium theatre down. Instead, having the vision to see the potential of this new fashion, 'television', he went to the other extreme. He paid fabulous sums of money to the cream of the world's entertainment to bring them to the Palladium stage. Everything that was to appear at the theatre was to be the very best, even down to the dancers' costumes. He set a new standard with the lavishness in his productions. He even redecorated the theatre, adding new carpets and new seating, installing the most up-to-date lighting equipment and also a lift in the orchestra pit. It was a big gamble that paid off.

VAL PARNELL
PRESENTS
Sunday Night
at the
LONDON PALLADIUM
One Hour of Entertainment
from
THE WORLD'S GREATEST VARIETY THEATRE
Produced by Bill Ward
SUNDAY, 25th SEPTEMBER, 1955
Doors open 7 p.m.
No admission after 7.30 p.m.
PRODUCED BY THE INCORPORATED TELEVISION PROGRAMME CO. LTD.
FOR ASSOCIATED BROADCASTING COMPANY LTD.

17

RESERVED

STALLS

Nanci, this little town adored you,
Nanci, now let the world applaud you,
Maybe you'll remember
Though we let you go,
we loved you so.

Dear Nanci we're gonna miss you sadly,
Nanci but wish you luck, and gladly,
promise we'll be happy, when you make your name
win through to fame
For every hope you cherished we have shared with you,
there never was a girl to be compared with you,
You could do 'most anything you cared to do,
pretty as a picture – your head always in a whirl,

Dear Nanci, we're saying 'Heaven bless you'
Nanci but may as well confess though you climb,
to the big time,
to the folks at home you'll still be their own
Dear Nanci – and a smalltown girl.

These simple words, written by Phil Park and set to music by Eric Rogers, were sung by the cast in the popular 1955 Norman Wisdom show, *Painting the Town.* It was to become the most famous signature tune of any popular TV show in the 1950s and 1960s. The title of the music was 'Startime'. The talented Eric Rogers could play every instrument in his orchestra except the violin. The ballet scene was specially devised by the highly respected popular song and dance man, Dick Hurran. Dick's talents went back to the pre-war days of the Coconut Grove and the Windmill Theatre. The elaborate scene depicted Nanci Crompton as she left her little village by train for the big time; and 'Big Time' the Sunday night TV slot proved to be.

When commercial television came into being on 22 September 1955, Val Parnell was not only at the helm of the London Palladium, but he was also the Managing Director of Associated Television. He was given the job of producing a top variety show every week at 8.00pm and, naturally enough, he gave it the title *Sunday Night at the London Palladium.*

Such was the popularity of *Sunday Night at the London Palladium* all over the country, the viewing public were changing their daily habits so as not to miss what was to become an institution in the history of British

TV. Stop anyone in the street today who remembers the 1960s and hum the first few bars of that tune, 'Startime', and they will instantly recall the revolving stage that was used to end the show, where the complete cast would assemble and wave goodbye. Or maybe they will recollect Bruce's immortal words, 'I'm in charge', or 'You have sixty seconds to Beat the Clock and re-assemble these words to make a famous phrase or saying.' In order to retain his parishioners, one vicar in Surrey even re-scheduled his evening service to start half an hour earlier, allowing enough time for the parishioners to get home to view the show. Such was the popularity of this much loved and greatly missed era in the history of television. The talking point on everyone's lips on a Monday morning was, 'Did you see the Palladium show last night? What did you think of the top of the bill, and weren't The Palladium Dancers good?'

Viewing figures in the form of ratings were vital, and the Palladium's Sunday offering, when not actually *top* of the ratings, was *always* in the top ten. Whilst some were naturally still loyal to the BBC, viewers now had a choice. The first and second shows managed to catch seventy-eight per cent of viewers, and by December eighty-four per cent of UK viewers were tuning into the Palladium show. In the early days it was only the viewers in the London area who could receive the programme, but by February 1956 the viewing figures had increased because ATV The Midlands had been included. A mere 100,000 viewers on the opening night had increased to an estimated twenty-two million by the end of 1960. By then television licences had reached the ten million mark, and this number had doubled since 1955.

Billed in the *Television Times* for the day, the timetable was always as follows:

7.40pm: 'Palladium Preview': A visit to the star's number one dressing room at the London Palladium to meet Val Parnell, the Palladium's Master Showman, who will personally introduce the top of the bill for the Palladium show for the night.

Then at 8.00pm precisely, Eric Rogers would raise his baton and that famous piece of music, 'Startime', would begin. It would haunt the viewing public for some four hundred performances over the next twelve years or so.

The real day had begun some twelve hours earlier. Now, at 8.00am on a Sunday morning the Palladium is normally dark, quiet, lonely and vast in its emptiness, but in those days, it was full of noise and movement. Preparations for the show had begun in earnest! The lighting riggers had been in the night before, but all through the day the Sunday camera crews and technicians took over the Palladium with cables, cameras and lighting, discreetly transforming the theatre into a giant television studio. In all, four cameras were used. One was on a trolley moving up and down the stalls gangway, another was placed in the dress circle and a third provided the high overhead shots from the upper circle. The fourth camera was used on stage, sometimes in the wings, to give a profile shot of the performer. On occasion it was placed at the back of the stage facing the theatre audience. Sometimes you were able see the back of The Tiller Girls, looking out over the heads of the orchestra into the audience, then the next moment you could see their faces, with no camera in sight. The explanation for this was that the camera at the back of the stage was deliberately hidden from view in the scenery and so could not be seen from the front.

In the orchestra pit, conductor Eric Rogers prepared the music and his talented musicians for the day's rehearsal. Such was the high expectation of the demanding Parnell that, apart from a lunch break, eight solid hours of preparation went into just one hour's performance. One week it would be The Tiller Girls, the next week George Carden would be grouping his Palladium Dancers in readiness for their complicated precision routines. Costumes would have to be organised for the dress rehearsal, and pressed to perfection.

Seated in the middle of the stalls would be Val Parnell with his personal assistant and secretary, Miss Wood. He would listen to the music and the acts, and watch every movement and every detail of the show in its rough rehearsal, ironing out problems that would occur and adding his own personal touch to the presentation. After frequent consultation with stalwart Charles Henry, his Chief of Production, he would then decide that the final dress rehearsal could take place. Taking into account that the show was broadcast live in the early days, each act was meticulously timed to the split second as the show could not possibly overrun. Woe betide you if you did.

SUNDAY NIGHT AT THE PALLADIUM

Notice To Artistes

FOR THE FINAL REHEARSAL WITH THE ORCHESTRA THIS AFTERNOON, IT IS ESSENTIAL FOR LIGHTING AND CAMERA PURPOSES THAT YOU WEAR EXACTLY WHAT YOU PROPOSE TO USE FOR TRANSMISSION.

Thank You

As well as receiving a very strong dressing down from Parnell, you would probably never work the theatre again. Ever!

In the first show that went out live, the joint tops of the bill were our very own Gracie Fields, who sang her famous 'Sally', and Guy Mitchell, who had already appeared live on that very same stage to packed audiences in regular Variety. His rendition of 'She Wears Red Feathers' and 'Truly Fair' brought the house down, as one would expect from such a popular and frequent visitor from the United States. Channing Pollock, that suave and sophisticated sorcerer, made doves materialise from silk scarves and produced cards from thin air in his own unique and inimitable style. Once produced, the doves then vanished in a cage just as mysteriously as they had appeared, which ended his all too brief performance.

BEAT THE CLOCK

It was his famous stage presence that had made him unequalled in his own particular branch of the magic profession, and he was one of the most highly paid speciality acts. Those whirlwind equilibrists The Christianis, The Theda Sisters and The George Mitchell Choir completed this historic variety bill, along with The George Carden Dancers who added glamour, precision, tempo and skill. The only name that could link them all together was that of Tommy Trinder, who had seemingly been in almost permanent residence at the Palladium for nearly twenty years. The master ad-libber with an almost unquenchable thirst for jokes was the compère for the whole show for a number of years.

The format of the Palladium show would be as follows. The first third would be made up of the world's top variety artists and speciality acts and then, after a commercial break, the second third would take over with *Beat The Clock*. This was an idea that had been imported from America, devised by Goodson and Todman, whose names are still synonymous with game shows to this very day, with *What's My Line* perhaps being their most recognisable show. *Beat The Clock* was compiled of a series of games, using members of the public who were chosen at random just before the show went on air. They were invited to attempt seemingly impossible tasks, all to be accomplished within sixty seconds, with valuable prize money at the end. If the prize was not won, an accumulator came into operation. The highest amount not won was £1800, which eventually ended up being divided between four charities.

Centre stage was a large clock, with the sweep hand ticking away the seconds. In one game, contestants did their very best to bounce a ball off a bass drum onto a snare drum and then onto a cymbal, before their partner tried to catch it. For eighteen weeks this one particular game proved impossible, although consolation prizes of either a hairdryer or an alarm clock were always on hand. Complaints were made that the game was impossible, but after a summer break when the show returned, the game was played again and was won first time!

It should be pointed out that most of the games were devised by Jim Smith, the Senior Studio Manager at ATV. They were tried out first by him on the Monday which preceded the live show on the following Sunday. They were again tested during the rehearsals by Fred Pearson, the Palladium Stage Manager, and perhaps a Tiller Girl acting as his 'wife', just to make sure that the ideas would work. Those that didn't work never got as far as the show. Easier games were created to put the contestants at their ease. 'Rearrange the words behind the screen', Trinder would say, revealing some simple phrase like 'A bird in the hand is worth two in the bush', except it would read as follows: 'worth the hand bush is in a the bird two in'. It looked comparatively easy to the viewer sitting comfortably at home in his own armchair and viewing at a distance. Being close up to the screen and knowing that possibly twenty million people were watching you, the nervousness did take the simplicity of the problem away and made it appear harder! In the early days, each participating male and female contestant was given a specially designed *Beat the Clock* tie and silk scarf respectively.

After another commercial break, the final third of the show would be allocated to the top of the bill. This was preceded by a contribution by the hardest working members of the cast, the dancers. The Tiller Girls alternated each week with The George Carden Palladium Dancers; twelve bodies and twenty-four legs in precision routines which were expertly choreographed.

Tops of the bill have included over the years almost every foremost name from all corners of the entertainment profession. The Palladium has seen not only pop singers and comedians, but also stars from the world of opera and ballet, film stars and TV personalities; a cast

covering the whole gamut of show business. They have ranged from the queen of jazz Ella Fitzgerald, to Judy Garland, Bob Hope, Jack Benny, Errol Garner, Oscar Petersen, Pat Boone, Eartha Kitt, Roy Orbison, Johnnie Ray, Lena Horne, Jane Russell, Jane Morgan, Markova, Nureyev and Fonteyn, Liberace, Fernandel, Patachou, Pearl Bailey, Rosemary Clooney, The Platters, Cliff Richard, Frankie Laine, Jayne Mansfield, Larry Parkes, Mario Lanza, Diana Dors, Tony Bennett, Frankie Vaughan, Max Bygraves, Harry Secombe, Eric Sykes, Frankie Howerd, Shirley Bassey, Dave Brubeck, Eric Morecambe and Ernie Wise, Arthur Askey, that delightful little Italian mouse Topo Gigio, Sabrina, Roy Castle, Alma Cogan, Allan Jones, Frank Ifield, Tommy Steele, Xavier Cugat, Petula Clark, Pete Seeger, Ethel Merman, Peter Paul and Mary, Tom Jones, The Springfields, Tommy Cooper, Cilla Black, Charlie Drake, Norman Wisdom, and Nat King Cole. The list is almost endless, but they were all worthy of that top spot.

TOMMY TRINDER

No. 6   CHANNING POLLOCK
SUNDAY NIGHT AT THE LONDON PALLADIUM

SERIES No. 1

SERIES N

SERIES N

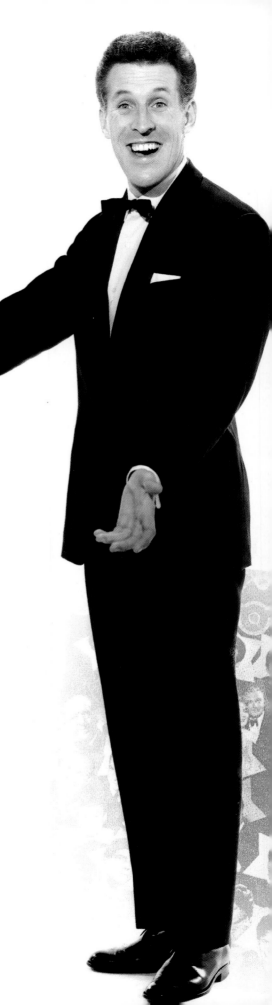

After the top of the bill had finished his or her act, the heavy red velvet curtains would swish to a close, allowing them to take a well earned bow. This gave the stage crew only just enough time to reset the stage for the whole cast to stand on 'the revolve', waving goodbye until the next time, with the music 'Startime' playing the show out. By this time the hearts of all those taking part would be beating fast. It was an emotional time.

Then it was time to take the make-up off, grab a quick bite to eat and go to bed for a well earned rest. Another show over maybe, but rehearsals would begin all over again the next day, as Monday morning saw the start of the final planning of the following week's show.

The list of compères over the years ranged from Tommy Trinder to the avuncular Robert Morley, Dickie Henderson, Hughie Green, Bob Monkhouse, Don Arrol, Alfred Marks, Dave Allen, Des O'Connor and Ted Rogers. And although they were only there for one night, the names of Arthur Haynes and Roy Castle should also be included for completeness. When the last series came to the screens in 1974, it was hosted by all-round actor Jim Dale. These were some of the names of the regulars, but apart from the ubiquitous Tommy Trinder, the names which were most frequently on the lips of the more latter day viewers were the ever popular Bruce Forsyth and of course Jimmy Tarbuck.

The hundredth production of the Sunday night spectacular took place on 2 March 1958, and a top show was lined up with Buddy Holly and The Crickets. This was to be this star's first and only appearance at the Palladium. Bob Hope, who was by now a regular visitor, and the world famous ballet star Markova completed the line-up. The compère on this occasion was Robert Morley.

In 1960, Cliff Richard was seen by an estimated nineteen million viewers in 6,853,000 homes. By 1961 Val Parnell had notched up his 200th edition, and the stars appearing that night were Bruce Forsyth, Mel Torme,

Bruce Forsyth

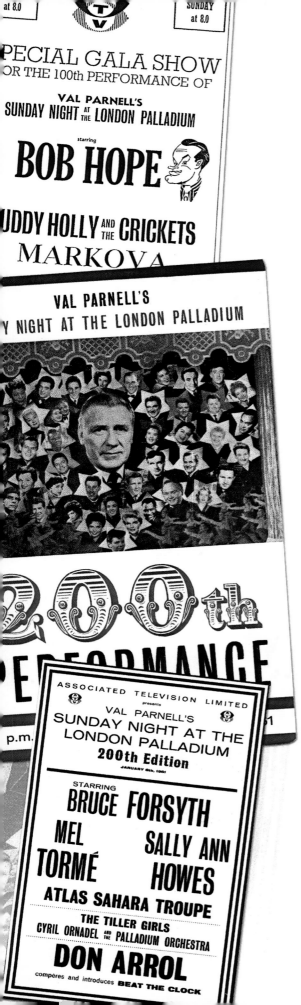

Sally Anne Howes, and The Atlas Sahara Troupe. The omnipresent Tiller Girls completed the bill, and Cyril Ornadel conducted the London Palladium Orchestra. By this time, Don Arrol was the compère. *Sunday Night at the London Palladium* had been in the top ten ratings for all but seventeen of the previous 199 performances. Quite an achievement! On 15 April 1962 the 250th edition had Harry Secombe as top of the bill, with Eric Sykes assisting in the merriment. The viewing figures had by now increased to an estimated twenty-one million.

In late 1961, due to a dispute between the actors' union Equity and the Independent Television Companies, the regular *Sunday Night* show could not go ahead. In its place, Norman Wisdom and Bruce Forsyth just went ahead and did the show themselves. A simple two-man show. Such were their joint talents it was no problem for them to fill in the time, so much so that their performance has since become a classic to this very day.

Val Parnell once stated that he built the show around the headliner and then chose other acts to complement the star. 'Our policy for the Palladium is to make the viewer feel one of the audience. The bulk of the television audience is from the provinces and they perhaps never get the opportunity to get to a big West End variety theatre and that is why, once a week, I give them the best seat in the house at the greatest music hall in the world.'

As the show was always live in the early days, unforeseen things would often happen. When a complete power failure occurred just before transmission, Tommy Trinder was left to entertain the specially invited audience for nearly two hours in the theatre. When power was finally restored, Trinder still had the strength to say, 'Welcome to Monday morning at the Palladium!' Later, in more troubled times when the talented Bob Monkhouse was compère, a bomb scare once prevented the show going out to the waiting public.

Costs had risen from £8,000 per programme (at around £135 per minute) to £20,000 a programme by 1965. Lew Grade, who succeeded Parnell as Managing Director of ATV, was budgeting £50,000 per show in the 1970s. Dickie Henderson used to say, 'If Val Parnell was there he always had something to say about presentation and about material and *anything* in bad taste was most definitely out. He was very astute!'

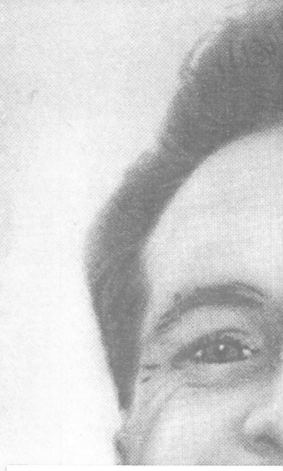

By the late 1960s colour TV had arrived, and although by this time *Beat the Clock* had gone, a faster moving show altogether took place, which was more in keeping with the times. When the show was reprised in 1966, Jonathan Winters, Fess Parker, Roger Moore, Hugh O'Brien, and Lorne Greene all took over the role of host and linked the show together on separate occasions for the American export market.

One could fill a book with hilarious stories concerning various incidents during the run, but one true story concerns Errol Garner, who made his first appearance in October 1963 and then again in 1966. His playing was certainly never overshadowed by his height. In order that he might reach the keyboard, the Stage Manager added two London Telephone Directories to the piano stool! In those days the complete London Telephone Directory was in four volumes; A–D, E–K, L–R and S–Z. Two volumes were sufficient to raise him to the correct height in order that he could reach the keyboard to do his act. Just before the live show was about to go on air, he went over to the Stage Manager, Jack Matthews, and complained that he couldn't go on, and wouldn't go on! Seconds were ticking by, and Jack tried to calm him down, as by this time it would have been impossible to find a replacement top of the bill. Some of the stars were temperamental, and they had to face the enormity of appearing live at the world's most famous theatre. But this was cutting things a bit fine! Everything had been perfect at rehearsal. Just what was the problem? Unbeknown to the stage crew, Errol Garner was something of a practical joker (maybe to lighten the nerves). He said that during rehearsal he had been given A–D and E–K in order that he could reach the keys from his piano stool, and now he was being offered L–R and S–Z, and he wouldn't go on until the same directories that had been used at rehearsal were used for the show. As the directories were of equal thickness, it could hardly have mattered that they had been swapped!

Another story concerning Errol was when the Stage Manager, Jack Matthews, indicated to compère Bruce to carry on talking. After a while he was given the all clear and introduced the top of the bill. On entering the wings Bruce asked Jack whatever had gone wrong? Jack said, 'look at the piano!' It appeared that whilst setting the piano centre stage the leg had given way, and not having

No. 48   SERIES No. 1
BRUCE FORSYTH
SUNDAY NIGHT AT THE LONDON PALLADIUM

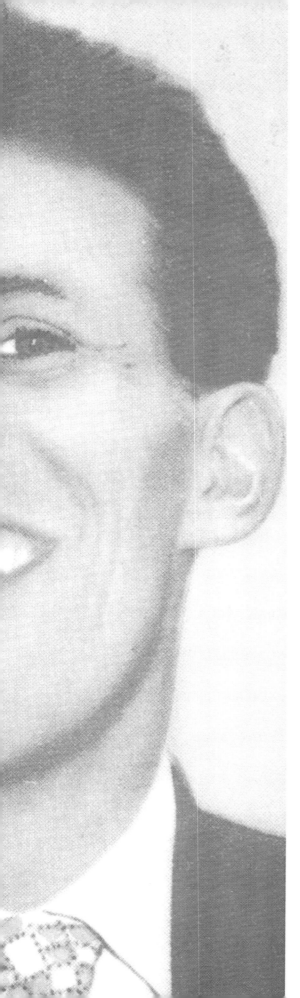

another piano they quickly had to fix the one they had got. Remember it was a live show! They located a beer crate (I wonder how they found one of those backstage?) and covered it with black velvet and propped up the piano that way. Very elegant indeed, but I am sure no one noticed.

This was actually Bruce's first appearance at the Palladium. He had been appearing at the Hippodrome in Eastbourne the week before, and he drove up to London on the Sunday morning. When he arrived in London and was ready to park his car, he was so nervous at the thought of his first appearance that he drove around the block three times!

There are a multitude of other stories as one would expect, but there are one or two that I feel are particularly worth repeating. I was privileged to be present during the first colour recording in April 1966, primarily to witness Robert Harbin present his famous 'cutting a lady into three' Zigzag illusion in colour. One of the items in this full variety show was being presented by radio 'Goon' Michael Bentine. It was a typically English sketch with Benny Lee, Alfie Ravel, Derek Guyler, Leon Thau, Maurice Gibbons and Thelma Taylor. The scene was a quintessential English village pub. As one would expect from the pen of Bentine, it was only understood by those who were au fait with his brand of humour. It was very funny to watch, but when the American distributors viewed the sketch they didn't really have a clue as to what was going on and it was cut. To fill in the time, Bentine had to come up with another idea pretty fast so that it could be edited in and the show could then be sold to the United States and around the world.

This was the scene that was finally considered acceptable; twelve Paddy Stone Dancers, who had been working in Blackpool the night before, travelled down to London especially to appear in the scene. Michael came out in front of the famous 'house tabs' to announce, 'No show would be complete without a dancing troupe. Here on the show tonight we have The Paddy Stone Dancers!' The curtain began to rise, revealing twenty-four pretty legs suitably dressed with tights and silver shoes, each left leg moving in unison and in time to the music and then each right leg similarly moving as the curtain continued to rise. As soon as the curtain reached about waist height though, it stopped, but the dancers continued to kick, professionals that they were. Michael looked anxiously into the wings to the Stage Manager for help as to what was happening to prevent the curtain from continuing in its upward path. By this time, realising that there was a problem, the dancers had stopped dancing. The curtain had really got stuck. 'Well,' said Michael, 'they have come a long way to present this routine and have spent hours perfecting it. It would be a shame to waste their talent!' And so they completed their routine.

What the public never knew of course was that the whole thing was a set-up. Even the dancers were in on the joke. The curtain was meant to get stuck, so much so that the dancers were only dressed correctly from the waist down with the appropriate stage fishnet tights and shoes, as this was the only part of their bodies that would be seen. On their top halves, they were wearing just cardigans, normal street clothes and no stage make-up. This was typical Bentine humour which lost nothing in the translation to the US screens and the rest of the world. A lovely, talented man and a much missed sense of humour.

Some weeks the format of the TV show would be Variety, some weeks it would have a classical theme, and on one show a headlining opera singer had been booked. It reached the time for the dress rehearsal and his voice went completely. With not too much time to spare, a replacement had to be found, but where, and more to the point how quickly? It was a live show, remember! Someone had a friend in Surrey who loved opera and he was phoned to ask his advice. He just happened to have someone staying with him, who, although unknown, had a superb voice. It was worth a try. He was speedily brought up by car to Argyll Street and whilst he was en route his music was located. It turned out to be a superb show and his singing was sensational. He later found fame as Luciano Pavarotti!

Once, Oscar Petersen had finished his act but rather than stand up from the piano to take his bow, he did so sitting at the piano. This was puzzling to the Producer and Stage Manager, who had expected him to stand up at the end as rehearsed. What they didn't know was that one of the piano legs had given way and he was holding up the piano completely with it sitting on his knees!

Val Parnell

presents

Sadly, little remains today on tape or film of those wonderful days. At the time, the powers that be decided in their wisdom that with the cost of the video tape running at £1,000 for the hour, they would re-use the tape as no one would want to watch the programmes again. How wrong they were!

Val Parnell had a policy:

A television set is another front door to your house: open it and you admit someone into your home. In sending people to your front door we shoulder a delicate responsibility. Our audience grows each day and with it our responsibility to maintain a service of entertainment which will hold the public's preference.

YOU, our audience, are the people I'm aiming to please. YOU are the people who make this whole vast industry possible. YOU are here to enjoy yourselves, and for our part we intend to do our best to make that possible.

Chapter Fifteen

THE 'SPESH' ACT

Part One: A Circle of Magicians

There were at least sixty music halls in London alone in the 1900s, and sometimes an act could manage three appearances in three different theatres in one night! Any well-balanced bill would nearly always contain a 'spesh' act as it was affectionately known, 'spesh' being short for speciality. The speciality act would often be a magician or perhaps a ventriloquist, a juggler or maybe a protean 'quick change' artist. In the first part of this chapter I will attempt to list just some of those magicians who have graced the Palladium stage.

The first known magician to appear in Argyll Street was Buatier de Kolta, who performed in 1897 when the Palladium was still operating under the Hengler banner and was the home of The National Skating Palace. De Kolta, a Frenchman born in 1845, was educated in a seminary and intended for the priesthood by his parents. However he was more interested in manipulating cards, and soon his interest began to grow towards bigger things.

He was the inventor of many famous illusions that are still presented today by top TV wizards, most notably the one where a bird is seen in a small cage held between the fingertips of the magician, whereupon after the count of three the bird and cage disappear into thin air without trace. On this occasion in 1897, on a special stage built on the ice rink, de Kolta performed his latest 'Marvellous Illusion': the 'Ascent and Miraculous Disappearance of a Man in Mid Air'. Twice daily, de Kolta would dress up as a fireman and climb a vertical ladder that was fixed to the stage. When he had almost reached the top, literally in a split second he simply disappeared! On an earlier visit to London his magical prowess had earned him a Royal Command Performance before Queen Victoria, and he will long be remembered as one of magic's top inventive names in the late nineteenth and early twentieth centuries.

In 1911, although billed as the 'Egyptian Mystic', Rameses was really Albert Marchinski, a one-time Yiddish actor who was born in Poland as the son of a clothing manufacturer. Having decided that the stage was for him and having purchased magician's props with an Egyptian flavour, he travelled to Egypt to completely research his 'character'. So successful was he that he was engaged to tour the United States and then to return to the Palladium, where he appeared many times in Variety. He had the distinction of appearing in the very first special Royal Performance programme in 1914 in aid of the rebuilding of the Chelsea Hospital for Women. This was undoubtedly a coup for Charles Gulliver, for it was the first time that Royalty had consented to attend a variety performance. The gracious presence of the King and Queen was the turning point in the future success of the Palladium.

Within six months of the theatre opening, an appearance by an American (who was of Scottish and English parents) in the guise of a Chinese man allowed one of magic's most loved and revered artists to show off his colourful and dangerous feats. Chung Ling Soo was born William Ellsworth Robinson in New York in April 1861. 'Billy' Robinson, as he was then known to his friends, learned his trade in the US working for such famous names as Kellar and Herrmann the Great. Billy made his British debut as Chung Ling Soo in 1900 when he appeared at the Alhambra in London. One of his

famous tricks was to catch live goldfish on the end of a fishing line. His persona as a 'Chinaman' was carried to the n'th degree, for when he was 'Soo' he spoke no English, and needed an interpreter present when he gave a press interview. What brilliant subterfuge! His performance of fifty-five illusions in almost as many minutes in a lavish setting provided the public with a superb and colourful evening's entertainment.

Sadly, his name will be better remembered as a result of a tragic accident. He had perfected a special presentation known as 'Catching a Live Bullet.' During the years of the First World War it was almost impossible to obtain gunpowder, but due to his charitable works for the armed forces and wounded soldiers sent home from the front, he had acquired friends in high places. This enabled him to obtain the necessary explosive ingredients to present this item twice nightly. A previously marked bullet was loaded into a musket and fired at Soo. Night after night he continued to excite the public by catching the marked bullet in his teeth. Then, on the night of 23 March 1918 at the nearby Wood Green Empire, something went tragically wrong. The loaded gun was fired at Soo as always by his trusted assistant Jack Grossman, but this time he fell to the stage mortally wounded. Although attempts were made by medics to save his life, he died the following day in hospital. A truly traumatic ending to one of the most colourful characters in Variety.

Another terrible incident involved The Great Lafayette. He was born Sigmund Neuberger in Germany in 1872. As the brilliant Lafayette, he would undoubtedly have been employed to entertain Palladium audiences had he not tragically died in a fire in May 1911 at the Empire Theatre, Edinburgh. The stage setting for one of his most famous presentations, 'The Lion's Bride', was the interior of a circus tent. One should visualise a real African lion pacing back and forth in a cage centre stage. A beautifully gowned lady climbs into the cage, the lion roars, the lady screams. The beast rears up as if to pounce on his prey. Suddenly, the animal skin falls away, only to reveal The Great Lafayette, who just a few moments earlier had been standing outside and helping the lady into the cage. As well as presenting illusions, Lafayette was known for his protean skills. On the night of 9 May 1911, during the second house Lafayette came forward after his presentation of 'The Lion's Bride' to acknowledge the well deserved applause from the near capacity three thousand-seater house, when tragedy struck. An oriental lamp high above the stage inside the tent burst into flames, setting the tent on fire. The fire curtain was quickly lowered and the audience was ushered out to safety. Sadly, backstage it was a different story. Everything was destroyed. One or two of his key staff managed to escape, but Lafayette perished in the raging inferno. To protect his secrets, Lafayette had clauses in his contract that no one other than his assistants was allowed backstage during the performance, and all doors leading to the stage were to be locked.

Although this sad incident had no direct connection with the Palladium, it is mentioned here because the Empire was to have been the venue for the first Royal Command Performance to be held on 11 May 1911. This had been organised to coincide with the visit to Edinburgh by King George V. This Command Performance did eventually take place the following year in London at the Palace Theatre. It was the first of many such performances that would eventually be held, almost exclusively, at the Palladium. The relevant footnote to the fire incident was that *The Great Lafayette Show* did actually take place at the Palladium in September 1911, but with his lady friend, Miss Lalla Selbini, in control of the stage. It was to Lalla that Lafayette had bequeathed his estate and rights to the show, and this she carried on in his memory with a full cast of twenty-six performers. Methinks such was his popularity, he would already have been contracted to appear at the Palladium long before the fire. If he had gone to the trouble and expense of fireproofing all his scenery, this tragedy could so easily have been avoided.

With magic being truly international, the next act to grace the stage in Argyll Street was that of Hang Pin Chen presenting 'The Peking Mysteries'. A real Chinese man this time, with authentic assistants, who produced magic with water in every conceivable way. Chen would somersault across the stage and upon landing on his feet he would be seen to be holding a bowl that was brimming over with water. Considering that the bowl and water had been on his person during the somersault, it made the feat even more remarkable. A couple of toy ducks were then

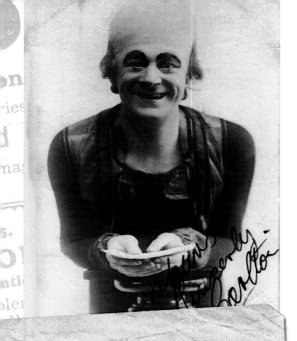

THE PALLADIUM

Engagement Extraordinary at Enormous Expense of

THE "ONLY"

GOLDIN

The Royal Illusionist.

Presenting in Three Series

"The Old and the New—and a Tiger too."

The most stupendous exposition of magic ever produced on any stage.

FIRST SERIES.

"A REVUE OF CONJURING"

From the Fifteenth to the Twentieth Centuries.

In which Goldin provides a happy blend of the Magic and Protean Arts, impersonating the following Conjurors—

HORACE GOLDIN
1. BAUTIER DE KOLTA.
2. SIGNOR ANTON BLITZ.
3. ROBERT HOUDIN.
4. CHING LING FOO.
5. HERMANN.

SECOND SERIES.

HORACE GOLDIN'S

Twentieth Century "Miracles"

Performed with that Remarkable Celerity and Precision, that has caused Goldin to be known as "The Whirlwind Illusionist."

THE MYSTERIOUS SEDAN CHAIR.
THE RAJAH'S LUNCHEON.
THE GORGEOUS BEDCHAMBER.
WEIGHED IN THE BALANCE.
LIVING SHADOWS.
THE MAGNITTO MYSTERY.
THE BEWILDERING DOUBLE CABINETS and
THE MUSICAL FLIGHT.

Goldin's Latest Masterpiece, in which a Real Piano with a Lady are made to mysteriously vanish into thin air in full view of the audience.

THIRD SERIES.

Goldin's Latest and Greatest Creation, a Pantomimic Spectacular Production :—

THE TIGER GOD

A Moorish Mystery, by Horace Goldin.

Costumes by Clarkson.   Scenery by Bruce Smith.

A weird and awe-inspiring Story of Eastern Mystery, reminiscent of all the wonderful legends of "The Land of Islam," culminating with a bewildering and incomprehensible Illusion with

A LIVING TIGER.

The whole produced amidst scenes of Oriental Splendour and Magnificence never before attempted.

placed upon the water and the whole affair covered with a shawl, and in a flash the bowl was gone, water and all. After Chen had taken his well deserved applause, to climax the routine the bowl was then reproduced, complete with a real duck swimming on the water!

The first British born wizard to appear at the Palladium was Carlton. 'The Thinnest Conjuror Extant' was his bill matter, and he was also known as 'The Human Hairpin'. He was probably Britain's first comedy magician. His tall lean figure, accentuated by a false domed bald head and wig, together with 'lifts' on his shoes, made him look grotesque. An apocryphal story tells of a lady and child watching Carlton, and the child is overheard asking the mother, 'What are those wires?', to which the mother replies rather embarrassingly, 'Those aren't wires dear, those are his legs!' He had a kind of Professor Wallofski character about him. He was often assisted by a very fat man and a dwarf, which only added to his bizarre appearance. Whatever magic he touched, it turned to laughter, much in the same way as his later counterpart, Tommy Cooper. I can best quote one critic who, full of praise, said:

> Carlton continues on his merry way and rocks his audience with mirth in his absurdity, which for sheer unadulterated nonsense will take a lot of beating. He has created more laughter than the rest of the bill put together which is doing the company no discredit, for Carlton's burlesque is hypnotic in more senses than one and he manages to entrance his audience even more successfully than he entrances his subjects during his mock hypnosis act.

A natural clown indeed, and in addition to being highly paid, he was well respected amongst his fellow professionals.

Next on the scene chronologically was Polish born Horace Goldin. His bill matter was 'The Whirlwind Wizard'. As the title implied, he performed a series of fast moving miracles in rapid succession in a short space of time. Don't blink or else you will miss a trick! The element of danger, especially with wild animals, was a feature of many a Palladium prestidigitator, and Goldin's presentation of 'The Tiger God' in 1913 was no exception. A real Bengal Tiger was seen pacing up and down inside a cage centre stage. A beautiful young maiden was thrown into the cage, whereupon Goldin saved the girl by making the tiger disappear the moment the girl was seen inside the cage. His many appearances on the Palladium stage coupled with his world travels testified to the popularity of the performer. Goldin appeared before Royalty many times, performing before King Edward VII at Sandringham, and later appearing before the Queen of Saxony and the King and Queen of Siam. Always with an eye for publicity, he began calling himself 'The Royal Illusionist,' a well deserved title.

Later in the 1930s, Goldin was famous for 'The Magic Saw', and such was his popularity in the United States that he had half a dozen different touring companies presenting this one illusion. Goldin always had the advantage on his rivals though. He had an ambulance parked outside the theatre with a well placed sign: 'In case the saw slips!' Always searching for something new, he went one better and had the lady sawn 'in half' by a fearsome *circular* saw. Tremendous publicity ensued and he was held over for a second week. The jewels that had been presented to him by Royalty never outshone this truly wonderful, many faceted performer. *However*, it should be remembered that earlier, in 1921, the inventor Selbit the Magician had presented his original 'Sawing Through a Lady' at the Palladium. A pedantic detail maybe, but Selbit was the first to accomplish this illusion! Both presentations were entirely different, but the play on the words 'in half', where he was seen to saw a lady in half and then *separate* the halves, perhaps gave Goldin the edge.

Percy Thomas Tibbles was an unlikely name for a top illusionist, and so by reversing his surname and dropping the second 'b', he became Selbit. He was truly a master illusionist and inventor and will always be remembered for being the first person in the world to, in effect, 'saw a lady in half!' He first introduced this in London at the Finsbury Park Empire in January 1921, and within five months he was booked to appear at the Palladium. It was truly a miracle! A young lady was placed in a long wooden box, and secured at the wrists and ankles by individual lengths of rope that were passed though corresponding holes in the sides of the box. These were held taut by volunteers from the audience, who acted as committee men. When the lid was closed, padlocks

secured the whole affair, imprisoning the lady inside with no means of movement or escape. Three panes of glass were thrust down through the lid of the coffin-like box, and two sheets of steel blades were also pushed from front to back. It seemed impossible for the lady to have survived the ordeal. The central piece of glass was then removed from the middle section of the box, whereupon Selbit, assisted by another volunteer, proceeded to saw the box and seemingly the lady in two with a menacing cross cut saw. 'The greatest riddle of the age'. It was without doubt a big sensation, so much so that Selbit was honoured by being asked to appear on the 1922 Royal Variety Performance with this very illusion. It was an accolade indeed as he was only the second magician to be given this high honour. Selbit helped to publicise this illusion by having his assistant pour a bucket of (simulated) blood into the gutter after his performance, to the obvious bewilderment of the passers-by in front of the theatre. This was a sure way of catching their eye and enticing them to view the next performance of this sensation! Such was the inventive brilliance of Selbit's mind that if he were to have presented all his inventions in one night, the performance could quite easily have lasted all evening and possibly well into the early hours of the next morning!

For someone who started life as an architect, Oswald Williams made many an impressive appearance on the Palladium stage 'Under Royal and Distinguished Patronage', his presentation comprised of 'A series of original mysteries presented in the most gorgeous settings ever seen on any stage.' One of the most puzzling was billed as 'The Quickest Thing on Earth'; 'A magical pantomime sketch entitled "Who's Who", incorporating a series of transformations and substitutions in which four people appear, disappear and change places in the most baffling manner, performing no less than seven distinct illusions in the space of forty-five seconds.'

Word of mouth, they say, is the best possible publicity. The following appeared in a magic journal in 1914:

> In recent conversations with brother artists we were pleasantly struck by their independent testimony to the comfort and attention shown to artists by the Palladium Management and it is a significant fact that in this, one of the most up-to-date Variety Houses in London, the cream

of the conjuring profession is constantly fulfilling return engagements. The Management are to be congratulated on the excellent arrangements in each department affecting the welfare of the artists appearing on the bill. It is in this way that all houses should help their artists and so forward their chances of success.

Soon after the Armistice was signed at the end of the First World War, the world renowned top American illusionist Carl Hertz (Leib Morganstern) appeared on stage alongside the top names of Variety. He was a brilliant performer and publicist, which was highlighted when, to promote his show in Melbourne, Australia, he advertised for 1,000 cats that he would set loose in the streets, and around their necks would be fastened paper collars advertising his show. However, Hertz' real claim to fame was that he was, and still is, the only magician ever to have given a magical presentation before a Select Committee in the House of Commons.

One of the items in the Hertz repertoire was the famous de Kolta invention, where a canary in a cage held between the hands of the performer vanishes in a split second, leaving no trace whatsoever. It is still being featured to this very day by magicians around the world, but, dare I say, not always with a live canary! Hertz, however, *did* use a real canary. Such was the speed of the disappearance, he was challenged that the canary was harmed and in some cases killed when the cage actually evaporated. Connie, his trained canary, was marked and placed in the cage which Hertz held between his hands, and just as before on hundreds, perhaps thousands of occasions, everything disappeared. In a nonchalant way Hertz tossed his jacket to the members of the Commons Committee before leaving the room. A few moments later he re-entered the room to the buzz of conversation with Connie perched on his outstretched hand. The canary was obviously none the worse for wear, happily twittering as if to say 'I know something that you don't know!' Those present who had witnessed the marking of Connie verified the markings again, and testified that it was the very same bird. Hertz confirmed that Connie had been disappearing twice nightly for almost a year; in fact, some of his birds had been used for up to six years. The publicity that ensued helped to swell the box office ticket sales wherever he went!

Another inventor and performer to grace the Argyll Street stage was Fred Culpitt. Culpitt is immortalised in magic circles for his invention of showing a small dolls' house, completely empty except for suitably sized furniture. Smoke would then begin to spiral from the chimney, and when the roof was lifted off, it revealed his assistant Miss Jan Glenrose, dressed in voluminous attire, who completely filled the house.

It became a well known fact that if you wanted to know if Culpitt had appeared at a particular theatre, all one had to do was to inspect the stage floor and if you found a hole that had been plugged by a cork from a wine bottle then you knew instantly. Allow me to explain. During his act he would display a solid walking stick, tapping it on the stage to verify its solidity. It really was a solid cane! He would then proceed to wrap it up in a paper tube, again tapping it upon the stage. After a few mystic passes he would proceed to tear up the paper, throwing the confetti into the air and proving beyond all doubt that the cane had completely dematerialised. How did he do it, you may ask? On a Monday when all the artists turned up at the theatre for their obligatory 'band call' for music rehearsal and lighting checks, he would wait until everyone had finished and the stage was deserted. Then with a brace and bit he would bore a hole in the boards of the floor of the stage which was wide enough to accommodate the cane to slip through unnoticed into the void underneath the stage. At the end of the week, after the last performance had ended and the curtains had closed for the last time on the last act, he would then pop a suitably sized cork into the hole and no one was any the wiser. One popular but unverified story goes that unbeknown to Culpitt, at the time of his performance someone was under the stage at the point where he was about to vanish his walking cane. With a tap tap tap from above, the cane came down through the hole and hit this person on the head. Not realising quite what was going on above, he proceeded to push the cane back up through the hole to a puzzled Culpitt and a highly bemused audience!

Culpitt made several return engagements to the Palladium. His penultimate appearance in the late summer of 1936 prompted the powers that be to include him in the line-up of performers that the BBC would use in one of the first television programmes to be transmitted from Alexandra Palace in October of that year.

Culpitt also worked in close cooperation with another fellow artist and protean performer Henry MacPherson, whose stage name was Hymack. 'The Chameleon Comedian' was his bill matter and he certainly lived up to it. Bow ties, waistcoats, handkerchiefs, and gloves changed colour, disappeared and reappeared at will. His hat grew in height and his collar vanished, only to reappear again. Flowers flew to each of his lapels, gloves appeared again in green and yellow and frustration set in when after almost completely divesting himself, in a flash he was re-attired in complete wedding array of faultless grey, complete with trousers, jacket, waistcoat and topper, with every detail immaculately correct. The change was effected in full view of the audience and appeared little less than miraculous, considering the strenuous performance immediately preceding it. His work was distinctly original in conception and wholly admirable in execution. Hymack even played the part of the Vizier in the Palladium pantomime *Aladdin* in 1926, with Culpitt in the list of credits as the inventor of the illusions that had been specially constructed for this season. Hymack's chameleonic act would not have been right for this particular occasion, colourful though it undoubtedly was.

Without doubt the most well known name of all in magic, even to this very day, is that of Houdini. It could be said that other names may have become more 'famous', perhaps through the medium of television, and as a result may have been seen by more people at any one given time, but the name of Harry Houdini will live on forever. 1874 saw the birth in Budapest, Hungary, of Erich Weiss, the son of a rabbi. He was taken as a baby by his parents when they emigrated to Appleton, Wisconsin, USA. Performing on a makeshift trapeze in a neighbour's garden before an audience of friends was his first encounter with entertainment. His father was on a very limited income and soon it became apparent that Erich, or 'Ehrie' as he was known to his friends, would soon have to supplement the family funds. The family moved to Milwaukee and later to New York, where Ehrie had a number of jobs, including that of a tie lining cutter. Magic was just one of his hobbies. He had a short muscular frame, was a good swimmer and diver and was always keen to improve his physical fitness as well as his knowledge. He happened to read a book by the famous French magician Jean Robert-Houdin. Houdin was the first magician to be honoured with a postage stamp in 1971, which was the centenary of his birth, and Harry was similarly honoured in the USA in 2002. Ehrie was so impressed by the contents of the book that he took the name Houdin, added an 'i', and overnight Ehrie became Harry Houdini. So began the legend that lives on today, and probably will do forevermore. He 'swallowed' some thread and a dozen or so needles, only to bring them out again neatly threaded along that same thread, he performed 'The Vanishing Elephant', and he apparently walked through a brick wall. However, he will be best remembered for his daring and often dangerous escapes.

To put into just a few words or a few lines the immense life story of this champion of showmanship is impossible. More books have been written about him than any other magician. Hours of research went into every presentation. Every facet was studied in great detail, for his life would depend on a speedy exit from whatever the box, barrel or restraint might be. When thrown into the nearest river, not only did he have to escape from that secure unit but also the sack, chains, leg irons and handcuffs that had been added in an attempt to hold him. Nothing could, it would seem. He outwitted them all. No prison, no manner of fetter or handcuff could keep him down. When padlocked inside a milk churn that was full of beer and just barely big enough to contain him, he just managed to escape in time. The fumes nearly caused him to fall unconscious. It was something that he hadn't allowed for. Similarly, when a 'sea monster' (which resembled a cross between a whale and an octopus) had been washed up on a nearby beach in Massachusetts, he was challenged to escape from it. Suitably manacled, he was then forced into the carcass that had been embalmed before it was brought on stage at the local theatre. The slit was closed after him and the whole corpse was then entwined with chains to add to his problem. Within a quarter of an hour he was free, vowing never to undertake such a challenge again. He had almost been overcome by the fumes from the embalming fluid the taxidermist had used to douse the monster, which had been necessary to enable him to bring the creature on to the stage.

In the spring of 1919 Houdini appeared in his first Hollywood feature film for Paramount Artcraft Pictures, called *The Grim Game*. Quite naturally his prowess as an escape artist was much in evidence in the plot, with daredevil breathtaking scenes throughout. Although he made three other feature films though, he was happier with a live audience. His appearance 'in person' at the Palladium in 1920 was a great success, and it was reputed that his salary was just over $3,700. Bearing in mind that there were four dollars to the pound sterling in those days, the sum of over £900 made his salary the highest paid to a single performer.

Many stories have romanticised Houdini's untimely death, none more so than in 1953, with the Paramount film starring Tony Curtis and Janet Leigh. He did not die from drowning in the 'Torture Cell' as the film depicted. The upside down escape from a large tank of water with his ankles secured in stocks in the roof of the tank had long been a feature of Houdini's stage act. He always effected his escape from this watery prison. He would invite servicemen up to the stage to inspect the various items before he was locked in securely. In order to show off his physical fitness, he invited the men on the count of three to punch him in the stomach as hard as possible. Whilst he never seemed to flinch, he could withstand the hardest blow. Being very fit, he secretly flexed his stomach muscles to withstand the punch. However, whilst he was relaxing in his dressing room between performances one day, two university students came to interview him. One of them asked if it was true that he could withstand a heavy blow

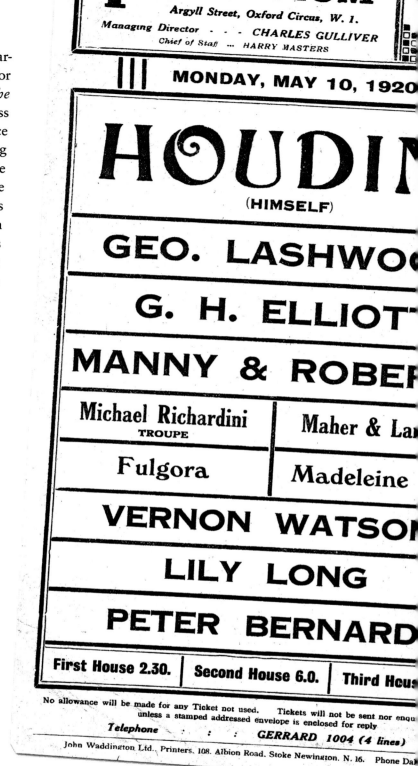

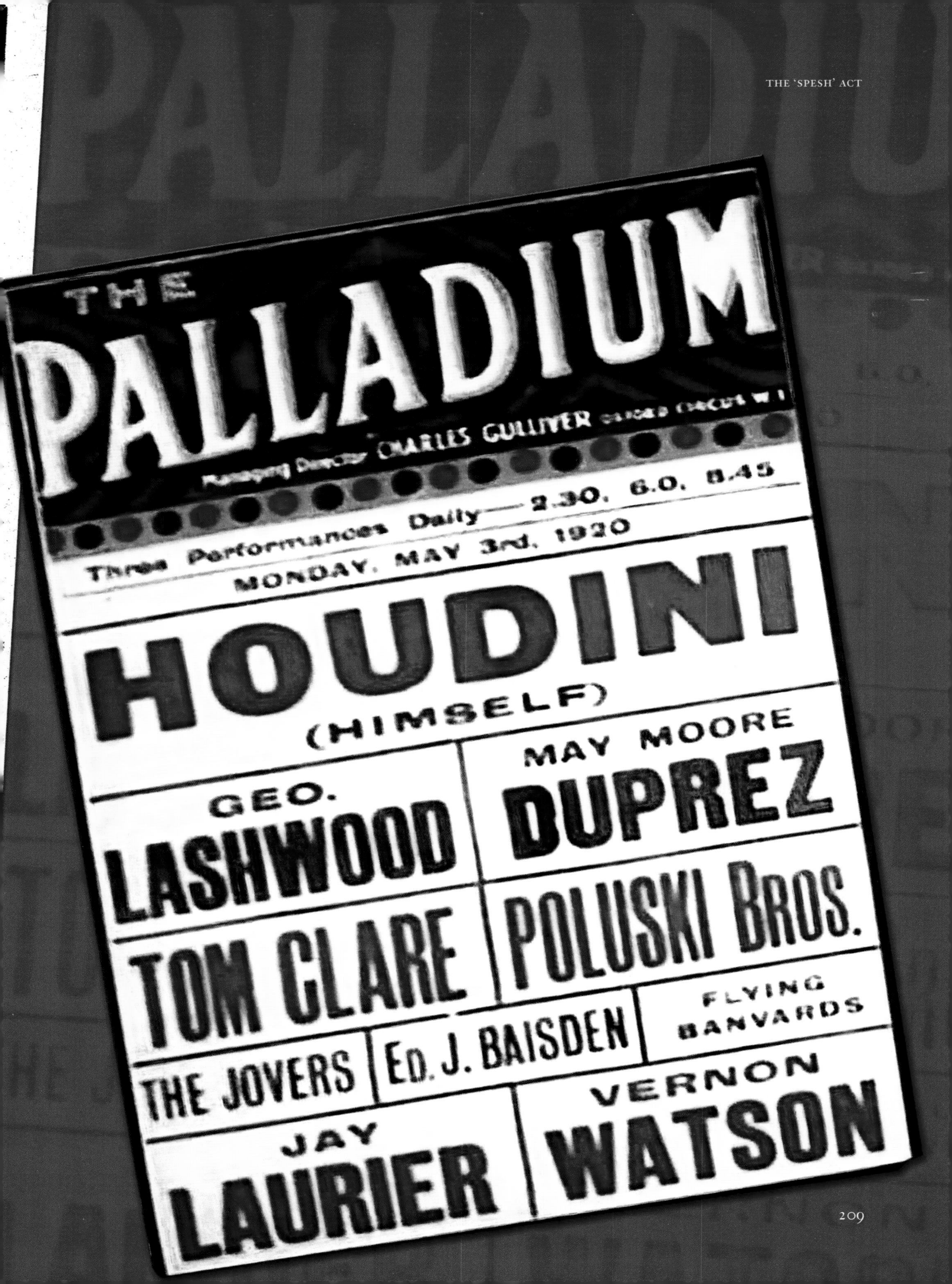

THE PALLADIUM

Managing Director CHARLES GULLIVER Argyll Circus W.1

Three Performances Daily— 2.30. 6.0. 8.45

MONDAY. MAY 3rd. 1920

HOUDINI
(HIMSELF)

GEO. LASHWOOD

MAY MOORE DUPREZ

TOM CLARE

POLUSKI BROS.

THE JOVERS

Ed. J. BAISDEN

FLYING BANVARDS

JAY LAURIER

VERNON WATSON

to the stomach without injury, and without any warning proceeded to hit him very hard four times, giving him no time to brace himself. He was in great pain for hours afterwards but managed to carry on with his performances. Unbeknown to anyone, his appendix had been ruptured, and he collapsed on stage after the curtain had been lowered. A surgeon was called who immediately removed his appendix, but the poison had been seeping through his body. After peritonitis developed, a second operation was carried out but the end was near and his condition worsened. He died on Hallowe'en, 31 October 1926. How sad that someone who had escaped death so many times thanks to his careful preparation, should die as a result of what was in effect just an accident. Or was it? There will always be a mystery about Houdini. He was truly a legend, not only in his own lifetime, but as a name that will live forever.

One of the other feature acts that played the Palladium in the 1920s was that of Carmo. Born in Australia of Scottish immigrant parents, Harry Cameron soon got the taste of show business when he visited the local variety theatre and witnessed Cinquevalli, the world famous juggler. He couldn't wait for the show to finish so that he could get home to practice juggling and one day be as good as his new hero. Carmo was phenomenally strong for his age and had superb muscle control, as well as the excellent coordination of hand and eye needed to be an expert juggler. With an inherent flair for showmanship and theatre, he had everything going for him.

I can best quote a critic of the day:

Carmo is probably our best versatile performer and his mastery of the various sections of his artistic field is complete. He is a fine juggler and an illusionist, a protean artist of considerable ability, a clever sleight of hand performer, and expert rifle shot and sharpshooter, and his feats of muscular strength would not disgrace Sandow himself. His consummate showmanship is largely responsible for his personal success, whilst his scenic arrangements go a long way to making his turns the success they undoubtedly are. To each of his performances, for Carmo is music hall in himself, he had a separate and appropriate setting, and each was really an individual entertainment in itself. His biggest illusion consisted of the evanishment of a full grown Forest Lion from an open cage

FRANK VAN HOVEN
THE MAN WHO MADE ICE FAMOUS

and brought an effective finish to a show which was full of versatility and originality.

Carmo made many return engagements to the Palladium in the 1920s, his greatest undoubtedly being in the summer of 1923 when, just after a successful four week engagement at the Alhambra in Paris, he presented 'The Most Gigantic Mystery Act in The World', complete with a veritable ark full of animals comprising lions, tigers, bears, horses, two elephants, a camel and forty assistants. Obviously, an act not to be missed. Packed houses proved his undoubted appeal.

At the other end of the scale, however, the American entertainer Frank Van Hoven provided smaller mysteries and became notable as 'The Man Who Made Ice Famous'.

> To see Hoven is to laugh, and it is needless to add that the Londoners are having their full measure of laughter for every minute he occupies the boards. Quite the finest compliment that can be paid to Van Hoven is that his brilliant success here notwithstanding, there has been no attempt to imitate him, which is as well they would, for this kind of thing cannot be successfully imitated even if one has the brains to originate anything near the mark, which is saying a good deal.

He would get three small boys from the audience to assist him. One was given a bowl of water, the second a large block of ice to hold, and the third received a lit candle. The antics which ensued created hilarity, with the boys, water and ice slithering all over the place. An exhausted and dishevelled Van Hoven finally slithered off stage to rapturous applause and laughter, riding atop the block of ice!

Richard Valentine Pitchford, better known as Cardini, was born in south Wales in November 1895. He was wounded during his time in the trenches in France during the First World War and returned to Southampton in England to recuperate. Whilst in hospital he asked the nurse for a pack of cards and a pair of gloves in order to practise tricks he had been learning in the trenches. When the physician who was treating him heard that he wanted gloves, he thought his patient was mad and sent him to a mental hospital in Liverpool! The staff there were kinder and encouraged Cardini to entertain them with his baffling card tricks.

After returning to good health and civilian life, he obtained a job at the famous Gamages store in Holborn, London, demonstrating behind the counter in the Magic Department. When travelling around the world perfecting his ideas and mastering his act, he appeared at the Tivoli in Australia and then proceeded onto New York to appear at the Palace on Broadway. Immaculately attired in full evening dress, the slightly inebriated man about town was assisted by his wife, Swan. The press called him the 'personification of grace, admirable showmanship and prestidigitatorial excellence.'

The compère would announce: 'Paging Mr Cardini, paging Mr Cardini.' He would enter on stage in a spotlight, a slightly tipsy, be-monocled gentleman. His wife Swan, the diminutive pageboy assistant, took the newspaper he was holding, and cards would be plucked from thin air in their dozens just as he had practised all those years ago in that hospital bed, the cards dropping into the newspaper Swan was now holding. Copious cigarettes would also materialise between his fingertips, and the flower in his buttonhole would whirl around in circles in amazement. Billiard balls appeared and disappeared, and they even changed colour, all deftly executed. More cigarettes appeared and then finally a cigar. By the end of the act, being 'satisfied' had sobered him up somewhat; having been astounded by his own antics, he was handed his cape, gloves, hat and cane and left the stage, puffing away merrily on a huge Meerschaum pipe! The ultimate in perfection, copied by so many since but never, ever equalled.

He always worked against a set of 'tabs' or curtains at the Palladium, which, for many moons after he had retired, became known as the 'Cardini Blues', such was their hue. Fame indeed, and for someone worthy of such an accolade. His one-week engagement in the 1930s resulted in further weeks, and even seasons with The Crazy Gang which lasted almost a year. The real pinnacle of his career at the Palladium was being invited to appear in the 1933 Royal Variety Performance before Their Majesties King George V and Queen Mary.

CARDINI

Many years later, another equally suave and dextrous deceiver by the name of Channing Pollock also worked in front of those Cardini Blues. Channing, an extremely handsome American, took Britain by storm in the 1950s when he first appeared on *The Rosemary Clooney Show*, when he produced beautiful white Java doves so effortlessly from nowhere. With charm and elegance, the birds materialised from silk squares, and he placed them in a cage one by one. The cage was eventually covered with a cloth, and the whole aviary just vanished. His booking and re-booking at all the top variety theatres ensured his continued popularity. He was in fact chosen to appear on the very first *Sunday Night at the London Palladium* television show in September 1955, and his British career culminated fittingly with an appearance in the November Royal Variety Performance in that same year. Such theatre has never been seen since. He was very different in his style of performance to Cardini before him, and he will long remain a 'one-off' in the history of magic. It is impossible to put into words as superlatives abound, but he was often billed as 'Splendour on the Stage,' which says it all. He could best be described as having true 'Star Quality'.

Just as Channing made his mark with doves, others had their own trademarks with different objects. Gus Fowler produced clocks and watches out of nowhere, which rightly earned him the title 'The Watch King'. Allan Shaw managed what you and I would like to be able to do, but none of us have yet found the secret. He could produce handfuls of coins and banknotes from the air with no apparent difficulty. Jack Le Dair succeeded in adding a new dimension to magic with his highly original idea of magic with giant safety matches. 'Matchic', as he used to call it.

'Mr Electric' deserves a special mention. Marvyn Roy and Carol appeared many times, not only at the Palladium but also every top nightspot in the world, including many seasons in Las Vegas. Marvyn would literally breeze onto the stage with the enthusiasm of a teenager and a passion for his work that thankfully is still with him today. He would produce fully lit electric light bulbs from a top hat that had previously been shown to be empty. First a yellow one, then a blue, followed by a red, and then finally a green one, all fully illuminating his unique and special talent. Small lit single bulbs were then unscrewed from their holders, with the lights going out. He then swallowed the bulbs one by one until at least a dozen were ingested. Then the wire followed them down. Lo and behold they all soon emerged from his mouth, threaded at regular intervals and fully lit, not just the dozen or so that he originally swallowed but maybe fifty or more, stretching right across the stage. Silk scarves appeared to produce a fully lit chandelier. Milk vanished, only to be found inside a previously lit large electric light bulb which shone white. The climax of his act was where he not only attempted, but always succeeded in lighting a 5000 watt bulb which he held in his bare hands. The huge electric light bulb was lit and then from the centre of the huge glowing bulb came the unexpected appearance of his superb and lovely assistant, Carol. It must be said at this point that there were no connections with hidden electricity points on stage for any of these items. Marvyn just used his bare hands. One should also give special mention here that Carol was without doubt one the best magician's assistants in the world, if not *the* best. They are happily retired now and living in Palm Springs, California. Not only was their act unique, it was honed to perfection, and this was obviously the reason why they were in constant demand around the world to appear with all the top named superstars of the day.

Another act, not so dangerous and dramatic but perhaps just as colourful, was provided by Sylvestre, 'The Sunshade Maker', who filled the Palladium stage with parasols of every shade and colour. Kardomah, on the other hand, produced flags of all nations until the stage was a spectacular, patriotic, colourful canvas.

To encourage newer generations of magic and to offer a springboard to the talented youth of the day, The Magic Circle in London inaugurated 'The Young Magician of The Year' contest in 1962. The first winner was a red haired youth who immediately shot to fame, and within hours of gaining the coveted title he appeared on *Sunday Night at the London Palladium*, plucking a spectrum of multicoloured budgerigars from the air. They danced amongst his talented fingers with enthusiasm, as he was obviously their best friend. Their happy antics let everyone know that cruelty played no part whatsoever in his presentation. His name was Johnny Hart, and he went

214

Marvyn Roy and Carol

Johnny Hart

Robert Harbin

on to rightfully enjoy many seasons at the Palladium, appearing with all the top names and then taking his magic around the world to *The Ed Sullivan Show* in New York, and top spots in Las Vegas. Truly an ambassador of British Magic.

The Wychwoods, however, preferred to conjure with their canine friends. Poodles appeared, disappeared, and changed colour. To climax their truly original act, seemingly dozens of poodles made their exit from a giant castle of cards that had been carelessly scattered on the stage mere seconds before. There were dogs everywhere! An applause puller if ever there was one. Mark Raffles took over the act and also appeared in 1997 with some of the original poodles.

'Think a Drink Hoffmann' poured any alcoholic potion and became the highest paid bartender in the world. Those who felt thirsty could call out any drink, and he would pour it from the same shaker. It was Giovanni, on the other hand, who preferred to pick pockets, and he was one of the best too. The Zomahs knew exactly what was going on in your mind with their two-person thought transference act. All the way from Spain came Frakson, who conjured cigarettes, as did Keith Clark from Paris. All were masters of deception in their own individual field.

Although born in South Africa, Robert Harbin will be remembered as one of Britain's greatest, if not *the* greatest inventor and performer of illusions. He first appeared the Palladium in 1948 in *The Jack Benny Show* and again in 1949 with George Burns and Gracie Allen. Billed as 'The Magic of Tomorrow', he always lived up to that title. Although he invented well over five hundred miracles, he will perhaps be best remembered for his Zigzag Girl Illusion. This illusion, still talked about today, was where his lady assistant was secured in a cabinet just about big enough to accommodate her, and then sliced into three by two metal blades. Bob, as he was affectionately known, would then slide over the middle section to one side on a shelf at the side of the cabinet. I was fortunate enough to be present at the Palladium when Bob first presented this wonderful and much talked about miracle on the first colour *Sunday Night at the London Palladium* in 1966. The audience proved beyond doubt by their tumultuous and instantaneous applause how great this illusion was, and remains so to this day.

Bob told me a true story which related to the appearance that he had made in 1948. A box was wheeled onto the stage to be shown as empty, before Dorothy, his wife, was magically produced from its depths. Luckily he turned to the wings, to see Dolly, as she was affectionately known, talking to one of the stagehands. Thinking on his feet, Bob said, 'This illusion is too good to show you at this moment. I'll show it to you later on in the act', and promptly wheeled it off and went on to the next miracle. The next time round, Dolly was ready in the box, and promised to pay attention in future. Bob died in 1978, but I wonder what further miracles he would have invented if his life had been spared. 'A Wizard if ever there Woz!'

Bob had learned his craft working for the Maskelyne family at St. George's Hall long before the war. John Nevil Maskelyne made a brief appearance at the Palladium in 1916. I am sure that he would have been proud of his grandson, Jasper, who not only went on to appear in many a season with The Crazy Gang but also in the prestigious Royal Variety Performance for 1932. He too had the unusual honour of having a set of black curtains named after him, as afterwards they were referred to as 'The Maskelynes'.

David Nixon made rare TV visits to the Palladium, although he never actually appeared in Variety as such. However, Tommy Cooper made more appearances than any other magician, appearing not only in variety shows, but also on TV, Royal Shows and many successful seasons too.

Billy McComb, 'The Leprechaun Wizard', who was originally from Belfast but was a long-time resident entertainer at The Magic Castle in Hollywood, California, appeared on *The Debbie Reynolds Show* in 1974. Until then his publicity was 'Billy McComb, currently staring at the London Palladium.' This was a very clever mis-spelling, and he little realised that one day he would actually stand on that very stage.

Billy always felt that the 1950s Mentalist Al Koran *should* have appeared at the Palladium, and so when he died Billy scattered Al's ashes backstage.

The Italian superstar Silvan appeared in *Doddy's Here Again* in 1967, a most successful season for all concerned. Silvan also appeared on *Sunday Night at the London*

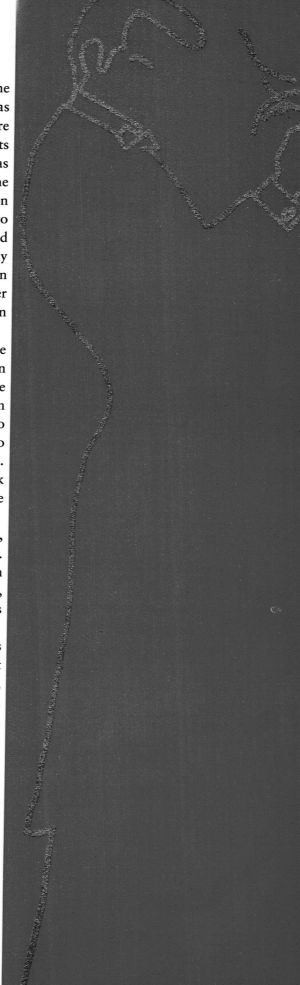

CHRIS VAN BERN

DISCOVERING THE APRON OF THE UNTIDY MAID

OF COURSE THE CIGAR BOX BECOMES A REFRESHER

WITH THE MYSTERIOUS ENTRE OF CHRIS VAN BERN

HE TURNS IT INTO A BRUSH

A LIGHTNING TRANSFORMATION IN DRESS

COMES A SERIES OF SURPRISES - HIS HAT AND STICK BECOME A TABLE

BUT THERES MANY A SLIP TWIXT THE CUP AND THE LIP

AND HIS WALKIN STICK HAS A WAY OF ITS OWN

CHRIS VAN BERNS IDEA IS THAT THE AVERAGE COMIC SINGER DOESN'T GIVE SUFFICIENT INTEREST

FLOWERS SPRING FROM VASES

TO ILLUSTRATE HIS THEORY - WHILE SINGING, MANY WONDERFUL THINGS HAPPEN

ONCE MORE A TABLE TURNS INTO HAT AND STICK

EVERYTHING FROM THE TOP OF THIS TABLE VANISHES

A WONDERFUL TRICK CHRIS VAN BERN CHANGES AN ORDINARY PILLAR AND BASIN INTO AN ELABORATE CHINA CABINET.

A CHAIR BECOMES HIS SUITCASE AND SO EXIT VAN BERN

Palladium in March 1966 and again for three successive weeks in 1967. He is truly a superstar performer, and a great magic ambassador of international repute.

For the sake of completeness, other magic names who cropped up on various occasions and need to be mentioned are: Chris van Bern, The Great Wieland, Claude Golden, Billy O'Connor, E.J. Moore, Oswald Bemand, The Great Leon, Servais le Roy, Rupert Ingalese, Cortini, De Biere, Chris Charlton, Brad Martin, Fred Brezin, Chefalo, Raymond Phillips, Paul Daniels, Wayne Dobson, Herbert Collings, Lucille, Glen Pope, Doc Marcus, Orson Welles assisted by Elizabeth Taylor, Donald B. Stuart, Benson Dulay, Richard Ross, Levante, Kodell, Richiardi, Galli Galli, Don Alan, Larry Parker, Terry Seabrooke, Laurence Leyton, Richard and Lara Jarmaine, Brian Miller and Audrey, Geoff Ray and Pat, Robert Grigor, Noel Brookes, Potassy, Michael Allport, Anna Lou and Maria, Bunny Neil, Romark, Shahid Malik, David Berglas, Terry Burgess, Harold Taylor, Geoffrey Durham as The Great Soprendo, Finn Jon, Ed Alonzo, Lance Burton, Shimada, Omar Pasha, Fay Presto, Wayne Dobson, John Lenahan, Stacey Lee and Julian, Richard de Vere, Brian Sibley, Lew Lewis, John Wade, Nicholas Einhorn, Ali Bongo, Duncan Trillo, Mike Caveney, Mr Blub, Tina Lenert, Paul Kozac, Len Lewis, Salvano Netcheporenko, Visiona (Vicki Lewis Thum), Fred Roby, Juliana Chen, Sabrina and Gena Kil, James Dimmare, Jorgen Samson, Darryl Rose, Philip Hitchcock, Paul Zenon, The Morettis, Christian the Magician, Scott Penrose, Paul Stone, Jeff Hobson, Kalin and Jinger, Soul Mystique, Jason Byrne, Vik and Fabrini, Luis de Matos, Johnny Thompson and Pam, Raymond Crowe, Norm Nielsen, and recently making a personal appearance all the way from Las Vegas were magic superstars Siegfried and Roy.

Part Two: An Even Bigger Circle

It would be possible to list all the other important speciality acts that had appeared at the Palladium, but there would be many dozens if not hundreds of names. In fact, a complete book in itself could be written on the subject! However, just to list some very different ones and

enlarge upon their own individual bill matter will, I hope, make it more interesting to read.

The advertising bills and programmes had to be printed each week for each theatre, and the Palladium was no exception. The artistes' position on the bill, size of typeface and bill matter were of extreme importance and were dealt with by the publicity department in Cranbourne Mansions in Leicester Square, London, who sent out the 'copy' to the printers. In the early days almost all of the poster printing was done by the firm of Tribe Brothers in St Albans. 'Bill matter' was how each act was described in the theatre programme and on the posters. The posters were mostly 20" x 30", known in the business simply as Double Crown. However, some were 20" x 12 ½" and called Folio, and Quad Crown posters were 30" x 40". There were box office cards too and these were 10" x 15". On occasions there were massive hoardings in and around London. One of the prime locations was in Leicester Square and these were known as '48 sheets'. Each letter was a single wooden block that had to be set by hand to make every word or phrase. It was a time consuming job, but it kept the printer busy week in, week out, that's for sure! Specially designed posters had to be created as well to go outside the theatre over the front entrance. This was and still is known as the Marquee.

On the regular smaller posters, the act and their bill matter had to fit into little 'boxes' within the poster. Sometimes the posters had a 'half tone' picture of the top of the bill. Another important aspect was that the smaller the name, the bigger the typeface within that box. For example, the word Houdini would need to be a much larger typeface to fit the top of the bill box than if he had been called 'Harry Handcuff King Houdini'. Perhaps the shortest name (and consequently the biggest typeface) to appear was on 18 January 1932, in the form of BuBu the Chimpanzee. With regard to The Minstrels of 1913 however, the longest name, even if it was only the programme matter, was without doubt 'Minstrolographiphoneymaticisms'.

During the 1950s, the Booking Control Manager, formidable and diminutive Cissie Williams, would agree the salaries and issue the smaller contracts to the support acts who were lower down the payroll, who were often referred to as the 'wines and spirits'. In the early days the prices for drinks sold in a music hall were given at the very bottom of the programme page. Usually the least important performers were also detailed on the same page in the programme, just above the drinks prices. Originally the expression was, euphemistically, 'oh, he is down amongst the wines and spirits prices', which lead to the less successful, but equally important performers being labelled as 'a wines and spirits performer'. When paid for a small, one-off concert, the artist would be paid, say, two guineas (two pounds and two shillings) with 'a crackle and jingle', meaning paper money and a couple of coins that would jingle. 'Has the ghost walked?' is another phrase often used even today by artists. 'The ghost' was a mysterious character that no one ever saw, but somehow you were paid. Some used to say that it was a reference to the ghost of Hamlet's father.

It is said that in Elizabethan times, when one attended a play there were three prices for admission: one was for standing, the second was for a seat and the third was for a seat with a cushion. A man would pass amongst the audience with a box on the end of a long stick collecting the appropriate coins. Once all the money had been collected it was placed safely in the office; hence the term 'box office'! Another common expression is 'See you on the green', green being short for greengage, cockney rhyming slang for stage, hence the 'green room' just adjacent to the stage. There is such fascinating lore connected with the theatre.

One of the earliest and most unusual speciality acts was that of Bert Wickham. Under the banner of Hengler's he appeared at one of the Austin Fryer circus presentations. Billed as the all-round Welsh Athlete, his speciality was 'Man Versus the Motor Car', in which 'He will resist the force of any motor car of any make from 16 to 22 horse power. Owners may bring their own cars driven by their chauffeur. Mr Wickham also tears asunder ordinary tennis balls and breaks horse's shoes in twain'. Obviously not a man to pick an argument with on a dark night!

According to his bill matter, 'the World's Greatest Protean Actor' was R.A. Roberts. He appeared in 1911 in 'A Comedy of Deception' which was written, invented and acted by Roberts himself. A note in the programme detailed the following information: in the course of the sketch, 'Mr R.A. Roberts impersonates eight different types of humourous Character-Drawing, the longest change occupying four seconds and the shortest, one and one tenth of a second: The whole sketch is acted by himself without the aid of accomplices, trick dresses, or illusions of any kind.' Dick Turpin and the legal scene and 'Ringing the Changes' were two more of his popular presentations, also with eight changes of character.

In the Christmas period of 1911–12 a presentation by the name of, naturally enough, *Yuletide Revels* appeared. Whilst not maybe strictly a 'spesh' act as such but worthy of a mention here, 'a beautiful ballet divertissement' took place in one scene, invented and produced by Madame Haley and with incidental music by James Sale. It introduced a corps de ballet of fifty charming girls, a production replete with sparkling dainty music and magnificent scenery. 'A feast of colour, grace and art'.

Living portraits of Listz, Hollman, Paderewski, Joachim and Gounod were all portrayed as early as 1912 by the wonderful personality and genius of Lamberti. By 1937 Lamberti was still appearing at the Palladium in a musical presentation, this time playing the xylophone. Was this a case of having to move with the times?

On 10 June 1912, 'Sandow, The Human Pony' made an appearance. Whilst the handsome mustachioed strong man Eugene Sandow sadly died after he overexerted himself trying to lift a motor car out of a ditch, here we had his namesake in the form of a pony who was almost human!

Another animal act was provided by Gobert Belling and his Four Legged Comedians. The funniest and cleverest exhibition of animal training ever presented 'the only singing donkey in the world,' 'the football playing mule', and 'the burlesque Spanish Bull Fight' which introduced a real dwarf bull. Yes, they all appeared on the Palladium stage!

On 2 December 1912 (J. Robert) Pauline, 'The World Famous French American Hypnotist' appeared. Billed as 'America's Greatest Sensation', the poster stated that Pauline's performance 'has been acclaimed the Most Remarkable and the Most Mystifying, the Most Entertaining in the history of Vaudeville.' It was reputed that he earned $2500 a week.

Joe Boganny's Royal Lunatic Bakers had 'Fun in an Opium Den', (as performed in the Royal Command Performance) and they also had 'Fun in a Bakehouse'. In fact, there was fun wherever he and his company chose to go!

On 4 August 1913, Harry Edson and his wonderful Musical Dog Comedian, 'Doc', the dog with the human brain and gold teeth, made a successful appearance.

The prize for the most unusual name surely belonged to American Apache violinist Ywaxy, who performed in 1913. Also appearing in 1913, perhaps ahead of their time when it came to their name, were Les Videos, with wonders on wheels, featuring Leoni the Junior Marvel who had appeared before the King. Another name for the scrabble championship was that of The Great Zylbastrians, who were 'Novelty Instrumentalists'. If you look this name up on the internet, it does come up, and they were apparently from Kent.

On 28 July 1913, Victoria Monks and her Twelve American Beauties appeared in her latest song scena, 'John Bull's Girl'. Interestingly, a programme note for this show stated that,

> His Master's Voice, the most wonderful Musical Instrument in the World, prices £4–£50. Dealers in Free Concerts. The Instruments in various parts of the house supplied by the Gramophone Co., Ltd., 21 City Road London EC. Illustrated catalogue Free.

In 1914, it was the turn of La Somna to fill the speciality slot. The programme declared:

> La Somna. The Most Wonderful Woman in the World. Demonstrating powers beyond the mind of man to fathom...Ask La Somna any question you like and judge for yourself. Questions can be asked direct or written at home and kept in the possession of those who write them. La Somna does not employ confederates or use any special pads or papers.

Between 1914 and 1918 Franco Piper and his Spinning Banjos certainly provided another very unusual act. Piper played fifteen instruments whilst the banjos were spinning at 250 revolutions a minute. His letterheading stated that he had several other acts. *The Times* can be quoted as saying, 'Franco Piper is the

Paderewski of the Banjo.' Other papers supplied further compliments, such as 'What Paganini is to the violin, Piper is to the Banjo' and 'Franco Piper has revolutionised the banjo leaving all others standing'. It seems that Franco could juggle four or five banjos and still play a melody by plucking the strings as he caught and then tossed them!

Somersaults it seems were of a different kind in 1914 with Silbon's Cats, who presented the greatest comedy cat act in the world. 'Tillie' was the only cat who could loop the loop. Tillie must surely have had the X factor!

On 14 July 1919 it was the turn of Billy O'Connor and his Fifty-Two Assistants. When one saw this billing one might have thought that the stage would be littered with people, only to find that the 'fifty-two' referred to a pack of cards. Nevertheless Billy's skill at entertaining with many laughs along the way far outweighed any possible disappointment.

On 3 May 1920 Houdini, billed simply as 'Himself', provided the 'spesh' act. Although Houdini has already been discussed at some length in a previous chapter, it is worth mentioning here that it is thought that 'Himself' referred to the fact that Houdini had just starred in several self-produced films for the early cinema, and by stating 'Himself' it inferred that audiences would be seeing the real thing, not a celluloid image. I suppose today one might say 'In Person'.

Winston's Water Lions and Diving Nymphs appeared on 24 January 1921, to delight audiences with 'The Aquatic Marvels of the Twentieth Century'. 'During their performance the Water Lions will emulate all the feats performed by the Misses Farry and Wood, Gold Medalists of the swimming and diving world.' Even a high dive of twenty-five feet was successfully attempted. Later on in the bill for that occasion was an act called Warzan and his Apes.

Owen McGiveney was a protean artist who gave a dramatic rendition of the Dickensian sketch *Bill Sykes*, which originated in 1907, and in which he played all the parts. This was a strenuous act which caused Owen to be dashing back and forth, in and out of windows and doors, effecting the necessary changes to keep the storyline going. It seemed that it was impossible at times for him to be playing all the characters. But he did, as did his son Michael who inherited the act and appeared in the 1970s, supporting Johnny Mathis.

Owen McGiveney

One of the most unusual acts was that of Harry Hemsley. His billing was 'Child Impersonator', and through his success on radio, which was really his forte, he spent his time on stage behind a newspaper, talking to himself with all the various voices that were in his repertoire. 'Horace' was his main character, along with 'Winnie', who was Horace's sister. Success was his as he made at least a dozen or so appearances on the Palladium stage.

1923 saw an act by Pharus the Egyptian, who was described as 'A modern miracle man introducing the wonderful system of ZONERY. The master stroke of modern health agencies. A rediscovery of the greatest blessing to humanity. How to stop pain by simple nerve pressure.' A note written in pencil in one programme read 'Fakery!' However, if readers should wish to learn more about Zonery, there is a book on the subject which was written in 1922.

On 21 August 1933 Mr Christopher Stone appeared. Now Christopher was reputed to be the very first 'disc jockey' on radio presenting 'gramophone record recitals', as the BBC called them in those days. It was the *Radio Times* which called him 'The man with a million friends', such was his avuncular approach to broadcasting. As people had only heard him on radio, he was quite an attraction because they wanted to see him in the flesh. His appearance at the Palladium was a very unusual one in that he simply sat in an armchair next to a gramophone and played records, much to the delight of the audience!

In April the following year, 'The Girl who amazed Einstein', Gene Denis, made her first appearance in the UK. She was billed as 'The Psychic Marvel of the Age'. 'Ask her about your health, happiness, children, missing relatives, business troubles, lost property. She will solve your problems.' I bet she would be busy today if she was still alive!

Alphonse Berg's Fashion Show of 1935 took place on 21 May. Here was a really unusual act. A live model tastefully dressed in little but her outer garment would stand centre stage. Alphonse would then display a bolt of dress material. Within seconds of opening up the cloth he would design, drape, fold, pleat and with the aid of a few pins, create the most delightful garment you could imagine. He would often appear in The Crazy Gang Shows.

N.Y.
World's Fair
1939.

Walorf
Paris

with best wishes
to Leonard Lemon and
Sonia friendly
A Ratoucheff

In the mid 1920s and early 1930s, Ratoucheff's Russian Seven Lilliputians, 'The smallest actors, vocalists and dancers in existence', appeared for the first time. Their ages, the programme notes stated, ranged from nineteen to thirty-two years, and their heights were between two feet two inches and three feet four inches. If this was the 'smallest' act to appear on the Palladium stage, then in 1938 during the all too short season of Fats Waller, another unusual act appeared for the first time, in the shape of Lowe, Hite and Stanley. Hite, as his name might suggest, was naturally the tallest. He stood seven feet ten inches tall. He was only twenty-three and weighed some 286 lbs. He ate six good meals a day alongside his diminutive partner Stanley and Lowe, who was of medium height. They showed off their talents in a knockabout act that was very well received. On the journey over to England by sea, Henry Hite slept in two cabins at once, with a specially cut hole in the dividing wall between enabling him to sleep. That really is the truth and not just a tall story!

Willie, West and McGinty proved to be a huge hit with 'A Billion Building Blunders.' One has to wonder: are they still in business today?

When it came to Henri Vadden and his Famous Cartwheel, of all the unusual acts ever to appear on any stage, this must surely have been one of the most dangerous. Henri would begin by donning a Kaiser-style helmet that had a huge spike on the top of it. A very large, authentic, heavy wooden cartwheel would be spun on the top of a six foot pole. The pole would then be balanced on Henri's chin with the spinning cartwheel atop. While the wheel was still spinning, after a brief moment, he would knock the pole away, leaving the cartwheel spinning momentarily in the air. Thanks to gravity taking over, it would fall, only to be caught on the spike of the helmet with a resounding thud (and a huge jolt to Henri's neck, I wouldn't wonder). It is reported that he got shorter by the week! He certainly must have looked forward to his day off on Sundays!

The Three Barbour Brothers and Jean were stilt-walkers. They made several appearances in Royal Variety Performances and in later years Roy Barbour appeared again with his daughter, carrying on the family tradition in *Barnum*, the circus spectacular that starred Michael

Crawford. Michael was no stranger himself to dangerous stunts in the role of the hapless TV character Frank Spencer.

One person who must surely have made the most appearances over sixty-five years was the late Johnny Hutch MBE. He first made an appearance at the Palladium in September 1928 as a child in an acrobatic troupe called The Seven Hindustans. This was a pyramid balancing act with strongman Harry Prescott at the base and little Johnny at the top. This act was so popular in the late twenties that it went on to be invited to appear in the 1930 Royal Variety Performance. The act then became known as The Royal Hindustans. During his days in the army gymnastic section, he spotted that every time anyone vaulted over the horse and accidentally fell, all those around turned their heads to snigger. This gave him the idea for a comedy act using a vaulting horse. The Thunderbolts, The Halfwits, The Seven Volants; they were all Johnny Hutch acts with routines specially devised by him for inclusion in dozens of pantomimes and variety specials. Truly a one-off!

American born George Carl was another act in the old vaudeville tradition. Just to say he was a mime act would be doing him a very great injustice indeed. He had that great comedic quality with expert timing which is rarely seen today. For the unacquainted, his act consisted of juggling with his hat, getting the microphone cord caught up in his jacket, and playing a harmonica which finally burst open to reveal umpteen items of cutlery. Finally, he was seen walking off stage with his legs apparently getting shorter and shorter. In the space of a few short minutes he would have every audience in stitches with his wonderful clowning that had him constantly employed around the world in all the top nightspots, from The Crazy Horse in Paris to all the best Las Vegas venues. He rightly had his place in the 1974 Royal Variety Performance, and this honour was repeated in 1983. Again, a truly one-off speciality act.

Another of the acts that the British viewing public took to its heart was that of Topo Gigio, an Italian puppet that had a shy but loving personality. This lifelike 'stick' puppet mouse with huge ears would appear against a black cloth and would be worked by three puppeteers from behind. One would work the head, the second the

Joan Rhodes

Gaston Palmer

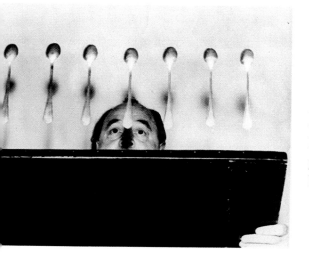

body, and the third would work the arms and legs. Topo appeared many times on *Sunday Night at the London Palladium*, always returning by popular demand.

A good example of traditional string puppets that were worked by one or two people from above was provided by porcine puppets 'Pinky and Perky', who were ably assisted by Jan and Vlasta Dalibor. Having made a big hit with the public in their own mini TV series, they appeared in the Royal Variety Performance for 1963 and also many times on *Sunday Night at the London Palladium*. They were enjoyed by children and adults alike.

Another animal act, a live one this time, was Tanya the Elephant. In today's politically correct world it would perhaps be considered unacceptable to a have a performing pachyderm on stage, but Tanya made many a Palladium and TV appearance, and she is still alive and well and enjoying life in a winter circus home in Mexico.

There have been 'strong men' but very few, if any, 'strong women'. Joan Rhodes, 'The Mighty Mannequin', proved to be the exception when she appeared in 1955 on *The Dickie Valentine Show*. Her act consisted of tearing a telephone directory in half, bending an iron bar in her teeth and breaking six inch nails literally in two. She was always popular with audiences, and a great addition to any variety bill.

Other assorted 'spesh' acts which all deserve a mention were Leonard Gaultier's 'Animated Toy Shop', H. Franklin and The Standards, and The Living Rubber Balls. Colonel Gaston Bordeverry, who was 'The world's greatest pistol and rifle shot' appeared on 17 June 1912. Tom Edwards, 'The Hunstman Ventriloquist', appeared in an entirely new 'Ventriloquial Bloodless Surgery'. Then came Hiawatha and Minnehaha, the astounding educated Chimpanzees. Takio and his '£1000 Film Introducing The Living Jungle' made an appearance, as did Fred Cooper, billed as 'The Famous Australian Bushman and Company', in a sensational exhibition of stock whip manipulation. Gaston Palmer presented 'All the Spoons in all the Glasses'. In 1923 Enrico Rastelli, 'the world's greatest juggler', did a speciality slot. Sherkot, the continental eccentric dancer of extraordinary skill, also obliged, and his 'goalkeeper' burlesque was a brilliant example of pantomimical nonsense. In 1932, on one of the early visits by Mr Bud Flanagan and Mr Chesney Allen, an act joined them which was called 'Mr Joe Peanuts with his Simian Gigolos'. Monkey business was afoot for sure!

Various ventriloquists who appeared were: Fred Russell and Coster Joe, Coram and Jerry, Edgar Bergen and Charlie McCarthy, Saveen and Daisy May, Peter Brough and Archie Andrews, Robert Lamouret and Dudule, Bobbie Kimber and Augustus Peabody, (they appeared in the 1947 Royal Variety Performance, and she was the very first female impersonator ventriloquist to do so), Arthur Worsley and Charlie Brown, Denis Spicer and James Green, Terry Hall and Mickey Flynn, and then later with the loveable but shy Lenny the Lion, ('Oh, don't embawwass me!'), Harry Worth, (yes, Harry started off as a 'Vent'), Ray Allan and Lord Charles, Senor Wences, Jay Marshall and 'Lefty', Shari Lewis and Lamb Chop (who appeared in the 1969 Royal Variety Performance), Roger Carne, Ward Allen and Roger the Dog, the hilarious Neville King, Fred Roby, Roger de Courcey and Nookie, Rod Hull and Emu, Jose Louis Marino, Philippe Genty, Dawson Chance, Pepe and Friends, Steve Hewlett and not forgetting Jim Henson's Muppets, who appeared in the Royal Variety Performance of 1977. These were just *some* of the Vent acts that appeared!

The numerous jugglers who made appearances were Teddy Peiro, Rob Murray, Valente Valente, Stetson, Bobby May, Rudy Horn, talented Mark Robertson, and Nino Frediani. Boy Foy, the 'Juggler on the Unicycle', also did an act. Billed as 'England's youngest juggler', Foy, the son of Jack Melville of the Juggling Melvilles, appeared many times, not only at the Palladium but also at all the top theatres around Britain. He was honoured to be chosen to appear in the 1935 Royal Variety Performance.

Unusual bill matter, in no particular order, (but so descriptive!) was as follows: Mr Hymack – 'The Chameleon Comedian', Perci Honri – 'Concertina-turn', Carlton – 'The Human Hairpin', Zellini – 'The Human Chimney', Roxy la Rocca – 'Wizard of the Harp', The Delfont Boys – 'Eccentric Dancers', Stetson – 'With a few old Toppers', Gaston Palmer – 'All the Spoons in all the Glasses', Gordon Freeman – 'The World's Worst Inventor', Ben Blue – 'All American Half Wit and his Nit Wits', Will Morris – 'A Merry Wag on Wheels', Donald B. Stuart – 'The Tallest Conjurer in Captivity', Tex McLeod – 'Spinning Ropes and Yarns', Master Freddie

Bobby May

Craig – 'The Boy with the Index Brain', The Hazel Mangean Girls – 'Four Speeds No Brakes', George Prentice – 'The Punch and Judy Show. That's The Way To Do It!', Wilson Keppel and Betty – 'Cleopatra's Nightmare', Sherkot – 'The Goalkeeper Continental Eccentric', Ray Huling and Seal – 'The Sea-Going Taxi', The Ganjou Brothers and Juanita – 'Romance in Porcelain', Max Wall – 'Irresponsible', and 'The boy with the obedient feet', Giovanni – 'The man who baffled Scotland Yard', Kafka Stanleys and Gray Sisters – 'Aerial Revuette', Wences – 'I'm Not Afraid', Florence Desmond – 'The Worlds Greatest Impressionist', Ted Ray – 'Fiddling and Fooling', Trixie – 'The Five-Year-Old Juggler', Chief OsKeNonTon – 'The Mohawk Singer', Joe Termini – 'The Somnolent Melodist', The Six Gridneffs – 'Balancing on Unsupported Ladders', Sylvestre – 'The Sunshade Maker', Joe Besser – 'Just Crazy', 'Captain Tommy Kayes And His Lions in the World's Smallest Cage', Joe Davis – 'Wizard of the Cue', The Dollinoff and Raya Sisters – 'Dancing Dollusions', The Cairoli Brothers – 'The World's Greatest Clowns', El Granadas – 'With Rope, Whip and Unicycle', The Zoris – 'The Leopard and His Prey' and Bob Bromley – 'The Biggest Little Show on Earth'.

No Variety show is complete without a speciality act, who sometimes can steal all the applause!

HAROLD DAVISO
PRESENTS

AN
EVENING
WITH
JUDY
GARLAND

LONDON PALLADI
1960

Chapter Sixteen

THE SWINGIN'
SIXTIES

eslie MacDonnell was now the Managing Director of the London Palladium and in full charge of policy and bookings. He opened the new season with Liberace, who was to make yet another appearance early in 1960 with his *Music Box Show*. Although television was proving popular, not everyone had a set, and the general public were still content to visit the theatre to see a live show in colour, rather than stay at home to watch something in black and white. Leslie Mac, as he was affectionately known, then continued with the long running show *Stars in your Eyes*, starring newcomers Cliff Richard, Des O'Connor, Russ Conway, Joan Regan, Edmund Hockridge, Billy Dainty and David Kossoff. This had a most successful run which ended in a Grand Gala Charity Night in aid of The St John's Ambulance, in the presence of Her Royal Highness the Queen Mother. The Gala, with excerpts from the show, was strengthened with additional special appearances by Bruce Forsyth, Max Jaffa, and Judy Garland. Sandwiched in between all this

was a late summer engagement with the legendary Judy
Garland, who made a special one-off performance with
Norrie Paramor and his Orchestra. It was such a sell-
out that another concert was quickly arranged for the
following Sunday. The first pantomime of the decade was
Dick Whittington, with Norman Wisdom and Yana in the
lead roles. Norman had certainly come a long way since
his early days, having already had tremendous successes
at the Palladium in 1954, 1955, 1956 and 1957. In those
days, it seemed as if the pantomimes ran forever.

In May 1961 a two-week run of a variety presentation
starred Frankie Vaughan with speechless ventriloquist
Arthur Worsley, Tony Fayne, Gladys Morgan and
Company, and Joe Church, who was always a popular
visitor. The Allisons and Kenny Ball and his
Jazzmen complemented the strong bill. This was
followed by another Robert Nesbitt spectacular
revue, *Let Yourself Go*, with Harry Secombe,
Roy Castle, The King Brothers, Marion Ryan,
Eddie Calvert, Audrey Jeans, and, in very small
print, the newcomer Ronnie Corbett. Charlie
Drake finished off the

season in traditional style as the Merriest of Monarchs with the new pantomime *Old King Cole*. This co-starred Jeanette Scott, Jackie Rae and Gary Miller, as well as pantoland stalwarts Jack Francois and The Johnny Hutch Seven Volants, with Bert Brownbill and Billy Danvers adding their own spirit to the occasion.

1962 commenced with a short variety season which featured the electrifying star Shirley Bassey. She was accompanied by The Temperance Seven. (Just to confuse everyone, there were really nine of them, and from all accounts the Dog and Trumpet across the road enjoyed their company on many an occasion!) The show also included the rising topical comedy star Ted Rogers, and brilliant artistic magic was provided by Richiardi. Paul Andrews created quite an impression, further humour was provided by Mike and Bernie Winters and showing us all how he could 'Twist' was the new dance sensation, Lionel Blair. Two weeks later the schoolgirl songstress Helen Shapiro topped the bill. She also went on to top the bill on the Sunday night TV show too and was one of the youngest artists ever to do so, seeing as she was still at school! She was accompanied in this variety season by The Magic Circle Young Magician of the Year, Johnny Hart. Also on the well balanced bill was the singing star Matt Monro, along with the 'Girl of many voices', Joan Turner, and eccentric dancer Billy Dainty.

These four preliminary weeks of variety heralded the start of yet another very long season with *Every Night at the Palladium*, which starred Bruce Forsyth. Bruce had learned his trade at the Windmill Theatre as well as on countless summer seasons around Britain. He was the rightful top of the bill, as by now he had established himself firmly in the hearts of television viewers. He appeared alongside Morecambe and Wise, Eve Boswell, and Pear Carr and Teddy Johnson in yet another tremendous box office success. This lasted until December when *Puss in Boots* gave the children their taste of traditional pantomime, with Frankie Vaughan, Dick Emery, and Jimmy Edwards playing the lead roles.

Sammy Davis Jnr entertained very professionally for a brief season, along with supporting acts The Dallas Boys, and the humourist Pat Henry, who was from the USA. A sell-out Sunday concert with Shirley Bassey, Matt Monro and Woolf Phillips and his Orchestra was followed by *Swing Along*, starring Arthur Haynes. Illness in the form of a heart attack would ultimately rob Arthur of his long running show, but this did allow a rare stage appearance by an artist who was known to millions by his lugubrious television personna. His name was Tony Hancock. He was assisted by the comedy foil Nicholas Parsons, and musical tastes were well catered for with Frank Ifield, Susan Maughan, Ken Martin and Joan Savage. They appeared in the Robert Nesbitt *Ring a Ding* revue.

By 1963, space was very much in the news with sputniks and cosmonauts, and so a specially written seasonal offering was put on. It was called *Man in the Moon* and featured Charlie Drake. Who would have guessed on seeing the show that six years later, man would actually land on the moon? After this, Matt Monro and Kathy Kirby appeared on stage for a special concert on Good Friday, in *A Song for Europe* with host Bob Monkhouse. They were all accompanied by Bob Miller and his Millermen. Then, on 13 October, the streets were thronged like never before and every seat in

At the famous
LONDON PALLADIUM

LESLIE A. MACDONNELL
presents

CHARLIE DRAKE

in ROBERT NESBITT's
SPACE AGE MUSICAL

OPENS DEC. 23RD
DEC 23 & 24 at 7.30
SUBSEQUENTLY
2·45 TWICE **7·30**
DAILY

THE MAN IN THE MOON

Based on a story by
JACK DAVIES & ROBERT NESBITT

WITH
Andrew LAURENCE · Michael HAWKINS
Geoffrey WINCOTT · James OTTAWAY
SYDNEY   DAVID   TOM
VIVIAN   DAVENPORT   GILL
Jack FRANCOIS · PeterDARE · Sonny WILLIS · Peter VERNON
The BILL SHEPHERD SINGERS
Reed de ROUEN · Jose CLEWS · Barry SHAWZIN

Songs by TOM SPRINGFIELD
Book by CHARLIE

INTRODUCING
THE RISING GENERATION
THE STARS OF TOMORROW
BARBARA EVANS
THE BAKER TWINS
ANNA DAWSON
ERIC FLYNN
VICKI MITCHELL
ELIZABETH BELM

235

the theatre was filled to capacity. For the viewers, it was just another *Sunday Night at the London Palladium*. Well, almost. Bruce Forsyth, the compère, announced Des O'Connor, and Des is the first to admit that the audience were shouting their heads off, not for him but with cries of 'We want The Beatles!' Bruce hosted *Beat the Clock*, but the audience could not have cared less that it stood at £200. They wanted The Beatles. Following the second commercial break, all Bruce had to do was announce: 'Here they are!' and the rest could not be heard through the roar of the fans in the theatre. Their pop heroes were live on stage and it was a memorable, magical night all round.

As 1964 came along, the fabulous Lena Horne entertained next, with The Bachelors, Arthur Worsley, The Three Monarchs, and Des O'Connor supporting. The big show of the year was *Startime*, starring Frankie Vaughan, and co-starring Audrey Jeans and Peter Goodwright. With the further additions of the hilarious Tommy Cooper, Liverpool's lady of pop Cilla Black, and The Fourmost, it proved to be yet another box office success. In a show that was once again produced by Harold Davison, Judy and Liza appeared in November in what was to be a very special Sunday concert. It was originally scheduled to be a one-time performance, but yet again, following the 1960 precedent, such was the success of the show that a second concert was hastily organised for the following Sunday. This too was a sell-out before it could even be advertised. It was a historic occasion for mother and daughter, and made for a truly memorable night for all those present. In December of that year, Cliff appeared with The Shadows, who had created two dozen new songs and the lyrics for the specially written pantomime, *Aladdin and his Wonderful Lamp*. Arthur Askey was in his familiar role as his 'mummy' Widow Twankey. Appearances were made by Una Stubbs, David Davenport, Alan Curtis, Billy Tasker, Charlie Cairoli, and The Johnny Hutch Seven Volants, all pantomime stalwarts in their own right, and Kirby's Flying Ballet also featured. The show's success was fully merited.

Staged by Robert Nesbitt, *Doddy's Here* took place in 1965 with The Kaye Sisters, The Barron Knights and ventriloquist Clifford Guest. All the reviews agreed that

it was a rib-tickling show for all the family. During the summer, a special one-off concert featured The Rolling Stones, who filled the theatre as well as the nearby streets with fans trying to get tickets. Once again, extra police had to be brought in to keep the crowds under control. With music and lyrics once again by The Shadows, *Babes in the Wood* ended the year in grand panto style, although this time The Shadows were appearing elsewhere in Britain. However, Frank Ifield, Sidney James, Roy Kinnear and Kenneth Connor did appear, along with the irrepressible Arthur Askey, who played the Dame once again as Big Hearted Martha.

The majority of the pantomimes and spectaculars during this period displayed the names of Albert Knight, who staged them, and Pamela Devis, who choreographed all their movements. In most if not all of the revues and pantomimes, the shows had the added benefit of The Ross Taylor Dancers and

The Bill Shepherd Singers, as well as The Aida Foster Children and The Peggy O'Farrell Children. Tod Kingman invariably designed the sets, and the costumes were designed by Cynthia Tingey. It was just one big team effort.

Following the long and successful Christmas offering and commencing on 6 May 1966, Leslie MacDonnell and Bernard Delfont presented *London Laughs*. It starred Harry Secombe and it certainly lived up to its name. It co-starred Russ Conway, Jimmy Tarbuck, Freddie Frinton and Thora Hird, and Anita Harris. The spectacular show was devised and produced by the doyen of the stage, Robert Nesbitt. Support came from Tony Sympson, Nicky Henson, The Mike Rabin Group, Dave Armour, Diane Smith, Jack Francois, and The Palladium Orchestra, which on this occasion was conducted by Billy Ternent. The choreography was by Douglas Squires.

Cliff Richard as Buttons and The Shadows were back in residence again at Christmas time, and they kept Edwin Shaw and his box office staff very busy indeed with a specially written *Cinderella*. Playing the Ugly Sisters were Terry Scott and Hugh Lloyd. The Francois and Tasker partnership was also in evidence and they were aided and abetted by Jack Douglas. As with most seasonal offerings, the speciality act was what most attracted the children, and this year was no exception. With keeper Jenda Smaha, the adorable Tanya, the petite pachyderm, almost stole the show! And they say never work with children or animals! This was also one of the first productions to use minute radio microphones, and the press criticised heavily, aghast that the star should 'mime' his songs, not realising that the new technology was in use and no visible microphone was in sight!

When this pantomime finished in the April of 1967, a short season of Variety was thought appropriate. Once again presented by Leslie Mac and by arrangement with Leslie Grade and Bernard Delfont, Frank Ifield, The Seekers and Tom Jones topped their own full supporting bills respectively, with backup comedy provided by the loveable Mike and Bernie Winters throughout this period. Johnny Hart with his well-trained budgies mystified everyone once again, and the somewhat larger Tanya made a quick return. All this was coupled with Sid Millward's Nitwits, Des Lane and his penny whistle, and

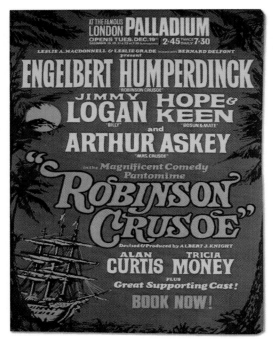

funny man Frank Berry. The bills were completed with The Tiller Girls working hard, as always, with their precise routines. In June 1967, *Doddy's Here Again* was in residence at the Palladium with the glamourous Bluebell Girls, the songstress Rosemary Squires, The Bal Caron Trio, Roy Budd and his Trio, South American speciality The Peiro Brothers, and Italy's elegant magician Silvan. They were all supporting the irrepressible Ken Dodd. What a line-up! What a show!

With the book by David Croft, *Robinson Crusoe* was the chosen pantomime which finished off this busy year for the box office. The supporting acts were Jimmy Logan and Hope and Keen, with Engelbert Humperdinck playing the title role. In the storyline Robinson Crusoe was captured by the natives and placed in a cage, only to sing 'Please Release Me Let Me Go!' However, it was a more memorable pantomime for other reasons that his 'mother', Arthur Askey, would never forget. A trapdoor used in one of the scenes was to be used one time too many in the production, as Arthur fell through with painful consequences. This left him out of action for

quite a time, which allowed talented Billy Tasker, his understudy on many an occasion, to step into Arthur's boots and striped socks, not to mention his copious frilly drawers, with only three hours' notice. He gave the performance of his life! The show must go on they say, and it did!

The hot ticket Tom Jones was back again for a limited season in 1968 with the fabulous Shadows, Ted Rogers and Michael Bentine. Midsummer of that year brought back the legendary Sammy Davis Jnr in the boxing musical *Golden Boy*. It co-starred Gloria de Haven and Lon Satton with Ben Vereen. Owing to the death in the USA of Robert Kennedy and as a personal tribute, a special charity performance was cancelled and re-scheduled later in this all too brief run. The *Autumn Show* had the ever popular Cliff and The Shadows topping once more, with Mike Yarwood not far behind with his incredibly lifelike and brilliant mimicry. The always popular Joe Church and Jimmy Marshall added the comedy, and Spanish supremo ventriloquist Senor Wences completed the bill along with The Paddy Stone Dancers. Finally, Jimmy Tarbuck headlined in *Jack and the Beanstalk* with Arthur Askey, now fit and well once again, playing his 'mother'. As Jimmy has often said, dear Arthur had more children in show business! The original book, music and lyrics were by the talented duo Ronnie Cass and Peter Myers. With Kirby's Flying Ballet, David Davenport and Jean Bayless, Audrey Jeans and Charlie Cairoli and the Tasker and Francois duo, it had all the ingredients of a success. And indeed it was, as the box office receipts proved.

1969 began, as in previous years, with brief variety seasons, this time with Val Doonican and Max Bygraves headlining their own individual shows, with Sandie Shaw, Jackie Trent and Tony Hatch supporting respectively. Ted Rogers, Dev Shawn and Des Lane, Will Gaines, Dailey and Wayne, and Arthur Worsley also added their own exceptional talents to the bills.

Des O'Connor was *Here and Now* at the London Palladium in May 1969 in a very long running season, with Mike and Bernie Winters giving able support when necessary. Clive Lea and The Rockin' Berries, ventriloquist Jack Beckett, juggler Valente Valente, Luis Alberto del Parana and Los Paraguayos and The Ukranian Cossacks

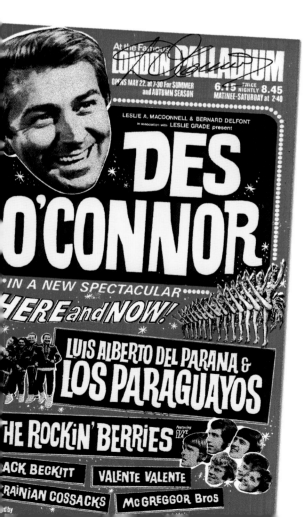

all highlighted the show. Johnny Wiltshire provided the musical backing throughout. It was here during one night on stage that Eamonn Andrews appeared with his big red book to surprise an unsuspecting Des with the famous words: 'This is your Life'. That was surely a night Des will never forget!

The spectacular and lavish pantomime of that year, *Dick Whittington*, starring Tommy Steele and Mary Hopkin, was to be Leslie MacDonnell's last presentation. It was a fitting tribute to a man who had brought the very best entertainment from all corners of the globe to the discerning theatre-going public. Her Royal Highness Princess Margaret took her two children to see the show, and Prince Rainier and Princess Grace also attended a regular performance. Later in the week, Princess Alexandra and her children also visited this family occasion, accompanied by the Duke and Duchess of Kent. It was a right 'Royal' pantomime in every sense of the word! Billy Dainty, Alan Curtis and Rupperts Bears and the combination of Francois, Tasker and Bertie Hare all added to the show's success.

Reflecting upon the decade, there were many special Sunday concerts. The annual charity show took place with *The Night of a Hundred Stars* and literally hundreds and hundreds of pounds were raised for The Actor's Charitable Trust. The Variety Club held their almost annual spectacular, *Fall in the Stars*, and another *Save Rave* pop concert took place for needy children.

The Beatles *and* The Rolling Stones appeared on *Sunday Night at the London Palladium*, though not on the same bill. Crowd control could never have coped! Extra police were drafted in as it was to try and keep the teenagers under some form of control. Beatlemania had arrived in Argyll Street at last.

For one night only in the new year of 1968, Maurice Chevalier made his farewell appearance and stopped off at the Palladium to say *au revoir*. Diana Ross, The Beach Boys, Liberace and Henry Mancini also appeared on their own shows too.

Although the Royal Variety Performances had been televised from the Palladium since 1960, the year of 1969 was to be a very special occasion, with the first colour production of the Royal Variety Show.

What a decade!

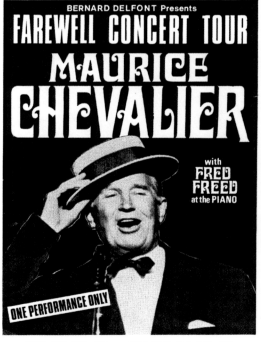

Chapter Seventeen

THE SUPERSTAR SEVENTIES

In 1972 the Environment Minister for the Government made a most important decision. Acting on the advice of the Historic Buildings Committee and following the recommendations of the Historic Buildings Board of the Greater London Council, he declared that he would 'list' the Palladium so that it could never be pulled down. The Palladium was chosen because of its architectural and historic merit. The theatre had been saved from the greed of developers. An office block? Never!

It was a new decade and there was a new man at the top. 'Benji' was now elevated to the post of Managing Director and in full charge of bookings. 'By Arrangement with Louis Benjamin' appeared on all the posters. It was almost time for another American invasion, but that would happen somewhat later in the decade. British tops of the bill still dominated the advertising boards outside the theatre and the likes of Bruce Forsyth, Max Bygraves,

Val Doonican, and Freddie Starr continued to entertain, as did Gallic heart-throb Sacha Distel, who was followed in turn by Tony Bennett, Engelbert Humperdinck and Peter Noone.

Dorothy Squires played a very special Sunday concert in 1970. She had always felt that her work was worthy of a dream appearance at this prestigious venue, but this wish had remained unfulfilled until this point. So, to cock a snook at the various managements who had missed their opportunity, she set about hiring the theatre herself at a personal cost of £5000. Although she was prepared to make a loss on the event, such was the devotion of her fans that it wasn't necessary! In fact, the tickets went so fast that they were all were sold within twenty-four hours. At the end of her show, 2,300 adoring fans gave her a standing ovation. Having proved her point, Dorothy was back again the following year *and* the year after that! In 1974 she was even headlining in a fully-fledged variety show, and this was repeated in 1975 too! Her determination had paid off.

The first year of the decade came to a close with the spectacular pantomime *Aladdin*, which starred Cilla Black, Leslie Crowther, Terry Scott and Alfred Marks. Support came, 'Boom Boom', in the unlikely shape of Basil Brush!

On the home front in the late spring of 1971, The Society for Film and Television Arts had their Annual Dinner at Grosvenor House, which was preceded by the Awards held on stage at the Palladium. The event was compèred by David Frost. However, the year was not without US influence in that Californian born Rod McKuen delighted his fans with selections from his vast repertoire. On another occasion later in the year, Andalusia was well represented by Raphael.

1971 saw Benjamin's first spectacular revue, *To See Such Fun*. Staged by Albert Knight, it starred the great clown and comedy conjurer Tommy Cooper, with talented Russ Conway, Anita Harris, and 'grandad' Clive Dunn. It ran for six months and was then followed by fortnightly variety seasons with Cliff Richard, Val Doonican, Des O'Connor, and Dorothy Squires, with supporting acts Dora Bryan, Olivia Newton-John, The Shadows, Mike Yarwood, Norman Vaughan, Larry Grayson, Roy Budd, and Henny Youngman. Jack Parnell

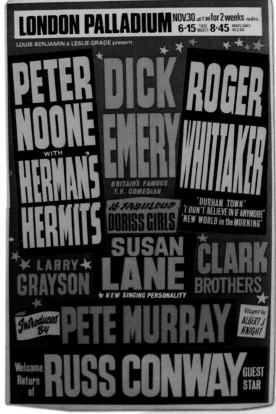

was also rarely away from Argyll Street during this deluge of talent.

In association with *The People* newspaper, Butlin's held the first of many Annual Grand Finals of their National Talent Contest. Mike Reid had reached the finals but was unplaced. Bobby Crush, however, came second. Comic Joey Kaye was judged the winner and understudied Ronnie Corbett in the pantomime that followed.

The ever popular *Cinderella* was the chosen festive offering with Ronnie Corbett as Buttons, Clodagh Rogers in the title role, and singing star Malcolm Roberts as the handsome Prince. Terry Scott and Julian Orchard played the Ugly Sisters, whilst David Kossoff was the Baron who was always hard up. The Patton Brothers were the Broker's Men.

Special Sunday concerts included one in aid of the RSPCA, another with Nina Simone from North Carolina, and one more with Amalia Rodrigues and Antonio Mourao from Portugal. In midsummer there had been a literally star-studded occasion in memory of Dickie Valentine, Sidney Boatman and Dave Pearson. Presented by Leslie Grade and staged by Albert Locke, the heart of show business appeared, with individual contributions from Lita Roza, Dennis Lotis, Labi Siffre, Olivia Newton-

John, Roy Castle, Frankie Vaughan, Cliff Richard and The Shadows, and Bruce Forsyth. Norman Vaughan acted as compère. With Jack Parnell conducting the orchestra, it was a night of nights for all those present. Then, in the presence of Her Royal Highness the Princess Anne, a Royal Performance took place in aid of The Variety Club with the usual star-filled cast of *Fall in the Stars*.

In 1972 Johnny Hamp's original Granada TV formula, *The Comedians*, was brought to the stage. It starred Ken Goodwin (who had appeared in the 1971 Royal Variety Performance), Bernard Manning, Charlie Williams, Mike Reid, Dave Butler and Joss White. Shep's Banjo Band provided the music, and The Pamela Devis Dancers added the glamour and precision. This was probably the most that the Palladium audiences had laughed at a group of funny men since The Crazy Gang. After six months the sides of the Palladium were beginning to split from too much laughter, and the successful season came to an end. During their long run and in the presence of Her Majesty the Queen and the Duke of Edinburgh, The Comedians all appeared in a special Royal Gala Royal Variety Performance that was organised to raise funds for the British Olympic Team. Other top names from around the world also appeared. At that time, US television's *Laugh-In* presenters, Dan Rowan and Dick Martin, were on a rare visit to London, and they acted as hosts for the evening. Additional appearances were made by Richard Attenborough, Michael Caine, Roger Moore, Larry Grayson, Philippe Genty, The Osmonds, Des O'Connor, Lily Tomlin and Liza Minnelli. Jack Parnell conducted the orchestra and Dougie Squires' Second Generation added energy and excitement to the occasion with their well planned dance routines.

Tom Jones, Jack Jones, Engelbert Humperdinck and Des O'Connor each had their own short variety seasons, as had happened in the previous year. Jerry Stevens, The Rocking Berries, Dickie Henderson, Keith Harris and Orville, and Mrs Mills added their support over the season.

Babes in the Wood was the winter offering, with TV star Edward Woodward in the starring role as Robin Hood, Derek Nimmo as the Good Robber and Bill

Maynard as Jasper Snatchem. Adrienne Posta was Maid Marion, whilst Alan Curtis was the Sheriff trying to keep everyone in order. An impossible task when there was a wild Emu on the loose, closely followed by Rod Hull. A mixture of music and mayhem ensued!

During this long, successful season, several special concerts were held. One was in aid of the Stars' Organisation for Spastics, and another was for The British Heart Foundation, and was entitled *We'll meet Again*. Appropriately, it starred Vera Lynn, and she was supported by Morecambe and Wise, Kenneth McKellar, Harry Secombe, Arthur Askey, Pete Murray, Syd Lawrence and his Orchestra, and The Beverley Sisters, with Dickie Henderson acting as host. This was a Billy Marsh and Leslie Grade production, which was once again staged by Albert Knight. The music and national dances of Romania were represented in a one-off occasion, and Johnny Mathis and Vicki Carr appeared on two separate Sundays in the summer. A family act called Gladys Knight and the Pips came from Atlanta, Georgia, and from Turkey came Erol, who also had their own special occasion during the busy year, not to mention another RSPCA Gala. It was a truly international year.

Continuing the policy of the previous years, fast moving Variety was very much in evidence in 1973, commencing with Tommy Steele, who starred in his own show with June Bronhill, Joe Church, José Moreno, and the canine conjuring team, the Wychwoods. The following month, Bruce Forsyth headlined in *Palladium '73*, supported by Kenneth McKellar, Mona Richardson and Los Indianos. Dougie Squires' Dancers were on hand too with their energetic routines.

In September, a show was produced which was simply entitled *Cilla*, with the Liverpool lass herself accompanied by Roger Whittaker, and with funny man Johnny Hackett. Philippe Genty and his Parisian puppetry, Gil Dova, and The Schaller Brothers complemented this particular bill, with Irving Davies providing the superb dance routines. It was another successful season for everyone concerned.

Gilbert O'Sullivan, Jack Jones, Engelbert Humperdinck and Tom Jones all had their own short seasons with supporting acts such as Little and Large, Jerry Stevens, Lennie Bennett, Rostal and Schaeffer, Peter Kaye, Dana, and Francis Van Dyke. The Young Generation energetically danced their way through them all.

Butlin's held their finals again. Whilst the judges made up their mind this time, the tuneful trio The Bachelors entertained the waiting audience. Another name to make them laugh was none other than ex-competitor, Mike Reid.

The magnificent pantomime that year was *Jack and The Beanstalk* with Frankie Howerd as Simple Simon, and Dora Bryan, Alfie Bass, Mark Wynter and Calli in the lead roles. Pantomime stalwarts Michael Kilgarriff, Leon Greene, and Berti Hare were aiding and abetting. As always, a speciality was included, and this time it was ventriloquist Beryl Calvert, who had been spotted on the previous Butlin's Finals.

In April the following year a special show was presented for deprived and handicapped children, with The Variety Club's annual *Fall in the Stars*. Tony Bennett, Red Buttons, Gladys Knight, Jack Benny, Gary Glitter, Jim Bailey and Buznea Piaff concerts all took place during the year.

1974 was another year to be packed full of popular names, including Cliff Richard, Frankie Vaughan, Howard Keel, Dorothy Squires, Mama Cass Elliot, and Debbie Reynolds, along with her entire Las Vegas company including Carrie Fisher. From Paris came Josephine Baker and Vic Damone, and Broadway's Ethel Merman also appeared. Ken Dodd had a tickle in, and in *Grayson's Scandals* was 'Shut that Door' Larry himself. They all had their own limited seasons. They were supported by a host of wonderful and popular acts, such as Moira Anderson, Diz Disley, Little and Large, Freddie Davies, The Rockin' Berries, Rod Hull and Emu, Billy Dainty, The Grumbleweeds, the hilarious ventriloquist Neville King, Peter Goodwright, Russ Conway, Arthur Worsley, Paper Lace, Mike Reid, Bobby Crush, Arthur Askey, Roger Kitter, Millican and Nesbitt, Springfield Revival, Wilma Reading, George Carl, Keith Harris, and Noel Gordon, to name but a few! ...Phew! Once again, The Second Generation were very much in evidence.

The Christmas offering for 1974 was *Hans Andersen*. It was produced by Harold Fielding, who was about to begin a very special and lengthy relationship with the Palladium. He presented this wonderful Copenhagen fairy tale with his long-time friend Tommy Steele playing the lead role. This show was highly successful in that it was a spectacular which combined the fairy tales and had memorable tunes known to all. This was certainly no ugly duckling; it was a swan of a show!

The Variety Club presented a very special one-off concert in the spring of 1975, which starred the relaxed Perry Como, with Hope and Keen, Roger Kitter, and Rod Hull and Emu supporting. On this occasion, the London Palladium Orchestra was under the direction of Gordon Rose. Slim Whitman made an appearance too in his own

Tommy Steele

251

show, *Springfield Revival*, later in the year. The Colin Charman Benefit Gala also pulled out all the stops, with Ronnie Barker, Cilla, Ronnie Corbett, Dana, Dick Emery, Bruce Forsyth, Cliff and The Shadows, Harry Secombe, the ubiquitous Second Generation, and Ronnie Hazlehurst and his Orchestra all giving their services to this very worthy cause. Matt Monro appeared in his own show with a handful of stars including Max Wall and Tommy Trinder. George Hamilton IV with Micky and Griff, and The Ted Heath Orchestra directed by Stan Reynolds both did special one-off Sunday contributions, as did Red Buttons with Mimi Hines, and Gene Pitney. In the presence of Her Royal Highness the Princess Margaret, Countess of Snowdon, a Royal Ballet Gala took place, with Natalia Makarova, Lesley Collier, Wayne Eagling, and Merle Park featuring amongst others.

Whilst *Hans Andersen* continued almost throughout 1975, other top acts appeared on Sundays during the year. Exploding onto the scene was child star Zena Zavaroni, and other more established names like Bill Anderson, Caterina Valente, Glen Campbell, Kamahl, Gilbert Becaud, Helen Reddy, The Drifters, Wayne Newton, Johnny Cash, Charlie Rich, Roy Orbison, Charles Aznavour, Stephane Grapelli, Sacha Distel and Dorothy Squires all enjoyed their one night of deserved success. The Greatest Swing Band in the World stopped off on their autumn tour, and Perry Como came back again to triumph once more.

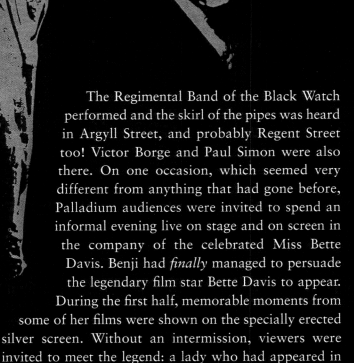

The Regimental Band of the Black Watch performed and the skirl of the pipes was heard in Argyll Street, and probably Regent Street too! Victor Borge and Paul Simon were also there. On one occasion, which seemed very different from anything that had gone before, Palladium audiences were invited to spend an informal evening live on stage and on screen in the company of the celebrated Miss Bette Davis. Benji had *finally* managed to persuade the legendary film star Bette Davis to appear. During the first half, memorable moments from some of her films were shown on the specially erected silver screen. Without an intermission, viewers were invited to meet the legend: a lady who had appeared in no less than eighty-four films. It was, without doubt, a night to remember! Let us also not forget *The Concert* with Count Basie, Sarah Vaughan, Pat Henry, and 'Ol' Blue Eyes' himself, Frank Sinatra. Yes, they all appeared in one show. They did it their way. What a year that was!

GREAT ROMANTIC SINGING STARS

EDDIE FISHER

With – also from AMERICA

Daughter of Judy Garland!.. Sister of Liza Minnelli!..
above all a star in her own right...
DYNAMIC! EXHILARATING! EXCITING!

LORNA LUFT

Plus – from ENGLAND

your Crackerjack favourite
DON MACLEAN

A powerhouse group of
singing, swinging
impressionists
FIDDLYGIG

ME!
st TV idol
to be at
um too!
xciting!

The great Ted Ray and the whole panel (as well as
the viewers' panel) of TV's New Faces last Saturday
UNANIMOUSLY voted

ROGER de COURCEY
The winner's winner.

and me too...
Come and see us all in one
great programme.

NDON PALLADIUM
NS MAY 17 to JUNE 5 / NIGHTLY AT 9.0 pm WEDS & SATS AT 6.20 pm

HAROLD DAVISON for M.A.M. in association with LOUIS BENJAMIN
presents

Shirley MacLaine

MUSICAL DIRECTOR
DONN TRENNER

SPECIAL GUEST STAR
VINCE HILL
AND
LENNIE BENNETT

Box Office Now Open Tel: 01·437 73

The year of 1975 came to an end with the Robert Helpman production of *Peter Pan*, with Lulu in the title role. Ron Moody was the awesome Captain Hook and Mr Darling. Mrs Darling was played by Rachel Gurney, Tony Sympson was Smee and Wendy was played by Tessa Wyatt. A further addition to this strong cast was Peter Bland in the role of James Starkey.

1976 followed a similar pattern in terms of a host of star names, although they were all different from the previous year. So successful was she at the box office that Shirley MacLaine appeared on two separate occasions, as did multi-talented Bruce Forsyth in his one-man laughter show. From the USA came Eddie Fisher and Lorna Luft, and Spanish heart-throb Raphael set hearts a-fluttering. The popular recording artists John Denver, The Stylistics, Frankie Valli, and The Three Degrees all appeared on the Argyll Street stage. Sacha Distel was accompanied by Mike Reid, Marti Caine, Kerry Jewell, and Brian Coshall. There were performances by Manhattan Transfer, Tony Bennett and Lena Horne. Harold Fielding presented Julie Andrews with Michael Bentine too. From the successful film *Cabaret* came Joel Grey again, who had made a

HE MUSICAL EVENT OF THE YEAR

Tony & Lena sing!

ONY BENNETT & LENA HORNE
in a spectacular musical evening.

Director
E ZITO

Music Director
LOU LEVY

he LONDON PALLADIUM
by arrangement with LOUIS BENJAMIN

RIDAY APRIL 30th and SATURDAY MAY 1st
and SUNDAY MAY 2nd.
nd 9.00 p.m. TICKETS: £6·50, £5·00, £4·00, £3·00, £2·00
from the LONDON PALLADIUM
K OFFICE 437 7373)or all leading ticket agencies

LONDON

LOUIS BENJAMIN and HAROLD FIELDING present

On stage again in London for the first time in 17 years!...

JULIE ANDREWS

returns to the

LONDON PALLADIUM

bringing you the songs she made famou from THE SOUND OF MUSIC... My FAIR LADY... Mary Poppins... Camelot... and a host of wonderful new tunes!

OPENS JUNE 9th at 7.30 UNTIL JUNE 19th 14 Performances C
JUNE 10,14,15,17 & 18th at 8.0pm JUNE 11,12,16,19th at 6.30 and 9.0

BOOK NOW! write call or phone 01·437 7373 and al

comparable hit when he had appeared at the Palladium twenty-one years earlier in Variety. George Burns appeared in June on a special Royal Gala Charity night with Pam Ayres and Toni Dalli. Later in the year there was even a tribute to Paul Robeson with Valentine Pringle.

Bing Crosby always maintained that he would never perform in Variety. As a film man, he said that the necessary discipline of the theatre did not attract him. However, it was the thought of golf during the day that ultimately tipped the balance when he finally said 'yes' to Benji. It was Bing's Fiftieth Anniversary tour, which took in Scotland and Ireland as well, at places which all

sported lovely golf courses! Rosemary Clooney and Ted
Rogers appeared with Bing and his family. In fact, he
loved the Palladium theatre so much that he appeared
again the following year. I wonder if any other theatre in
the world could boast of that? In actual fact, Bing had
already made a surprise and unprogammed visit during a
live Sunday night TV show when his 'Road' partner, Bob
Hope, was top of the bill. Only Val Parnell knew that
Bing would make the briefest of appearances. At a specific
time the Stage Manager was asked to go to the stage door
and meet a man who he would present with a workcoat
to wear and a brush to sweep the stage with.

HARRY BELAFONTE
and his full International
Broadway Company

LONDON PALLADIUM

Tuesday, 16th November –
Saturday, 20th November

This Bing did as planned, right in the middle of the act of a totally unsuspecting Bob. He just smiled and looked up briefly at the camera, to Hope's total amazement. What a well-kept secret! With no written ad-libs for once, it left Bob speechless!

In July of 1976, Harold Fielding presented The Australian Ballet in the British premiere of the ballet version of Lehar's *The Merry Widow*. Johnny Ray, Billy Daniels, Frances Faye, and The Ink Spots all appeared in a special US show. Sammy Davis, Billy Eckstine and The Nicholas Brothers all appeared in another special Royal Gala. Ray Charles, Andy Williams, Freddy Starr, Charles Aznavour, and Vicki Carr all made appearances too. In late October, Max Boyce was able to return home to his beloved Wales to shout out, 'I was there!' Charlie Pride, Marvin Gaye, Vicki Carr, and Harry Belafonte could all do the same! With his unique style of comedy in music, and all the way from Denmark, came Victor Borge. The Carpenters and The Drifters appeared too, although not on the same show! The talented David Essex and Barbara Dickson also added their names to the long line of celebrities. At the other end of the music spectrum, The Grimethorpe Colliery Band made a one-off appearance to celebrate their visit to the US Bi-Centennial celebrations. It was another year to remember!

The year was rounded off with the traditional pantomime, *Cinderella*, starring TV favourites Richard O'Sullivan, Yootha Joyce and Brian Murphy. The ventriloquist Roger de Courcey was interrupted by Nookie, and Fiona Fullerton played Cinders. She was aided by the Broker's Men played by Gordon and Bunny Jay, and The Peggy O'Farrell Children completed the cast. This lavish production was staged and produced by Albert Knight.

It was getting harder all the time to find new faces though, and 1977 had an identical format to previous years. However, the Management still succeeded in procuring new names from TV and films to entertain Palladium audiences. The country music star Faron Young opened a strong season with Hank Locklin and JoAnne Steele, and they were followed by The Stylistics. Bruce Forsyth was back again 'in charge' of his one-man show, and he was aided and abetted by long-time accompanist Don Hunt. Glen Campbell, Jack Jones,

Frankie Valli, and Sacha Distel all made appearances, along with newcomer magic man, Paul Daniels. In the presence of Her Royal Highness the Queen Mother, The Variety Club had their *Fall in the Stars*. Johnnie Mathis was backed by funny man Jerry Stevens, Koffee 'n' Kreme, Neil Sedaka, Steve Lawrence and Eydie Gorme. Chita Rivera was supported by Paul Daniels who had made a speedy return after his first appearance, and the master impersonator Jim Bailey was followed by Neil Diamond.

Almost 100 years had passed since the last event on ice before another ice show was to feature again at Argyll Street. In high summer of 1977, a specially constructed rink was assembled on top of the Palladium stage which had specifically been reinforced to accommodate all the weight of the rink and scenery. Larry Parnes presented *The Theatre of Skating II*, which featured John Curry, who stayed for the nine-week season and was a very great success.

For a two-week season, ballet of a different kind was then introduced by Roland Petit's Ballet de Marseille. The public then enjoyed a midnight feast with Tony Martin and Cyd Charisse. Ron Moody, Penny Lane, and Brian Stephens were also persuaded to stay up late.

Bing Crosby appeared once again with the Joe Bushkin Quartet between 26 September and 8 October. His support act, not that he needed one, was once again Rosemary Clooney and Ted Rogers, as well as members of Bing's family. Within seven days after the last night curtain came down, Bing sadly passed away on 14 October 1977.

Leo Sayer, Freddie Starr with Lynn Paul, Mike Goddard and Paul Ridgeway, Ray Stevens, Del Shannon and The Johnny Wiltshire Orchestra all appeared during this year. Dynamic music stars Cleo Laine and John Dankworth, Demis Roussos, Harry Belafonte, Captain and Tenille; yes, they all came too. Brotherhood of Man stopped off on their 1977 UK tour, and Slim Whitman and Gene Pitney also made successful one-night appearances. It was a busy time for the stage staff but they enjoyed the challenge.

LONDON PALLADIUM
SEPT. 26TH for 2 WEEKS ONLY
SEPT. 26 AT 7·30 · SUBS. NIGHTLY AT 8 P.M.

LOUIS BENJAMIN
By Arrangement with HAROLD DAVISON
presents

BING CROSBY
and Friends
including

ROSEMARY CLOONEY
THE JOE BUSHKIN QUARTET

BOOK NOW !! 01-437 7373

To celebrate the Silver Wedding of Her Majesty the Queen and the Duke of Edinburgh, a very, *very* special show was held on 21 November 1977. Presented by Lew Grade and Bernard Delfont in conjunction with Reg Swinson MBE, and produced by Dwight Hemeon and Gary Smith for US TV and the BBC, the show had a very strong trans-Atlantic appeal. With an estimated running time of four hours, Bob Hope was chosen as the host for the evening, and he introduced Julie Andrews, Paul Anka, Pam Ayres, Harry Belafonte, Brotherhood of Man, Tommy Cooper, Alan King, Cleo Laine with John Dankworth, John Williams, Little and Large, Shirley MacLaine, Jim Henson's Muppets, and Rudolph Nureyev. The Stage Director was Robert Nesbitt, who was no stranger to these events, and neither was Jack Parnell, who conducted the orchestra. The star of the evening in many people's eyes was octogenarian Olga Winogradsky, who presented Her Majesty with a special bouquet upon entering the theatre. Olga was the mother of sons Lew, Leslie and Bernard, who had all done so much to reshape the British entertainment industry.

At the end of the year, *Hans Andersen* was given a reprise with Tommy Steele featuring once again, although with a different supporting cast, this time headed by Sally Ann Howes and Anthony Valentine.

More top names came along in 1978 to give the box office a busy time, including Frankie Laine, Cliff Richard and The Shadows, and Manhattan Transfer, who stopped off on their World Tour. By arrangement with Tito Burns, Benji then presented the legendary silver screen stars Ginger Rogers and Donald O'Connor, along with Shoreditch born comedian Charlie Smithers. Showaddywaddy, The Stylistics, The Pasadena Roof Orchestra, The Supremes with Mary Wilson, a short season with The Liberace Las Vegas Show and The Dancing Waters, Diana Ross on her own, and Gladys Knight all provided great nights on stage.

On a Royal double bill, which was attended by Their Royal Highnesses the Duke and Duchess of Kent for the first performance and His Royal Highness the Prince of Wales for the second, a 'Super Night' was promised, and delivered. After an overture by The Royal Philharmonic Orchestra, and a prologue spoken by Anthony Quayle, Farrah Fawcett-Majors introduced dancers from The

Sadler's Wells Royal Ballet. Bob Newhart and Johnny Mathis closed the show. It certainly was a super night!

Elkie Brooks, Helen Reddy and Brian Marshall all appeared in popular special Sunday concerts too.

For the first time on any stage, Harold Fielding persuaded The Two Ronnies to join together in an evening of laughter. It had taken five years of negotiation but it was well worth all the sweat and tears. The sum of Corbett and Barker equalled pure enjoyment!

Nothing quite like The Golden Gala had been seen before. To mark the Fiftieth Anniversary of Equal Voting Rights for men and women, a Gala Event was produced by Wendy Toye and comprised a show made up entirely of ladies, with not a man in sight! Well, on stage anyway. In the orchestra pit, Jack Parnell was keeping his men in check. Well over 100 ladies appeared, all tops of the bill in their own right, and many thousands of pounds were raised for the appropriate charities. That was a unique night to remember for many a day. Mrs Pankhurst would have been delighted!

From Beirut came Fairouz for one night. Then Variety took up six nights, with legendary guitarist Bert Weedon, Marty Wilde, Iris Williams, and Bryn Philips, and top of the bill were The Dallas Boys. Max Bygraves, Bette Midler, Lena Martell, Lena Zavaroni, Dukes and Lee, Barry Manilow, Jack Jones, and Clodagh Rodgers; all took their turn to entertain. Sammy Davis also appeared with the very special guest Buddy Rich, then it was the turn of Smokie Robinson, Peter Skellern, Mary O'Hara, Cleo Laine, Demis Roussos, the legendary Liza Minelli, Darts, The Temptations and Tavares. They all enjoyed their own packed houses, as one would expect.

The extravagant Christmas offering for 1978 was the spectacular *Aladdin*, with Danny La Rue, Alfred Marks, Wayne Sleep, Dilys Watling, Bryan Marshall, Wei Wei Wong, David Ellen, and Johnny Hutch and The Half Wits. Gordon Rose conducted the Palladium Orchestra.

In 1979 the Liverpool comic Charlie Lea was the first man to hire the Palladium entirely at his own expense to present his own show. Appearing with Charlie were Johnny Mans and Joe Longthorne amongst others, and topping the bill was Charlie's fellow Liverpudlian, Ken Dodd. He couldn't fail, and he didn't!

Lou Rawls, Slim Whitman, Gloria Gaynor, Kate Bush, Tom Waits, Neil Sedaka, Don MacLean, Roger Whittaker; all wanted to appear on this famous stage. From India came Lata Mangeshka, and her following was so great that she filled the theatre on three consecutive Sundays. Lesley Uggams appeared with Bob Hope, and following his successful week he made a TV special for the home and US markets, alongside Leslie Leif Garrett and special guest star Racquel Welch.

In the presence of Her Royal Highness Princess Alexandra, The Variety Club presented their *Fall in the Stars*. Anthony Newley appeared with Juliet Prowse, Engelbert Humperdinck returned, and once again Cliff Richard appeared on two separate occasions during the year, as did Loudon Wainwright III.

The decade was fast drawing to a close and Benji could never be accused of not bringing the very best of the world's stars and superstars to the Palladium stage. There were very few left who hadn't been offered a contract. In fact, there were very few stars left to offer one to! It had been a veritable continuous galaxy of talent from all corners of the entertainment globe.

Perhaps it was a reversion back to the 1920s, but it was now time for a new formula; The Musical! And there was one star who had persistently eluded Benji. He had tried many times to entice Yul Brynner to appear. Every time, Brynner had said no. 'Getting to know you' must have been uppermost on Benji's mind, for he suggested that Brynner should just come and stand on the stage before he rejected his latest offer, and Brynner flew over on Concorde specially. He spent a short while in the darkness of the stage and said he had finally come to a decision. He said yes!

The original story of Anna and the King was set in 1862, and the show had not been seen in London since the 1950s. Planning for the staging of *The King and I* started immediately. The production co-starred Virginia McKenna, with John Bennett and The Rodgers, and Hammerstein's music came to life once again with Brynner in the lead role. Following the charity previews, it made its first appearance on 12 June 1979, and it ran until 27 October the following year.

It was a highly successful run and a memorable decade for Benji, something of which he could be rightly proud.

"Listen
very Carefully....
you will see this
Only once!"

Chapter Eighteen

THE EXUBERANT EIGHTIES

THE RETURN OF THE MUSICAL

The 1980s began on a high note with the continuation of the highly successful musical *The King and I*. The 1970s had seen the time of the variety superstar, but although superstars would still play a part in the 1980s, this period would be remembered as the decade of the musical.

Louis Benjamin led a hectic life of non-stop activity and he thrived on pace and pressure, jetting to and from all parts of America in search of new ideas and names that would attract and delight. By now, Benji was also producing the annual Royal Variety Performance, and his latest coup was to bring together Mary Martin and her son Larry Hagman for the 1980 Royal Performance. They had not been seen together in the West End since the days of *South Pacific* in Drury Lane.

After *The King and I* came to its natural end, Benji's first show of the new decade came in October 1980, in the delectable shape of TV's 'Wonderwoman' herself. Acclaimed in the US as the most exciting entertainer of the 1980s, Lynda Carter was certainly a lady you could listen to with both eyes. She was supported by Britain's funny magic man, Terry Seabrooke.

Benji then lined up the following top attractions: Max Bygraves and Chita Rivera, The Three Degrees, and Bruce Forsyth, who entertained as superbly as only he could. Ken Dodd presented his *Laughter Show* (an understatement if ever there was one!), and The Ted Heath Band also performed, as did Lena Horne with Ted Rogers. One of the thickest souvenir brochures accompanied Ray Donn's one night show, *The Publand Variety Show*. All proceeds went to The Entertainment Artists Benevolent Fund and The Adoption Society. Victor Borge and Peggy Lee, who were in town to appear in The Royal Variety Performance, both made special one-night appearances.

In support of The National Council for One Parent Families there was a Ballet Gala, devised and presented by Anthony Dowell and Anya Sainsbury in the presence of Her Royal Highness the Princess Margaret. Max Boyce was there again in November, and just prior to the pantomime came Matchbox and Ralph McTell.

The lavish festive production of 1980 was *Dick Whittington*. It cost £350,000 to produce and that year it was the West End's only traditional pantomime. It starred Jim Davidson, Mollie Sugden, Windsor Davies, Melvyn Hayes, Clive Dunn, Victor Spinetti, Jacqueline Reddin, Cherida Langford, Dino Shafeek, Derek Holt, and The Peggy O'Farrell Children, and with the Magic of Zee and Company *and* Lionel Blair, who also staged and choreographed, this was a *most* spectacular pantomime.

Bruce Forsyth

It was an occasion not to be missed, with something for all the family. Packed houses ensured that the box office was kept very busy indeed.

The spring of 1981 saw the first Children's Royal Variety Performance. The show was the brainchild of Rod Hull, the keeper of the incorrigible but loveable Emu. Thousands of pounds have been raised since for the NSPCC as a result of this particular venture.

The King's Singers, Christopher Cross and Anne Murray appeared later in the year, and then two of the greatest jazz exponents appeared together in the shape of Ella Fitzgerald and Oscar Peterson. They were in concert for six nights with The Jimmy Rowles Trio.

Liberace played another successful short season, together with The Magical Jeweller, Marvyn Roy and Carol. Then the Palladium moved from one of the world's great showmen to another, as Liberace made way for the musical *Barnum*, which told the story of possibly the greatest showman ever. It starred the gifted and multi-talented Michael Crawford and co-starred Deborah Grant and Williams C. Witter, with Sarah Payne, Jennie McGustie and Christopher Beck. This highly colourful and spectacular extravaganza opened to highly acclaimed reviews.

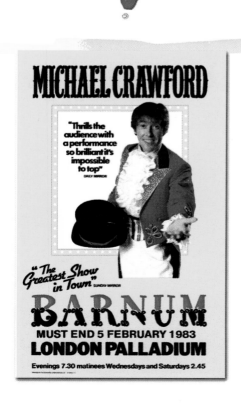

The show had everything for all ages, and Harold Fielding had come up trumps yet again. This was possibly the most colourful and spectacular show ever to come to this particular stage. It really was a 'Musical Amazement'; it traced the life of the scheming showman right from his early days of defending the noble art of humbug, and involved some really imaginative staging. Michael Crawford tackled every situation in the show with the enthusiasm he was so well known for. He clowned, juggled, sang, danced and acted his way through the very demanding part, and he was rarely off stage. He even walked the high wire! The whole show was beautifully costumed. *Barnum*, 'the Prince of Humbug', filled the theatre nightly. In the nicest possible way there was one born every minute to fill all the seats, and the show ran for a total of 663 performances. Yet again, another triumph for Benji!

As mentioned in an earlier chapter, Harold Fielding had brought together Messrs Corbett and Barker for the very first time in 1978. Ronnie Corbett had of course made many earlier individual appearances, but this had been the first time for Ronnie Barker. *The Two Ronnies* was written by Gerald Wiley (Ronnie Barker's literary pseudonym), with additional material by Eddie Braben, Donald Groves, Spike Mullins and Neil Shand. When the show was presented for a second successful season in 1983, one of the support acts was indisposed, so the talented, lugubrious magician Larry Parker stepped in as a replacement. The show ran for ninety-four performances. Once again it was written by Gerald Wiley, with other contributions by well-known scriptwriters Barry Cryer, Dick Vosburgh and David Renwick, and the whole show was again directed by Dick Hurran.

During the run of *The Two Ronnies*, a sampling of Turkish delight came in the shape of Bulent Ersoy, who had her own one-night Sunday concert appearance, as did Mari Wilson and The Wilsations and Ben Vereen.

MICHAEL CRAWFORD

"Thrills the audience with a performance so brilliant it's impossible to top"

"The Greatest Show in Town"

BARNUM

MUST END 5 FEBRUARY 1983

LONDON PALLADIUM

Evenings 7.30 matinees Wednesdays and Saturdays 2.45

However, what was perhaps Fielding's greatest achievement was yet to come. After many years of negotiation with MGM Studios, he finally convinced them to grant him authorisation to present *Singin' in the Rain* on stage for the first time ever. Once he knew he had it in the bag , he made a quick phone call to Tommy Steele with the opening statement, 'Tommy I've got it!' 'Got wot, Guv?' Steele retorted, to which Fielding replied, '*Singin' in the Rain.*' Steele immediately dropped everything and drove over to Fielding's office overlooking the Thames, and he stayed for several hours going over every possible detail. The press hailed it as 'bringing the lavish musical back to the West End with a vengeance.'

The logistics were far from easy. It was a mammoth task to redesign and strengthen the stage floor to accommodate the water scene, with huge header tanks above which allowed it to rain properly at the appropriate time. There was less room off stage than one might imagine to store the huge props needed for a show of this size. During the interval, the props that had been used for the entire first half, which had been stored on the left-hand side of the stage, were transposed to the other side. This enabled new scenery and props to be stored ready for use in the second half, especially the railway engine, which came apart for storage and was only assembled for its special scene.

None of this could have been done without the full cooperation of the stage staff, who Fielding said were 'better than first class. The show would never have happened without them and their dedication.' Such was the rapport that Fielding had with everyone who worked for him.

DEREK BLOCK PRESENTS
an evening with
BEN VEREEN

'THE MAN TO WHOM MICHAEL PARKINSON GAVE HIS T.V. SHOW'

STAR OF THE MOVIE "ALL THAT JAZZ"

'CHICKEN GEORGE IN ROOTS'

STAR OF MUSICALS PIPPIN & SWEET CHARITY

LONDON PALLADIUM
BY ARRANGEMENT WITH LOUIS BENJAMIN
SUNDAY 17th APRIL at 6.00pm & 8.45pm
Tickets: £10.00 £8.00 £6.50 £5.50 £4.00 BOX OFFICE TEL: 437 7373
TICKETS AVAILABLE FROM THEATRE AND USUAL AGENTS

Although Harold Fielding was to present *Ziegfeld* later in the decade, which involved a breathtakingly spectacular series of scenes, sets and costumes, he will most certainly be remembered best for his almost unbroken run of no less than fifteen years of producing shows at the Palladium.

During the long run of *Singin' in the Rain* Pearl Bailey and Brook Benton, Ralph McTell and Cannon and Ball all delighted Sunday concert audiences too.

Next, it was *Let's Hear the Applause* by Michael Freedland, and we did. Lots of it! In aid of respected Jewish charities, Michael entertained Palladium audiences with the veteran mouth organ virtuoso Larry Adler (who had first appeared on this stage in 1935), the bandleader Nat Temple, Joe Dindol, Sheila Steafel, Dennis Andrews, Debbie Arnold, master storyteller David Kossoff, Bernard Spear, and The Stutz Bear Cats. And this was only the first half! Jewish jocularity was provided by Alf Fogel, who was noted for his own musicals, and then Bernie Winters, magician Lawrence Leyton, irrepressible Ron Moody, and Frankie Vaughan all ensured that the demanding audience had their money's worth. They most certainly did, and more!

Entertainment generally knows no bounds and in the true spirit of ecumenism an Arabic Gala took place in 1984 with artists I would love to identify, but this is not possible as the programme was completely in Arabic!

The world of show business lost one of its greatest stars in 1984, with the death of Eric Morecambe. Eric had rightly earned his OBE for services to charity and the entertainment industry. Produced for Thames Television in aid of The Heart Foundation, a tribute show was arranged which was attended by His Royal Highness the Duke of Edinburgh. Those who gave their talents were his partner in comedy, Ernie Wise, who had also similarly earned his OBE of course, The Irving Davies Dancers, Max Bygraves, The Tiller Girls, and, in an old Jimmy James sketch, Roy Castle, Eli Woods, and James Casey. The Johnny Hutch Half Wits showed the audience how it should be done. Comedy arrived in the shape of Jim Davidson, and *Palladium Nights* were shared with Bruce Forsyth. Petula Clark delighted everyone, Bertice Reading sang with Kenny Ball and his Jazzmen, Lionel Blair danced with Suzanne Danielle, and in a show business salute to Eric were Jimmy Tarbuck OBE and, making a rare stage appearance, Benny Hill, along with Dickie Henderson, who had been many times before. Wayne Sleep and Cherry Gilespie, Bonnie Langford, Leslie Crowther, Mike Yarwood, Des O'Connor, Elaine Paige, Cannon and Ball, and Michael Parkinson all appeared too. The noted top table Toastmaster, Bryn Williams, had his work cut out to remember all those names on one show! As one would expect from a perfectionist though, he did so admirably. Without doubt Ernie and Eric were one of Britain's best-loved comedy duos, and they brought us all so much sunshine that they will never, ever be forgotten.

Dreamstar brought another helping of Turkish delight to the Palladium with Sezen Aksu and Ümit Besen. Then, noted for seeing into the future, Doris Stokes need not have worried, for it was a full house for her one-off special performance in 1984. Tickets were sold immediately to fans who were queuing right around the block.

Early in 1985, The National Jazz Festival took place in the presence of Her Royal Highness the Princess of Wales. All proceeds went towards the Jazz Centre in the heart of London, which was open all day, every day, for those with a passion for jazz. The event was compèred by Moira Stuart and David Rappaport. The National Youth Jazz Orchestra opened the successful show with their mentor and Director Brad Ashton MBE, and they were followed by Barbara Thompson's Paraphernalia. Will Gaines showed off his dancing talents, and Nigel Kennedy displayed the wonderful agility of his fingers. Chart-topper Alison Moyet closed the first half. In the second half, it was just another Working Week for a group of musicians who were called just that. Stan Tracey, a regular at Ronnie Scott's, John Patrick, a noted bebopper on the piano, and super cool Marion Montgomery from the USA delighted everyone present. Jazz enthusiasts were further thrilled with Jools Holland, Humphrey Lyttelton and Helen Shapiro, who closed the show. Jazz devotees are probably still talking about it even as I write.

The Home Farm Trust benefited from the 'Farm Yard Frolics' engaged in by Rowan Atkinson, Griff Rhys Jones, Mel Smith, John Sessions, Peter Cook, Frankie Howerd, Stephen Fry, John Wells and a host of others. The Great Soprendo was also amongst them. They all gave their services freely. The Trust's patron, Her Royal Highness the Princess Anne, must have had a laugh or three that night.

GILBERT & SULLIVAN

THE MIKADO
CENTENARY

To celebrate the Festival of British Jewry in 1985, Michael Freedland once again introduced us to previous regulars Alf Fogel, Lawrence Leyton, Larry Adler, Ron Moody and Frankie Vaughan, with new names added this time, in the shape of Lyn Paul, Georgia Browne, Patti Boulaye and Theodore Bikel. In a tribute to Hollywood, Geoff Morrow, Carl Wayne and The Dreamgirls also appeared. Davy Kaye made a guest appearance too. Ivor Raymonde was the Musical Director for this particular evening.

Singin' in the Rain ran for 898 performances, breaking the previous Barnum record. Whilst the cast, orchestra and crew were on their annual holiday, Harold Fielding brought his *Easter Festival* to the Palladium. Those dear ladies Hinge and Bracket brought their new stage presentation, *Our Lovely Days*. The Mantovani Orchestra entertained on Good Friday with the cascading strings for which it was so well known, then Louis Clark had us *Hooked on Classics* with The Royal Philharmonic Orchestra. This was followed by The London Savoyard's Centenary Celebration production of *The Mikado*. No one could say that Fielding didn't offer variety and good taste all at once. But then, he was a past master at knowing what the public wanted.

By now it was springtime in 1985, and a special concert in aid of Cancer Research, which was entitled *All on an April Evening,* was put on and hosted by Angela Rippon with Dame Anna Neagle and Lord Miles. Artists from The Ballet Rambert and The Royal Festival Ballet appeared, together with The London Pops Orchestra. Elizabeth Welch, who had made her debut at the Palladium in 1934, made a guest appearance too.

From India came Jagjit and Chitra Singh on 2 June 1985, and later that same month Dreamstar gave us Kucuck Emrah, Gokhan Guney, and Gulden Karabocek from Turkey. All of them were big recording stars in their own country.

The comic Charlie Lea repeated his earlier feat from 1979 by presenting a special concert which highlighted *Liverpool Startime.*

Singin' in the Rain ended its run on 28 September 1985, and the set was broken down and the stage returned to normal. The stage crew licked their wounds and gathered their thoughts in preparation for the winter onslaught.

Based on the popular BBC TV show, Wayne Sleep and his team presented *The Hot Shoe Show* for a short season in October, providing the very best that dance could offer. In the autumn, The English Tourist Board put on a special show called *England Entertains*, with their 1985 National Talent Contest. Paul Daniels compèred and the show was directed by the respected Dick Hurran.

At the end of the year, Des O'Connor was Buttons in the enchanting family pantomime *Cinderella*. With Sarah Payne as Cinders and Paul Nicholas as Prince Charming, not to mention special guest star Dame Anna Neagle as the Fairy Godmother, success was assured once again for breaking box office records.

Making their Palladium debut, the Kentucky duo The Judds hit London early in 1986. Hard on their heels were Nils Lofgren, Incantation, Nana Mouskouri, and John Martin. Next, one of the world's consummate performers, Liza Minnelli, enchanted a London audience once again in her own one-woman show.

In May, noted Producer Dick Hurran attended the first night of *La Cage aux Folles* and said that it was without doubt the glitziest event he had ever attended, and the show was the most spectacular he had ever seen. The settings and effects were out of this world. In spite of this, it had a short run of only eight months due to the show's subject matter and the public's attitude at that time.

In November 1986, the petite Pia Zadora was in concert with Robert Farnon and his forty-eight piece orchestra. Prior to its London showing, the *Los Angeles Times* declared it to be 'A musically impeccable evening'.

In December, the Palladium presented *Night of 100 Stars* in aid of Help the Aged in the charity's Jubilee Year, and it was televised by London Weekend Television.

However, with the unexpected end of *La Cage* it meant the theatre was 'dark' for a short time. This was a very rare occurrence indeed. In February 1987, Frank Ifield appeared on Valentine's Day, and in March The Children's Royal Variety Performance took place again. Later that month, there was *The Secret Policeman's Third Ball* held over four nights. Anarchy rules OK? Later still in that month, although this time far more sedate, came Paco de Lucia from Spain. In April, the public were entertained by the highly energetic and spectacularly colourful show of The Georgian State Dance Company, who came direct from the USSR with a cast of sixty musicians and dancers. In May, Gerry and The Pacemakers relived the *Solid Silver 60s* with the help of The Searchers and Peter Starsted.

Whenever a tragedy strikes, entertainers are always the first to offer help, and a huge industry swings into action for a one-off performance. Following the terrible Zeebrugge disaster, Jim Davidson set about organising a show in aid of the victims and their families. Dozens and dozens of names all offered their services for this worthwhile cause.

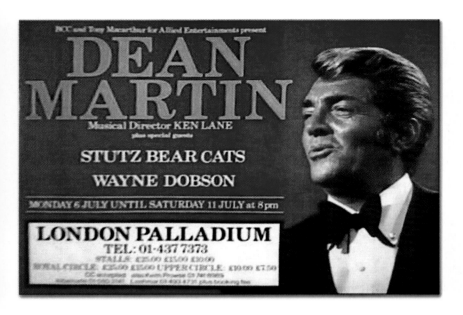

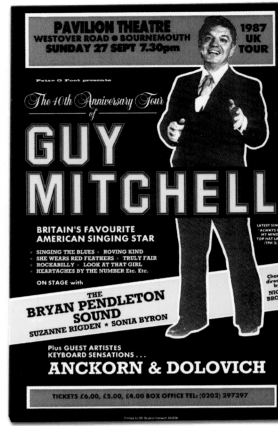

In June 1987 and to celebrate the Fiftieth Anniversary of the magazine *Woman*, a Royal Gala was staged and directed by Robert Nesbitt. It was attended by Her Royal Highness the Princess of Wales, and on the show (compèred by Noel Edmonds) were Cilla Black, Joe Brown, Bucks Fizz, the ever youthful Jess Conrad, broadcasters Gloria Hunniford and Derek James, Petula Clark, Ray Cornel and his Dancers, Barry Humphries in the guise of Dame Edna, Gerard Kenny, Elaine Paige, Paul Nicholas, Alvin Stardust, Roy Walker, Patricia Routledge, Wayne Sleep, and Mike Yarwood. The evening was generously sponsored by Louis Feraud, and it was a complete mixture of fashion and fun for all. Also in June, Jim Davidson came to fore once again with his merry band of friends to help The Sharon Allen Leukaemia Trust. They raised quite a few shillings that night as a direct result. In July, the legendary singer and entertainer Dean Martin made a most welcome return, with highly successful TV magician Wayne Dobson and The Stutz Bear Cats to help. Now this was class! Later that month, Steve Morgan paid for the hire of the theatre out of his own pocket for a religious crusade, attracting not too many people to his cause. He said that it was money well spent. In August, fifties songster Guy Mitchell appeared once more to packed houses. In that same month, Rudolph Nureyev and The Ballet Theatre Français de Nancy danced their way through *The Homage to Diaghilev*. The one-week offering was a delight to all lovers of exceptional ballet.

Something really unusual for the Palladium took place in September. There was a Thames Television *Silents Special*. The two films to be screened were *The General*, first shown in 1926 and starring Buster Keaton, and the original *Ben Hur*. Music which had been specially created by Carl Davis, the noted American composer and conductor, was added to the original silent films.

Winter was fast approaching, and Mary Coughlin, Loudoun Wainwright III and The Shadows all occupied centre stage. In December, a black-tie event was held for The Prince's Trust, attended by Their Royal Highnesses the Prince and Princess of Wales. The audience was offered a gilt-edged production involving Art Garfunkel, Robin Williams, Elton John, David Frost, John Ritter, Chris de Burgh, Sarah Brightman, Rowan Atkinson, James Taylor, Colm Wilkinson, Amy Grant, Belinda Carlisle, Mel Smith and Griff Rhys Jones, Rory Bremner, and Richard Digance. It was another night of nights! While London Weekend Television was busy each Sunday producing *Live From The Palladium*, Elaine Paige enchanted her audiences, as did Victoria Wood who brought her own show to the West End for several sell-out nights.

Babes in the Wood was to be the Christmas offering for 1987. There was an enormous cast headed by the popular Cannon and Ball duo, Marti Webb, John Inman,

Derek Griffiths, Cheryl Baker, Barbara Windsor, Peter Howitt, and Rod Hull and Emu. They were backed up by Sue and Peter Barbour, Nicholas Smith and The Santus Troupe, and The Peggy O'Farrell Children. The Producers, Duncan Weldon and Jerome Minskoff, were well known for their West End involvement. The Associate Producer was Peter Elliott, who was in the business for a long time as Manager to Dick Emery, but he is now Administrator to Brinsworth House. Peter is still advisor to The Royal Variety Performance when it is held each year. The pantomime was directed by Michael Hurll, who was always picking up awards for his work. It couldn't fail, and quite naturally it didn't. In fact, it was a great success, and full page adverts in *The Stage* newspaper endorsed the £1 million advance booking and £300,000 weekly gross, the largest in pantomime history. Following the show, there was another advert stating that it had been the longest running pantomime for the 1987–8 season, with a take of £1.6 million. Another record! 'The best pantomime I have ever seen', said the *Financial Times*. Praise indeed!

Early in 1988, the French heart-throb Richard Clayderman was on his *Valentine Tour*, and appeared at the Palladium to the delight of all his adoring fans.

To present the story of the famous showman Ziegfeld, with a sixty-strong cast and after a series of very many setbacks and costing a reported £3.2 million, Harold Fielding's most lavish production to date finally came to the stage in April 1988. It would require 100% capacity houses for some eighteen months in order to recoup its production costs.

The show initially starred Len Cariou and Geoffrey Hutchings who, following disagreements, left the show. Soon after, and to try to resurrect the falling demand, the show was redesigned and Topol was brought in to add some much needed chutzpah, but sadly the show still failed to attract the general public. Within minutes of hearing there was a problem, Fielding's old friend Tommy Steele was there to help in any way he could.

It was reported that it took two men working for a month to sew the beads on just one costume, such was

LONDON PALLADIUM
A Stoll Moss Theatre

the lavishness. The appearance of the show was astonishing, with every scene becoming more extravagant than the last, but alas, without a good storyline and catchy songs, it sadly didn't last. *Ziegfeld* was no more, and neither was Harold Fielding, who bowed out gracefully with the collapse of his company and losses of £2.5 million. 'Show business is a very precarious business,' he said, 'we have these ups and downs!' But with his usual indefatigable nature, he declared, 'I will dust myself off and I will be back!'

In September, The British Music Hall Society celebrated their Silver Jubilee with acts that were well known on the music hall circuit, from balladeer Bruce Trent, who had first appeared at the Palladium in 1939, to paper tearer Terri Carol, who appeared on The Royal Variety Show in 1947, and Roy Hudd, who was a champion of music halls any year. The show was organised by hard working President Jack Seaton, who as a boy had worked the limes in this very theatre. It was a popular performance and a great success.

Stopping off at the Palladium to highlight his own personal Silver Jubilee was Gene Pitney, on his hectic tour of thirty-three cities in as many days.

In August 1988, a report in the *London Evening Standard* had stated that Robert Holmes A'Court, an Australian businessman, was preparing to purchase fourteen theatres through his company, including the London Palladium. Times they were a-changing... Boy George made a rare one-off appearance on 14 December 1988.

'Now listen very carefully; I will say zis only once...' Another highly popular TV comedy show in the form of *'Allo 'Allo* came to the Palladium stage for a very successful season, and the year ended with a return engagement of all the cast. A double page spread in *The Stage* newspaper stated: 'Every record was smashed and £300,000 was taken in Christmas week with sixteen performances.' Advance bookings were in excess of £1 million, and this was only to be a very limited season, which proved the power and popularity of TV. Due to the cast's television commitments, the show closed in May 1989, but it was to return the following Christmas.

In September, and four months before the 'Allo 'Allo
show was due to open, all the tickets had been sold for a
special one-off production of *La Cage Aux Folles* in aid
of Action Research for Crippled Children. Barry Mishon
was in charge of production and David Jacobs, a long-
time champion of the Jerry Herman music, introduced a
line-up of Van Johnson, Denis Quilley, Robert Meadmore,
Josephine Blake, Linda Mae Brewer, and Donna
McKechnie.

In February 1989, we were invited to *Swing into Spring* for one night with the New Squadronaires, with Vince Hill, Tony Christie and Patti Gold. In April another black-tie affair and a Royal Gala in aid of The Prince's Trust took place once again in the presence of Their Royal Highnesses the Prince and Princess of Wales. Wet Wet Wet, Jerry Hall, Dame Edna Everage, Maureen Lipman, Debbie Gibson, Dame Kiri te Kanawa, Phil Cool, Mica Paris, Rosanna Arquette, Erasure, Paula Abdul, Rita Rudner, and Steve Coogan all appeared, delighting the packed charity audience. In June, in aid of the Living Earth Foundation, a grand gala was arranged and billed as a *Homage to Nijinski*. In the presence of Her Royal Highness Princess Michael of Kent, everyone witnessed a gala evening of ballet, starring Natalia Makarova amongst others. Also in June, the Palladium was infested by rats. What a headline that would have made! However, as with most stories this was not as one would have first imagined. The Grand Order of Water Rats celebrated their centenary, with stars coming from all four corners of the world just to appear for this unique, one-off performance. Exactly 100 stars appeared, the eldest being Nat Mills, aged eighty-six, who, with his wife Bobbie, had first appeared at the Palladium in the late 1920s.

Moving into July, The Street Entertainer of the Year Awards were held. Jimmy Roselli also appeared for one night. *Singin' in the Rain* took to the stage again, presented by Harold Fielding. It was produced by and starred Tommy Steele. This was for a short season of only 162 performances. Then Johnny Dankworth, Cleo Laine and George Melly entertained during the Soho Jazz Festival week in October, and in the same month Roger Whittaker made a most welcome return visit too.

In November, in aid of Action Research for Crippled Children, another gala took place. Organised by Barry Mishon and entitled *Stairway to the Stars*, it had a veritable galaxy of names to delight the audience. It was hosted by Van Johnson, and he welcomed The Nicholas

LONDON PALLADIUM
ARGYLL STREET W1
DAVID LINGWOOD

Manager

THE GRAND ORDER OF
WATER RATS

PRESENT

'RATS REVELS'
A CELEBRATION OF THEIR
CENTENARY
On SUNDAY 11th JUNE 1989 AT 7.30

(by kind permission of Louis Benjamin for Stoll Moss Theatres)

MEMBERS OF THE GRAND ORDER OF WATER RATS 1989:

Leslie Adams	Stanley Black	Bryan Burdon	Charlie Chester	Norman Collier
Bob Andrews	Lionel Blair	Terry Burgess	Peter Chester	Peter Colville
Peter Barbour	John Bouchier	Max Bygraves	Joe Church	Jess Conrad
Ken Barnes	John Boulter	Wyn Calvin	James Clark	Henry Cooper
Derek Batey	Bernard Bresslaw	Kenny Cantor	Stephen Clark	Mike Craig
Harold Berens	Peter Brough	Frank Carson	Bernie Clifton	Michael Crawford
David Berglas	Duggie Brown	Peter Casson	John Clive	Leslie Crowther
Jack Billings	Joe Brown	Dennis Castle	Con Cluskey	Toni Dalli
Joe Black	Billy Burden	Roy Castle	Dec Cluskey	
				Nigel Hopkins
Paul Daniels		Bruce Forsyth	Harry Gunn	Len Howe
Freddie Davies	Ted Durante	Dai Francis	Jan Harding	Roy Hudd
Les Dawson	Robert Earl	Alan Freeman	Keith Harris	John Inman
Roger de Courcey	Kenneth Earle	Serge Ganjou	Les Henry	Dave Jackley
Del Denester	Percy Edwards	Rusty Goffe	Vince Hill	Ken Joy
Pat Dodd	Peter Elliott	Ken Goodwin	Jimmy Hinchliffe	Dave Kaye
Lonnie Donegan	George Elrick	Peter Goodwright	Philip Hindin	Davy Kaye
Tommie Draper	Arthur English	Barrie Gosney	Mike Hope	
	Frederick Ferrari			Dick Ray
		Norman Meadow	Charlie Noble	Paul Raymond
Albie Keen		Nat Mills	Alf Pearson	Peter Regan
Barry Kent	Benny Lee	Pat Mooney	Jimmy Perry	Johnnie Riscoe
Paul Kidd	Johnny Lockwood	Johnny More	Bill Pertwee	Bobby Roberts
Neville King	David Lodge	Pete Murray	Jon Pertwee	Ken Roberts
Jack Kodell	Jimmy Logan	Billy McComb	Tom Plummer	Michael Robbins
Lew Lane	Len Lowe	Chas. McDevitt	Alan Randall	Cardew Robinson
Danny La Rue	Bill Martin	Ray McVay	Leslie Randall	
Johnny Laycock	George Martin			Billy Whittaker
	Johnny Maxim	Jerry Stevens	Ian Tough	Bryn Williams
		Albert Stevenson	Bruce Trent	Bernie Winters
Edmundo Ros	Alan Simmons	Ed Stewart	Tommy Trinder	Mike Winters
Freddie Sales	Keith Simmons	Clive Stock	Stanley Unwin	Norman Wisdom
Albert Saveen	Ronald Smart	John Stokes	Frankie Vaughan	Arthur Worsley
Billy 'Uke' Scott	Harold Smith	John Randolph Sutton	Malcolm Vaughan	Mike Yarwood
Harry Secombe	Charlie Smithers	Jimmy Tarbuck	Ben Warriss	Eric Yorke
Harry Seltzer	Don Smoothey	Harold Taylor	Bert Weedon	
Paul Shane	Judd Solo			
Don Shearman	Stan Stennett			

Appearances subject to professional commitments

ONE NIGHT ONLY ! EVERY HUNDRED YEARS !

TICKETS: Stalls £50; £40; £30; £20; £10 Royal Circle £50; £40; £30; £20
Upper Circle £10; £5.

Available from John Adrian, G.O.W.R., 328 Gray's Inn Road, London WC1X 8BZ (No credit cards please)

BOX OFFICE 01 278 3248

PROFITS TO THE GRAND ORDER OF WATER RATS CHARITIES FUND

Printed by G & M Chase Ltd. Willington, Bristol. Tc: 0934 860219.

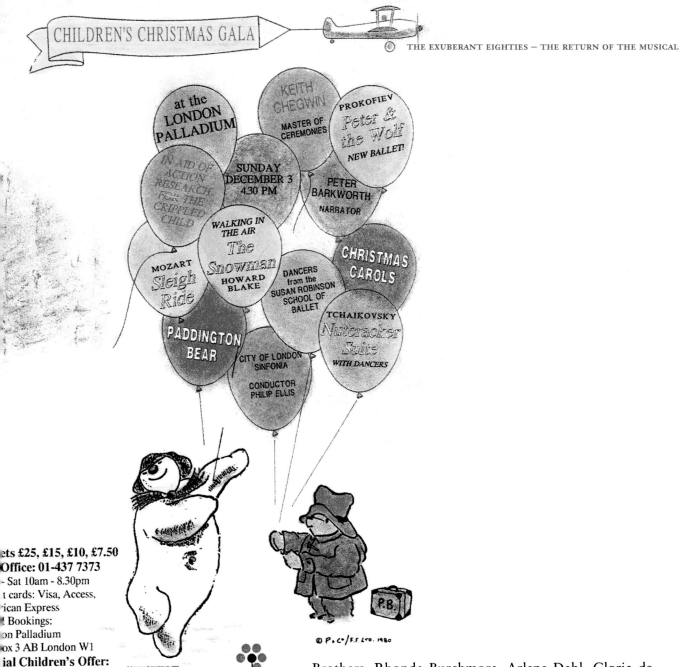

CHILDREN'S CHRISTMAS GALA

at the
LONDON
PALLADIUM

KEITH
CHEGWIN
MASTER OF
CEREMONIES

PROKOFIEV
*Peter &
the Wolf*
NEW BALLET!

IN AID OF
ACTION
RESEARCH
FOR THE
CRIPPLED
CHILD

SUNDAY
DECEMBER 3
4.30 PM

PETER
BARKWORTH
NARRATOR

WALKING IN
THE AIR
*The
Snowman*
HOWARD
BLAKE

CHRISTMAS
CAROLS

MOZART
*Sleigh
Ride*

DANCERS
from the
SUSAN ROBINSON
SCHOOL OF
BALLET

TCHAIKOVSKY
*Nutcracker
Suite*
WITH DANCERS

PADDINGTON
BEAR

CITY OF LONDON
SINFONIA

CONDUCTOR
PHILIP ELLIS

ets £25, £15, £10, £7.50
Office: 01-437 7373
– Sat 10am - 8.30pm
t cards: Visa, Access,
rican Express
Bookings:
on Palladium
ox 3 AB London W1
ial Children's Offer:
icket free with
y four purchased.

ACTION
RESEARCH FOR THE
CRIPPLED CHILD

© P.C./F.F.LTD.1980

Brothers, Rhonda Burchmore, Arlene Dahl, Gloria de Haven, Dolores Gray, Kathryn Grayson, Georges Guetary, Dorothy Lamour, Lorna Luft, Tony Martin, Dursley Mclinden, Gene Nelson, Virginia O'Brien, and Jane Russell, plus a twenty-nine piece orchestra, with The Stephen Hill Singers. The show was staged and directed by Irving Davies. Another name from yesteryear and still going very strong was Connie Francis, who made a brief appearance later in that month.

Once again in aid of Action Research for Crippled Children, there was a special Children's Christmas Gala Matinée. The event was presented by Keith Chegwin, and amongst other items was the very popular and timeless

'Walking in the Air', narrated by Peter Barkworth. It was now December, and Palladium audiences were invited to get ready to *Swing into Christmas* with the New Squadronaires and Frankie Vaughan, The Stutz Bear Cats, and Patti Gold. The *real* Christmas offering, however, was the return of *'Allo 'Allo*, which stayed for some ten extremely successful weeks, but then sadly had to say goodbye for the last time.

By then though, a new name was on the headings of Stoll Moss Theatre posters and programmes. It was Roger Filer. He was very much like George Black in that he was steeped in the entertainment industry because he also came from a cinema family. Roger had reached the pinnacle of his theatrical career by being made Managing Director of Stoll Moss, having previously been an Executive Director for some time. New ideas and new formulae were to come, albeit briefly.

A new decade lay ahead.

Chapter Nineteen

NEARING THE
MILLENNIUM

*I*t was 'curtain up' on a new decade, and once more there was a new man in the driving seat. Roger Filer, with his charm and his trademark bow tie, inspired enthusiasm in show business circles, the press, and the variety world in general.

Superstar Barry Manilow was first to appear on stage in 1990. The Golden Break Advertising Awards for 1989 were held and televised with host Jonathan Ross. The Really Useful Group presented a week of *The Music of Andrew Lloyd Webber*, with Sarah Brightman and The Royal Philharmonic Pops Orchestra. It was almost twenty-two years to the day that Tim Rice and Andrew Lloyd Webber first presented the show *Joseph and The Amazing Technicolor Dreamcoat* in a little known London school hall, and now he had conquered the world with all his shows and music.

Whilst helping to raise aid in *Relief Funds for Romania*, everyone on both sides of the footlights had a good time. Joan Regan, Chas and Dave, Joe Longthorne, The Drifters, Larry Adler, Edwin Starr, Donimo, Mike Carter, and The Romanian National Music and Dance Ensemble all appeared.

Jackie Mason is a master of humour, and during his performance at the Palladium the packed audience was in fits of laughter at his self-deprecating Jewish humour from the moment he walked on stage, and they were shouting for more when he left. Truly a genius of observation. It was a family show, with no suggestion of anything that might offend, unless you happened to be Jewish!

For a limited fourteen-week season, a new musical came to the Palladium with Gilbert and Sullivan's *The Pirates of Penzance*. It starred Paul Nicholas and Bonnie Langford. A decade earlier it had found great success on Broadway, and time had not changed that because packed audiences also ensued in London. Contained within the pages of the Palladium theatre programme of that time was a brief history of this famous theatrical venue, written by someone who was first encouraged to write its definitive story. And here it is, almost at an end.

The Solid Silver 60s Show with Duane Eddy, The Crickets and Tommy Roe had the audiences reminiscing and rocking in the aisles. Engelbert had the same effect the following Sunday, although in a more sedate way. Another Barry Mishon production was then presented in the shape of *Hello Dolly*, with perhaps the definitive 'Dolly' herself, Carol Channing, starring in this all-star special performance in aid of charity.

With few exceptions, from 1930 the majority of The Royal Variety Performances have always taken place at the Palladium. The complete list of artists who have appeared on all those shows has not been detailed here. However, the 1990 Royal Variety Performance needs a special mention. On this, the ninetieth birthday of Her Majesty the Queen Mother, a *very* special event was observed, with a Gala Tribute to her longevity. In the presence of Her Majesty, Her Majesty the Queen, His Royal Highness the Duke of Edinburgh, and Her Royal Highness the Princess Margaret, Countess of Snowdon, everyone enjoyed a wonderful show. A very special night at the London Palladium for a very special lady.

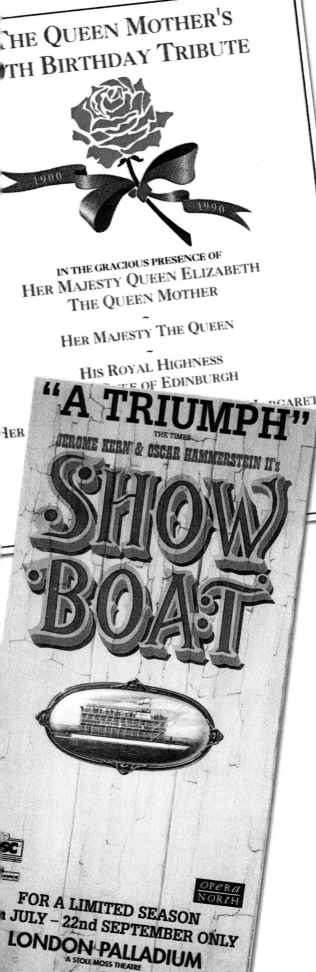

It must have been the birthday party to end all birthday parties. What a line-up, what a cast! Following the Birthday Tribute by Sir John Gielguid, and the Orchestra conducted by Harry Rabinowitz, the following names appeared; Liza Maxwell, Bonnie Langford, Hayley Mills, Angharad Rees, Anneka Rice, Lionel Blair, Christopher Cazenove, Mark Curry, Jeffrey Holland, Robert Meadmore, Jonathan Morris, Anita Harris, Jill Gascoigne, The Grenadier Guards, Major Watts, Eric Roberts, Geraldine McEwan, Pipe Major Spoore, Alan Harding, Wayne Sleep, Stephen Fry, Anthony Van Laast, Michael Denison, Dulcie Gray, Marilyn Hill Smith, Arthur Davies, James Galway, Bernie Winters, Leslie Crowther, Sir John Mills, Simon Cadell, Patricia Hodge, Robert Hardy, Dame Vera Lynn, Howard Keel, Willard White, Warren Mitchell, Roger Moore, Michael Caine, Dame Kiri te Kanawa, Rowan Atkinson, Cliff Richard, Sir Richard Attenborough, Darcey Bussell, Irek Mukhamedov, Dame Peggy Ashcroft, Sarah Brightman, Elaine Paige, and Placido Domingo. The choreography was by Norman Maen. What a cast indeed!

Showboat, another musical that had never been seen at the Palladium, was about to be launched. Opening in July for a limited season, *Showboat* was presented by Opera North and The Royal Shakespeare Company. Following the nine-week stay in port in Argyll Street, the show toured other major cities up until Christmas.

On 3 September 1990, tragedy was to strike the Stoll Moss boardroom with the untimely death of its Chairman, Robert Holmes A'Court. Rumours quickly started to circulate with stories of possible takeovers and acquisitions. However, the family had no desire or reason to let go, so Mrs Janet Holmes A'Court took full charge.

Later in September and after a ten-year absence, by arrangement with Billy Marsh, Roger Filer presented an all too short, six-week season with possibly the greatest court jester in Britain, Ken Dodd.

Prior to the show, during the press promotion in the foyer of the theatre, Michael Aspel appeared with his big red book to pronounce: 'This is Your Life!' For something like two and a half hours, Ken declared *How Tickled I Am!* with non-stop hilarity. 'A living Donald McGill postcard', one reviewer said. In fact, they all had nothing but praise for his work. Ken certainly believed in giving value for money, and you were lucky to leave without your sides aching from continuous laughter. Supporting acts The Williams Brothers, The Stutz Bear Cats, Omar Pasha and of course The Diddymen, along with Brian Rogers' TV Dancers, added to the variety of it all. During the run a special show was televised for Christmas

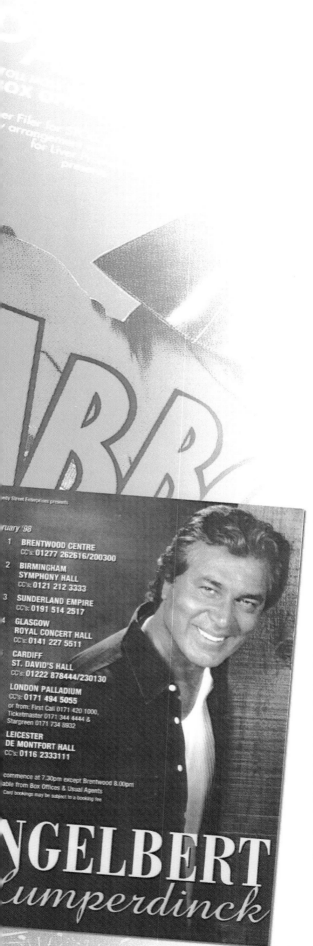

viewing later on. With all TV presentations, you are given a time by which you must be in your seat. No one dared to tell you when you would be able to leave! Most would have happily stayed all night though, just to witness the comic genius at work. Max Miller used to say in a self-effacing way, 'There will never be another'. This is most certainly true of laughter-maker Ken Dodd.

The 1990 Miss World contest was held in November, and to celebrate the fortieth occasion of the competition, Jason Donovan and Richard Clayderman were in cabaret while the judges made their almost impossible decision at the Finals.

On 12 December 1990, Roger Filer brought more comedy and variety to the stage. This time it was the TV favourite *Russ Abbot's Palladium Madhouse*, with comedic foil Bella Emberg, Lisa Maxwell, the talented young juggler Mark Robertson, and violin virtuoso Gary Lovini. Both of the latter two had come a long way since their earlier appearances on the very same stage in talent shows for Butlin's and *England Entertains* respectively. It was a young, vibrant cast and their energy showed through.

During that busy year, Helen Reddy and Engelbert Humperdinck had both enjoyed separate Sunday concerts and consequent full houses, as did Benny Green and his Jazz Collection, David Essex, Gene Pitney, and Julian Clary. In the presence of the Prince and Princess of Wales, Shirley Bassey appeared with Wayne Dobson on a Royal Gala Evening, once again in aid of The Prince's Trust.

Lerona Gelb was a special little girl who was severely injured in a car accident when she was five and suffered spinal injuries. With the unstinting help of Davy Kaye, a past King Rat of the Grand Order of Water Rats, who was later to be honoured with an MBE for his services to charity, a Grand Gala was organised in her name, and it was attended by Her Royal Highness the Princess of Wales. This was a grand night of sparkling stars, with Larry Adler, Jess Conrad, Joe Goodman, Neville King, Henry Kissin, Gerry Marsden, Tom O'Connor, Wendy Richards, Julie Rogers, Helen Shapiro, Wayne Sleep, The Stutz Bear Cats, Frankie Vaughan, Marti Webb, Bert Weedon, and Barbara Windsor. The original Tiller Girls were on the bill too. Don Shearman was on hand to make sure the music was just right. Introductions were by Davy

Kaye, and the surprise guests were Shirley Bassey and film star Robert Wagner. After the glorious event, Wendy Richards presented a cheque for £125,000 to the Spinal Research Trust in Barnet.

In a tribute to Light Entertainment, Producer David Bell arranged *A Gala Night of 100 Stars*, which was presented late in November. Those taking part were Russ Abbott, Maria Anderson, Michael Barrymore, Jeremy Beadle, Christopher Biggins, Cilla Black, Simon Bowman, Danielle Carson, Cannon and Ball, Brian Conley, Ronnie Corbett, Gemma Craven, Jimmy Cricket, John Dankworth, Jim Davidson, Bobby Davro, Les Dennis, Richard Digance, Wayne Dobson, Bella Emberg, Adam Fincham, Graham Fletcher, Rosemary Ford, Bruce Forsyth CBE, David Frost, Jill Gascoine, Gloria Hunniford, Henry Kelly, Matthew Kelly, Sarah Kennedy, Bonnie Langford, Diane Langton, Cleo Laine, Johnny Logan, Joe Longthorne, Kelly McAffer, Ruth Madoc, Jessica Martin, Robert Meadmore, Dennis Norden, Hilary O'Neil, Mike Osman, Billy Pearce, Shane Richie, Lea Salonga, James Smillie, Alan Stewart, Shakin' Stevens, Mike Sterling, Mark Walker, John Williams, and Gary Wilmot. The show was produced by Norman Maen. That Was The Show That Was!

On Boxing Day 1990, the London Palladium celebrated its eightieth birthday, and to mark this occasion a special show was presented for television on New Year's Eve. There was a real party atmosphere to celebrate this special event, and Max Bygraves, The Beverley Sisters, Russ Abbot and Jim Dale all joined in. So did Guy Mitchell and Charlie Cairoli, and recreating The Crazy Gang were Don Smoothey, Len Lowe, Joe Black and Barry Craine. Ernie Wise, Joan Regan, Roy Hudd, Michael Ball, There Were Five Guys Named Moe, Liz Robertson, Mark Wynter, Elaine Delmar, Dave Willetts, and Peter Goodwright all played a part, and Michael Williams, Polly Hemingway, Mike Yarwood, Gary Wilmot, Andrew O'Connor, Bea Arthur and Ian Smith were once again close 'Neighbours' on the stage. Graham Fletcher was Little Tich and giant Geoff Capes kept everything under control. Bobby Davro, Rustie Lee, Paul Shane and Suzie Quatro were there as well. It really was a party night! Don't you just wish you could have been there too? Those that couldn't get into the capacity

A STOLL MOSS THEATRE

Argyle Street London W1

LIVE FROM THE
LONDON PALLADIUM
NEW YEARS EVE – DECEMBER 31ST

TVS PRESENTS

HAPPY BIRTHDAY
A CELEBRATION – 80 YEARS OF THE LONDON PALLADIUM
HAPPY NEW YEAR

A STAR PACKED CELEBRATION –
80 YEARS OF THE WORLD'S GREATEST VARIETY THEATRE

BEA ARTHUR
MICHAEL BALL
THE BEVERLEY SISTERS
MAX BYGRAVES
MARTI CAINE
JIM DALE
BOBBY DAVRO
GRAHAM FLETCHER
PETER GOODWRIGHT
FRANKIE HOWERD
ROY HUDD

and lots of
surprise guests

DIANE LANGTON
GUY MITCHELL
ANDREW O'CONNOR
BERTICE READING
JOAN REGAN
LIZ ROBERTSON
DAVE WILLETTS
MICHAEL WILLIAMS
BARBARA WINDSOR
ERNIE WISE
MIKE YARWOOD

JOIN THE PARTY
LIVE ON ITV

BOX OFFICE: 071-437 7373 AND 071-437 2055

BRUCE FORSYTH

theatre were able to see it on their TV screens at home, so they could still get a taste of the magic.

1991 saw The Adeline Genée Awards, and later in January there was another one-night affair to aid Romanian charities, especially children, which was appropriately entitled *Kids at Heart*. 100 top names from the world of television and stage all came together to help this worthwhile cause.

Sponsored by *The Sun* newspaper, a Gala Concert was held on 24 February 1991 to help those who had fought in the Gulf War. It was very quickly and successfully organised by Mark Peters and with the help of forces' favourite Jim Davidson, plus a few friends, the evening was a tremendous success.

Bruce Forsyth 'gave us a twirl' and was once again at home at the Palladium with his one-man show, enjoying all those memories from the 1960s. In March, Jerome

WITH HIS PIANO AND ORCHESTRA

LONDON PALLADIUM

A STOLL MOSS THEATRE   ARGYLL STREET LONDON W1

OPENS Mon. 4th MARCH

FOR 1 WEEK   Evgs at 7.30

TEL: 071-437 7373   071-437 2055

FIRST CALL 071-497 9977 plus booking fee

Tickets £7.50, £10.00, £12.50, £15.00, £17.50

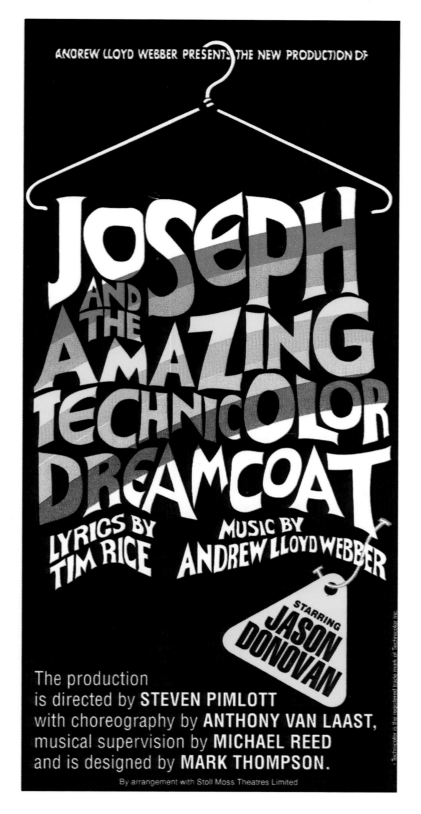

Kern and Oscar Hammerstein's *Showboat* berthed again for another short but successful cruise in Argyll Street. Barry Mishon presented yet another of his one-off spectaculars. This time it was the new Gershwin musical, *My One and Only*. It was hosted by Robert Kilroy-Silk, and included The Nicholas Brothers, David Soul, Bertice Reading, Clarke Peters, and lots more from the London stage.

From 1 June 1991, *Joseph and The Amazing Technicolor Dreamcoat* was the next offering to the Palladium theatre-goers. Once again extra police had to be engaged to control the crowds, who were swarming to see TV heart-throb Jason Donovan who played the lead. This sort of furore had not been seen since perhaps the days of The Beatles and Johnnie Ray. On the London buses, one would see posters advertising 'June, Joseph and Jason' emblazoned on the front. With superb casting, the show turned out to be a truly phenomenal success. Over the long run, others who played the lead were Philip Schofield and Darren Day, and Jason even came back for a final lap of honour. The box office was kept extremely busy for many, many, *many* months.

During the run of the show, which lasted for 1,095 performances, special seminars were occasionally offered in the mornings to London schools so children could witness how a show was actually put together, and the component parts were then discussed more fully. If a child was interested in the theatre, but maybe their talents did not run to singing, dancing or acting, he or she might consider a role in the wardrobe department or maybe the scenery construction, or sound and lighting. It was all detailed by members of the Lloyd Webber Really Useful team.

On 25 August 1991, the Palladium said *Welcome Home* to Bob Hope, who made a most welcome return with Danny la Rue, Roger Whittaker, Joe Longthorne and Maddi Cryer.

In November, the life of the much lamented Bernie Winters was celebrated by a terrific array of his friends. Bruce, Lionel, Les, Russ, Leslie, Jimmy, Bob, Ronnie, Anita; one only has to mention their first names to know who they were. Rising star Brian Conley was also there,

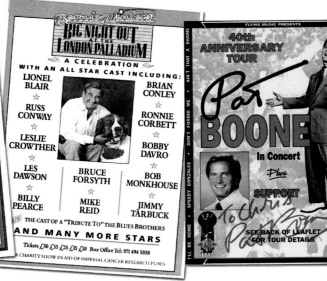

along with Bobby Davro, Mike Reid, Billy Pierce, Kenny Lynch, Roger de Courcey and Jess Conrad. Thanks to Bruce Vincent, The Tillers were there too of course. Numerous needed pounds were raised for The Imperial Cancer Research Fund.

In December, Paul Stone produced a very special, magical occasion. Paul Daniels and Debbie McGee, Ron Moody, Ray Alan, Les Dennis, Leonie Paige singing with the Band of the Scots Guards and a host of other stars made up this fine bill.

1991–1993 were the years when 'The Sunday Concert' came into its own. The Flying Music Company introduced us to many a performer, as did other promoters too. *The Magic of The Musicals* provided a great show, and Neil

Sedaka, Richard Thompson, Jimmy Jones, and Rose Marie all had performances. The Festival of Street Entertainers held their finals again. Tammy Wynette, Jack Jones and Engelbert all made a most welcome return, as did Jim Bailey who came back to give us his faultless impersonations of Judy Garland, Barbra Streisand and Peggy Lee.

Midsummer of 1992 saw the first lady of the theatre, Evelyn Laye, celebrating her ninety-second birthday. Helping her celebrate were so many of her friends. It was a 'bootiful' evening all round.

Popular 1950s stars Pat Boone and Kay Starr made a happy return to the Palladium on their *April Love* tour. Brenda Lee and Frankie Valli did the same, as did Sacha Distel and Rosemary Ford, who all enchanted their

supporters. Peter Casson demonstrated his hypnotic powers, *The Music of Hollywood and Broadway Years* was brought to us by Wayne Sleep and Lorna Luft, and Paul Jones and Elaine Delmar took us back to Hollywood itself. The top television comedy award winner Paul Merton also entertained for two weeks in 1993.

The London Society of Theatre, in association with American Express, held The Olivier Awards in 1994. As one would expect it was a glittering occasion, and it was filmed for TV by the BBC. This, along with The Children's Royal Variety Show, preceded a brief season of Topol in *Fiddler on the Roof*. Legendary songster Art Garfunkel made a brief Sunday appearance too.

'A Musical Masterpiece' was brought to the Palladium by Cameron Mackintosh. It was entitled *Oliver!*, and it starred Jonathan Pryce as Fagin. Russ Abbott and understudy George Layton also held the role for a brief period, as did Robert Lindsay, Jim Dale, and Barry

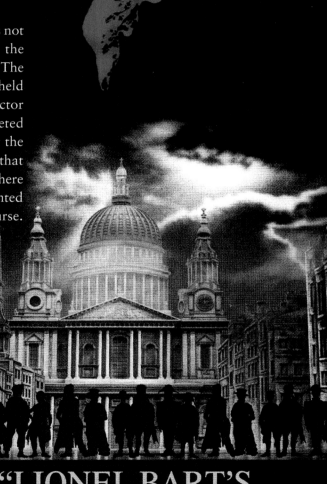

Humphries. They all 'picked a pocket or two', and in doing so they all added their own individual talents to the demanding part created by Lionel Bart. On the evening of 8 July 1997, your author was invited to attend the celebrations of the then longest running show, which at that point had notched up 1,097 performances. It was still running in February 1998, when the show finally came to its natural end.

Ironically, ardent research has proven that this was not the first time that *Oliver* had been presented on the Palladium stage. In the spring of 1936 and in aid of The Charing Cross Hospital, a Matinée and Pageant was held to celebrate the Charles Dickens Centenary. Noted actor Bransby Williams, appearing as Mr Pickwick, greeted everyone and introduced Sir Martin Harvey, who at the end of Act One auctioned off a pair of decanters that that had belonged to Charles Dickens himself. I wonder where they are today? The Dickens Fellowship then presented fifteen short excerpts, including *Oliver Twist* of course. No one could ask for more that night!

"LIONEL BART'S
MUSICAL MASTERPIECE
SUNDAY TIMES

LONDON PALLADIUM

If variety is the spice of life, then it most certainly goes on at the Palladium. In March 1998, a seventieth birthday was celebrated by someone who, more than anyone else, has become associated with the Palladium: Britain's much loved, top all-round entertainer, Bruce Forsyth. That week was some party! It culminated in a very special recreation of a live TV special of *Sunday Night at the London Palladium*. Some eight years later, Bruce would be honoured with a well deserved CBE.

Later in the spring, *Saturday Night Fever* took to the stage. Life was turning full circle, for had it not been that very fever which infected people on a Saturday night as they wondered what the next night would bring on TV with *Sunday Night at the London Palladium*? It would be the very best, that was for sure!

Max Bygraves OBE stated in his latest book that, 'whilst the Palladium has lost some of its sparkle by allowing commercialisation to bring to the stage some acts that perhaps were not worthy, it is still the greatest variety theatre in the world.' He should know; he has appeared there more than most.

As the hours ticked by to midnight on 31 December 2000, I wonder what lay ahead for the London Palladium?

The London Palladium: The greatest theatre in the world! All the stars said so.

Chapter Twenty

AND NOW
FOR SOMETHING
COMPLETELY
DIFFERENT...

*N*umber 7, Argyll Street has been the centre of all forms of entertainment, from circus and ice shows to opera and even ballet, right through the gamut of all branches of show business.

The Bioscope, as has been seen in another chapter, brought the world's news on film to the theatre-going public. In 1927 when talkies were all the rage, the Palladium was also the venue for Cine-Variety. After the successful musicals of the 1920s, talking pictures became the vogue, and in trying to keep in touch with the modern demands of the day a huge cinema screen was erected to be 'flown' away so that variety shows could be presented in between the films. In all though, only fourteen weeks were devoted to showing a double feature alongside top variety acts.

In 1927 Sir Edward Nichol, who was a great supporter of wrestling, took a team of a dozen wrestlers from Cornwall and they appeared three times daily for a fortnight as an additional act on a regular variety bill. Over the years, the London Palladium has also been home to religious talks, parliamentary discussions, product launches, and even Health and Strength displays on several occasions when the Mr Universe contest took to the stage late in the 1930s and later on again in the 1950s.

In the early 1960s yet another different form of entertainment took place on the Palladium stage, this time in the form of a cookery demonstration! Not the sort of thing that one would usually associate with the Palladium, but highly popular and entertaining nevertheless. After a variety show in the first half with acts like Cyril Fletcher, Pearl Carr and Teddy Johnson and Eric Delaney and his Band, the second half would be taken up with the highly entertaining and famous BBC cookery expert, Marguerite Patten OBE, who would proceed to show the audience how to make a flan or a soufflé. Dear friend Cyril, an expert on lots of things and knowing what made us laugh, would join in the merriment as Marguerite's assistant. With little or no rehearsal, they would perhaps make a trifle together in front of a specially invited audience, with lots of laughs along the way.

The Palladium building, as well as the stage itself, has been used many times as the location for films, product launches for Birds Eye Frozen Foods, TV commercials for floor cleaning liquid, and even an *Ed Sullivan* excerpt.

Then, in June 1963, it brought us the weigh-in for the Cooper versus Cassius Clay fight, which was held the following day at the Empire Stadium, Wembley.

In 1984 Charringtons the brewers launched their new lager to a specially invited audience. The launch was coupled with a specially produced variety show, in which Bruce Forsyth and Karen Kay and international illusionists Richard and Lara Jarmaine appeared. Later that year, the clairvoyant Doris Stokes hired the Palladium, which resulted in eager ticket applicants filing around the block in anticipation. All the tickets were sold in a matter of hours.

In 1985, the centenary celebrations of Gilbert and Sullivan took place at the Palladium, with a presentation of *The Mikado*.

In 1987 a property developer, Steven Morgan, hired the Palladium for a month at a reputed cost of £250,000. (Remember that in 1910 it cost just that to build!) He planned a Christian Crusade with four revivalist healing meetings held during the day. The first event attracted just seven people.

Having just launched their very first Gold Heart Day on 14 February 1991, in May of that year The Variety Club of Great Britain held a party in the Cinderella Bar at the Palladium to launch their £5 million Hospital Appeal Fund. Since the Club was formed in 1949, it has raised over 76 million pounds for worthy causes!

In 1992 the theatre was used as a venue when Air France, the French national airline, chose the Argyll Street location for their Sales Conference and incorporated the show of the day, *Joseph and The Amazing Technicolor Dreamcoat*.

A plaque at the stage door was unveiled to stage door keeper and long time employee Dave Grimley, who started his Palladium career as a music boy 'runner' for The Skyrockets Orchestra. In 1993 a memorial service was held at the Palladium for Bill Platt, who was the chief electrician for many years, and in 1995 a similar memorial service was held for the top agent and highly respected gentleman of the theatre world, Billy Marsh. In fact, his ashes were placed under the stage in a special location. It was ironic that it was in very close proximity to a 'No Smoking' sign. Billy was rarely seen without a cigarette between his lips!

More recently, with the change in regulations it is now even possible to get married on stage at the London Palladium. Whatever next, I wonder? When the rules on civil marriages were changed in the United Kingdom it allowed civil ceremonies to take place in locations other than a church or other religious building, and Stoll Moss spotted an opportunity that would allow their theatres to be venues for these special and memorable occasions. On midsummer's day on Sunday, 21 June 1998 a real *Cinderella* story took place on the London Palladium stage. Hilary Freeman and Steve Somerset said 'I do' and there wasn't a dry eye in the house.

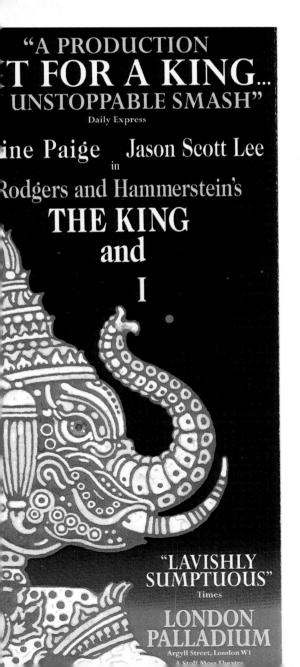

Chapter Twenty-One

CENTENARY COUNTDOWN

*I*n April 2000, East met West in a lavish production of *The King and I*, which opened with a cast of fifty and starred Elaine Paige and Jason Scott Lee. The new production of a show not seen at the Palladium since 1979 had originated in 1991 in Australia, before moving to Broadway for two years, where it won four Tony Awards. In London it took £8 million before the opening night. As is usual now with West End productions, to keep the production fresh a succession of other artists filled the title roles over time. Josie Lawrence and Keo Woolford completed the box office success after almost two years notching up 1097 performances.

In 2002, the old triple revolving stage from the 1950s *Sunday Night at the London Palladium* TV show had to be removed completely, but thankfully it has been preserved for posterity. The reason for its removal was that the complicated mechanism for the next big show needed the space beneath the stage.

301

With parking a continuing problem in the West End, the next show created little difficulty. The car simply flew onto the stage of the Palladium, and the Ian Fleming story of *Chitty Chitty Bang Bang* finally parked in Argyll Street. It starred Michael Ball as the inventor Caractacus Potts with Emma Williams as Truly Scrumptious. Anton Rodgers, Brian Blessed, Nichola McAuliffe and Edward Petherbridge were all there too on the opening night. Richard O'Brien was the first of many a Childcatcher. Other notables in this particular role were Paul O' Grady, Lionel Blair, Alvin Stardust, Wayne Sleep, Peter Polycarpou, Derek Griffiths, and Stephen Gateley, with each of them playing the dark side of this otherwise extremely happy show for four months each.

The film's original vehicle, the lovingly maintained and road-going car, GEN11, owned by Pierre Picton, made a visit to Argyll Street to help launch the show, much to the consternation of the area traffic wardens! No tickets were issued though, except from the box office! This event too was a sell-out success.

Any technical problems on stage in the run-up were quickly ironed out, and the child friendly, happy show just ran and ran. Russ Abbot and Christopher Biggins each supported Gary Wilmot and Brian Conley who filled the title role, and it was Jason Donovan, who had earlier played the lead, who flew over the stalls in the final journey in the car, which took place on 4 September 2005. The car was the star! Or that was the opinion of the press, anyway. The box office success show notched up 1,414 performances and this production now holds the record for the longest running show at the London Palladium. *Scrooge* was presented starring Tommy Steele in the title role, with special illusions created by Paul Kieve.

Ol' Blue Eyes was back in town with 'Come Fly with Me', in the show *Sinatra at the London Palladium*, which brought a revolutionary 2006 look to the old stage. Thanks to modern technology, with giant digital screens making it all possible, and with the family's full support, a mixture of unseen old footage from the Sinatra family archives, plus a twenty-four piece orchestra and a vibrant and energetic dance group of twenty on stage made Francis Albert come alive again. He sang with all the skill of yesterday to a modern orchestra. Others may have felt differently, but I was expecting him to come on at the end to take a final bow.

Days that used to be 'dark' were no longer, and some Mondays were filled with 'Sunday Concert' promoters in search of customers. Apart from the usual run of tribute rock and pop concerts that have been dominated by The Flying Music Company, other promoters have presented Art Garfunkel, Jack Jones, Petula Clark, Crystal Gale, The Chieftains, Stephen Triffitt, Jackson Browne, Engelbert Humperdinck, Dominic Kirwan, Joe Longthorne, Hank Marvin, Steve Hofmeyer, Omid Djalili, Jackie Mason, Aled Jones, Nana Mouskouri, Gene Pitney, Richard Clayderman, and Glen Campbell, and they have all made their mark on this wonderful stage. On a Sunday in

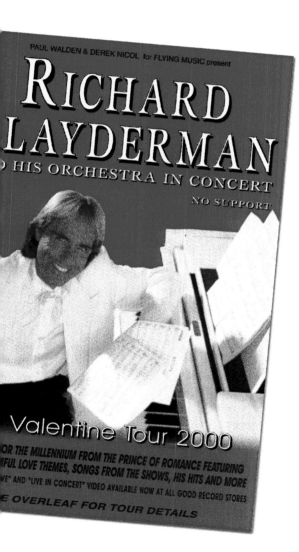

PAUL WALDEN & DEREK NICOL for FLYING MUSIC present

RICHARD CLAYDERMAN

AND HIS ORCHESTRA IN CONCERT

NO SUPPORT

Valentine Tour 2000

FOR THE MILLENNIUM FROM THE PRINCE OF ROMANCE FEATURING BEAUTIFUL LOVE THEMES, SONGS FROM THE SHOWS, HIS HITS AND MORE "LOVE" AND "LIVE IN CONCERT" VIDEO AVAILABLE NOW AT ALL GOOD RECORD STORES

SEE OVERLEAF FOR TOUR DETAILS

October 2007, a special show took place. *An Evening with Val Doonican and Friends* celebrated Val's sixtieth year in show business. And a great night was had by all!

One very special Sunday concert entitled *Lyrics by Don Black* took place in August 2008 to celebrate the special birthday and music of Don Black OBE. Mike Dixon conducted The Royal Philharmonic Orchestra and Sir Michael Parkinson CBE acted as host for the evening. He introduced, amongst others, Jonathan Ansell and Hayley Westenra, Marti Webb, Lulu, Maria Friedman, Mica Paris, Gary Barlow, Joe Longthorne and a whole host of other stars.

Another spectacular Sunday show took place at the end of September 2008. Paul Stone, who regularly presents Sunday concerts for charity, brought over from Las Vegas and from elsewhere in the world several magic superstars to star in *A Tribute to Siegfried and Roy*. Both Siegfried and Roy made a personal appearance, and they have done so much over the last thirty years and more to promote magic and illusion through their high quality shows, both in Las Vegas and throughout the world, so it was right and fitting that they were honoured in this way. It was a magic night of nights.

In October, the veteran star comedian Ken Dodd OBE made a one-off appearance in *Ken Dodd and Friends* in aid of the Entertainment Artists Benevolent Fund and Brinsworth House. I wonder what time the concert finished? Amongst Ken's special guest stars were funny men Joe Pasquale, Bernie Clifton, and Johnnie Casson. Sharon D. Clarke also appeared as well as Christian the Magician, The Laine Theatre Arts and Mark Evans. The music was provided by Trevor Brown and his Orchestra.

With just over two years to go before the centenary celebrations of the opening of the London Palladium, the recent brilliant pre-show publicity of the TV programme, *Search for Maria*, has once again put the Palladium on the map of the theatre-going public.

That highly successful film, *The Sound of Music*, has now been brought to the stage by Lord Lloyd Webber. Connie Fisher climbed many mountains in the TV heats and emerged from the search as a rightful star who was worthy of the lead role. Summer Strallen is currently appearing in the lead role. Long may the echoes of the sound of music in all its forms be heard in the corridors of the Palladium!

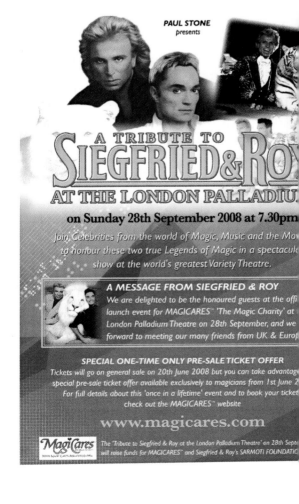

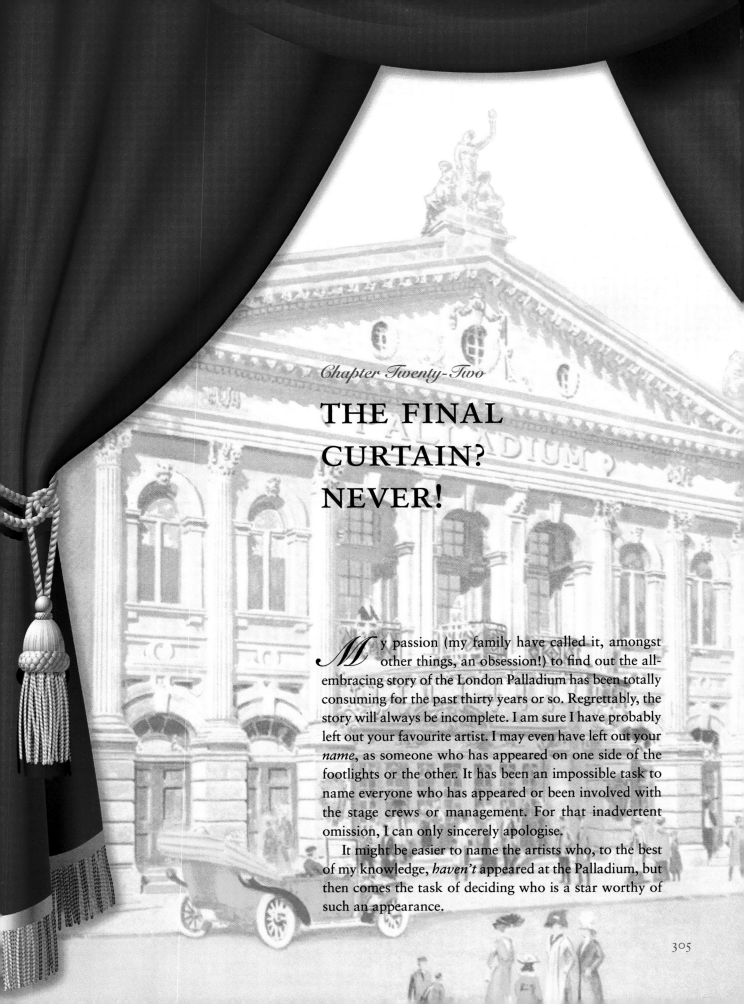

Chapter Twenty-Two

THE FINAL
CURTAIN?
NEVER!

*M*y passion (my family have called it, amongst other things, an obsession!) to find out the all-embracing story of the London Palladium has been totally consuming for the past thirty years or so. Regrettably, the story will always be incomplete. I am sure I have probably left out your favourite artist. I may even have left out your *name*, as someone who has appeared on one side of the footlights or the other. It has been an impossible task to name everyone who has appeared or been involved with the stage crews or management. For that inadvertent omission, I can only sincerely apologise.

It might be easier to name the artists who, to the best of my knowledge, *haven't* appeared at the Palladium, but then comes the task of deciding who is a star worthy of such an appearance.

305

The only names I cannot trace as having appeared on this stage are Charlie Chaplin, Marcel Marceau, Bob Dylan, and Phil Silvers. Elvis Presley never actually came to England, or did he? Although the Marx Brothers first appeared in the UK in 1922 at the Coliseum, and Chico and Harpo appeared at the Palladium in 1949, Groucho never made a personal appearance here to my knowledge. If I am wrong, please correct me! Al Jolson, however, *was* billed to appear in a show which was to be broadcast on radio, but the show was cancelled at the last minute and so he never made it into the list of luminaries.

Fred Astaire never actually appeared on stage at the Palladium as far as I know, but he did have his name in a programme once. It was a revue presented by Charles Gulliver and Laddie Cliff in 1927, which starred Jack Hylton and his Band with Charles Austin, Gwen Farrar and Billy Mayerl. The book was by Greatrex Newman, Clifford Grey, and Noel Scott. The music was by George Gershwin, Carroll Gibbons and Fred Astaire. The show was aptly entitled *Shake your Feet*.

Thankfully, the London Palladium is a Grade Two Listed Building, and so the curtain will never fall for the final time to make way for a supermarket trolley.

New producers, directors, choreographers, technicians, artists and managements will be born and will die, but the theatre will live forever. The Palladium is as much a part of London as Buckingham Palace and the Tower of London. It has always been synonymous with first class presentations and as long as the discerning public have that need for the very best, the owners, management and stage staff of the day will continue to provide it.

There have been many apocryphal stories, but there is one which I think best illustrates the magic and mystique of this theatre. Auditions were being held for a show, which particular one is really irrelevant. The Producer shouted, 'Next!' On walked a man in a raincoat. The Producer asked him, 'What do you do? Do you sing, dance, or what?' 'I don't do anything, sir', replied the man nervously. 'Then why are you here?' retorted the producer, angrily. 'I just wanted to tell my grandchildren that I had stood on the stage at the London Palladium.' He then walked off into the darkness and back out through the stage door into the street and disappeared into oblivion. To this day, no one remembers his name, but in his own eyes he had achieved something so important in his life, something that he could recount to his grandchildren, and say that he once stood on the stage at the London Palladium.

Having walked on that famous stage myself many times, I am thrilled that I can now tell the same true story to my grandchildren, Eliad, Rena, and Matan, together with Sophie and Benjamin.

It is almost impossible to put into words as to why the London Palladium is so special in the hearts and minds of so many people, not only the audiences and their happy memories, but all of the many artists who have appeared on that wonderful stage. It was best summed up, I think, by that consummate supreme artist Frankie Vaughan CBE who, in an interview in the Number One dressing room, said the following:

> It's magic! Because you've got a little lump in your throat, like I have now. And you think back to those very special nights, when it was expected from you that you top the bill and you leave the audience roaring for you. I mean those who have gone before us now, who were masters of their craft. The people poured all their talents into making this the number one.

And that's what the Palladium is – The Number One!

Amen Selah!

Long live the London Palladium!

HISTORICAL
HIGHLIGHTS

1864 The Duke of Argyll dies and Argyll House
      is sold and demolished.
1871 Corinthian Bazaar constructed.
1871 Hengler's Circus opens.
1885 Hengler's Circus rebuilt.
1895 National Skating Palace opens.
1908 Hengler's Circus demolished;
      Corinthian facade retained.
1909 Palladium Theatre under construction.
1910 Palladium Theatre constructed at a cost of
      £250,000.
1910 Opening night on 26 December.
1911 Variety.
1912 Variety, Captain Scott nears the North Pole
      on the Bioscope.

1913   Variety.

1914   The Royal Family visit a music hall for the first
       time. First World War begins.

1915   Variety.

1916   Variety.

1917   Variety.

1918   Variety, First World War ends.

1919   Variety.

1920   Houdini appears during May for two weeks.

1921   Variety.

1922   *Rockets* opens in February for
       500 performances.

1923   Variety.

1924   *Whirl of the World* opens for 627 performances
       with Tommy Handley, along with Nervo and
       Knox; 3 million patrons saw this show.

1925   *Sky High, Folies Bergère.*

1926   *Palladium Pleasures, Life.*

1927   *Apache* with Carl Brisson, Shaun Glenville
       and Dorothy Ward.

1928   Cinema begins, Cine-Variety, cinema ends,
       Variety recommences devised by George Black,
       The Delfont Boys appear in December.

1929   Max Miller, first appearance of Burns and Allen.

1930   First Royal Variety Performance on 22 May.
       First year of *Peter Pan* matinées.

1931   First appearance of Jack Benny on 10 August,
       first *Crazy Week* on 30 November.

1932   *First Crazy Month* in June.

1933   *Fourth Crazy Month*. Duke Ellington,
       Ramon Navarro and Louis Armstrong.

1934   First appearance of Cab Calloway,
       Sixth Crazy Month.

1935   *Life Begins at Oxford Circus,
       Round About Regent Street.*

1936   *All Alight at Oxford Circus, O-Kay for Sound.*

1937   *Swing is in the Air*, The Cotton Club,
       London Rhapsody.

1938   *London Rhapsody*, first appearance of
       Vera Lynn with Ambrose, *These Foolish Things.*

1939   *Bandwaggon* with Ernie Wise and
       Maureen Potter, *The Little Dog Laughed.*

1940   *Garrison Theatre* featuring Jack Warner,
       Top of the World with Pat Kirkwood runs for
       four nights only.

1941   Theatre Dark. *Applesauce* resurrected from
        the Holborn Empire fire. Bomb lands on
        Palladium roof, Able Seamen Wright and
        Bevan courageously defuse it. *Gangway* with
        Tommy Trinder.

1942   *Best Bib and Tucker* with Tommy Trinder,
        Variety.

1943   *This is the Army* with Irving Berlin.

1944   *Look Who's Here* with Cyril Fletcher, Variety
        with Max Miller.

1945   *Happy and Glorious* with Tommy Trinder.
        George Black dies, Val Parnell takes over.
        First Ted Heath Swing Session.

1946   *High Time* with Tessie O'Shea.

1947   Laurel and Hardy. *Here There and Everywhere*
        with Tommy Trinder. *Just William* matinées.

1948   Mickey Rooney, Danny Kaye, first post-war
        pantomime *Cinderella* with Tommy Trinder,
        Evelyn Laye and Zoe Gail.

1949   Harpo and Chico Marx, Benny Goodman,
        Big Show of 1949 with Charlie Chester.

1950   Dorothy Lamour, Max Bygraves, first
        appearance of Frank Sinatra, Ella Fitzgerald.

1951   Judy Garland.

1952   Bob Hope.

1953   First appearance of Morecambe and Wise.

1954   First Appearance of Norman Wisdom.

1955   *Painting the Town*, first *Sunday Night at the
        London Palladium*.

1956   Suez Crisis, Royal Variety Performance
        cancelled, *Rockin' the Town*.

1957   Ealing Film *Dunkirk* shot on stage at the
        London Palladium.

1958   *Large as Life* with Harry Secombe.
        First appearance of Bruce Forsyth in pantomime.

1959   *Startime* with Frankie Vaughan and Roy Castle.

1960   *Stars in your Eyes* with Cliff Richard,
        Des O'Connor, Joan Regan and
        Edmund Hockridge.

1961   200th edition of *Sunday Night at the London
        Palladium*.

1962   *Every Night at the London Palladium* with
        Bruce Forsyth, Eric Morecambe and Ernie Wise.

1963   Sammy Davis Jnr, The Beatles,
        Man in the Moon.

1964 Judy and Liza on BBC Television.

1965 The Rolling Stones, *Doddy's Here* with
Ken Dodd.

1966 *London Laughs* with Harry Secombe and
Jimmy Tarbuck. First colour *Sunday Night
at the London Palladium*.

1967 Tom Jones, *Doddy's Here Again*, *Robinson
Crusoe* (during which Arthur Askey falls
through the trapdoor).

1968 Farewell Tour of Maurice Chevalier, *Golden Boy*
with Sammy Davis Jnr, *Jack and the Beanstalk*
with Jimmy Tarbuck.

1969 *Here and Now* with Des O'Connor.

1970 *Dick Whittington* with Tommy Steele.

1971 *To See Such Fun* with Tommy Cooper,
Anita Harris and Clive Dunn.

1972 *The Comedians*.

1973 Tommy Steele. *Palladium '73* with
Bruce Forsyth.

1974 *Hans Andersen*.

1975 Frank Sinatra, Bette Davis, *Peter Pan* with Lulu.

1976 Shirley MacLaine, George Burns, Bing Crosby,
Sammy Davis.

1977 *Theatre of Skating II* with John Curry.
Neil Diamond, Bing Crosby.
(Bing died two weeks later.)

1978 Bette Midler, Barry Manilow.

1979 Bob Hope, Cliff Richard, *King and I* with
Yul Brynner.

1980 *Dick Whittington*.

1981 First Children's Royal Variety Performance.
Barnum.

1982 *Barnum*.

1983 *Barnum* ends after 663 performances.
Singin' in the Rain.

1984 *Singin' in the Rain*. Eric Morecambe Tribute.

1985 *Singin' in the Rain*.

1986 Liza Minelli, *La Cage aux Folles*.

1987 Dean Martin, Nureyev.

1988 *Ziegfeld*. British Music Hall Society
25th Birthday.

1989 *'Allo 'Allo, Singin' in the Rain*, Grand Order
of Water Rats Centenary.

1990 *Pirates of Penzance, Showboat*, Ken Dodd,
Russ Abbot's Madhouse.

1991 *Joseph and the Amazing Technicolor Dreamcoat* with Jason Donovan.

1992 *Joseph*.

1993 *Joseph*.

1994 *Joseph* closes after a record-breaking 1095 performances. *Fiddler on the Roof*. Olivier Awards. Lionel Bart's *Oliver*! opens 8 December.

1995 *Oliver!* Jonathan Price BAFTA Awards.

1996 *Oliver!* with Russ Abbot and Jim Dale.

1996 *Oliver!* with Robert Lindsay.

1997 *Oliver!* with Barry Humphries becomes the longest running show at the Palladium.

1998 *Saturday Night Fever*.

1999 *Saturday Night Fever*.

2000 *Saturday Night Fever* until February.

2001 *The King and I*.

2002 *The King and I* ends, *Chitty Chitty Bang Bang* opens.

2003 *Chitty Chitty Bang Bang*.

2004 *Chitty Chitty Bang Bang*.

2005 *Chitty Chitty Bang Bang*. *Scrooge* with Tommy Steele.

2006 *Sinatra*. *The Sound of Music* opens.

2007 *The Sound of Music*.

2008 *The Sound of Music*.

AFTERWORD

$\mathcal{D}$uring my early years, the London Palladium was always the spiritual home of Variety. I was first conjured into its confines when, as a star-struck boy of eleven, I won a competition in a children's comic weekly to be taken behind the scenes of Val Parnell's 1956 pantomime, *The Wonderful Lamp*. Our family archives still embrace photos of me sitting alongside producer Robert Nesbitt as he oversaw the production in the stalls, and then backstage in his dressing room with the star, Norman Wisdom, in a rare moment of calm in his overpoweringly hectic schedule. In later years, I returned many times to see the greats of that last true period of British Vaudeville score their triumphs on a stage which I would one day learn had unique magic qualities all of its own.

Inevitably, the memories come streaming back. The five whole minutes of laughter that accompanied Jack Benny's stare when the glamorous chorus girl who handed him his violin explained that the autograph she requested was only for her mother; the breath-taking athleticism of the world's greatest juggler, Francis Brunn;

the world-weariness of his comic counterpart, Rob Murray, as *sotto voce* he lived up to his billing, 'Juggling under Protest'; the warmth and humanity of Josephine Baker as she rolled back the years to sing her signature song, 'J'ai Deux Amours' and made everyone in the auditorium – male and female – fall genuinely in love with her in the process; the laughter that rolled towards the stage with such force that one felt the theatre might explode as Ken Dodd literally detonated his tickling stick in Argyll Street for the first time; the ease and lazy charm with which Max Bygraves provided a lesson in audience control that I shall never forget.

Many years later the agent Billy Marsh, who played such an important role in maintaining the Palladium variety tradition, explained to me the special quality of the venue; namely, the sheer intimacy it engendered for any performer who stood on its stage. When I later found myself producing a television documentary on the history of this theatrical gem, I took a moment of personal calm in my own hectic schedule to stand still and contemplate centre stage. It immediately became apparent what Billy had been trying to explain. It was as if one could reach up and touch the furthest seat in the house. One could understand how the likes of Danny Kaye and Gracie Fields had been able almost literally to hug their audiences to them. As I pondered the brilliance with which the architect Frank Matcham had achieved this, I enlisted my imagination to conjure up again the sounds of many of the ghosts that I like to think still linger in homage within its walls: 'Hello, playmates...', 'You lucky people...', 'Now, here's a bottle and here's a glass...', 'Say, "Goodnight," Gracie...', 'Somewhere over the rainbow...', 'There'll never be another...'

For this writer, the glory days have passed. There won't be another Palladium. Thank goodness for this book, if only in the hope that it succeeds in educating a new public to the diversity and greatness of the talent it missed before the musical-meets-television-reality-show express train came thundering down Argyll Street in its own singularly depressing way. If that seems a negative note upon which to end, it is only because the talent that serviced this theatre's greatest years was beyond compare, shining with an intensity that can never be completely dimmed.

JOHN FISHER

BIBLIOGRAPHY

40 Years of Television by Jane Harbord and Jeff Wright, Boxtree, 1992

A Career in Music by Lew Stone, Inchbrook, 1971

Acrobats and Mountebanks by Le Roux and Garnier, 1890

Alma Cogan: A Memoir by Sandra Caron, Bloomsbury Publishing, 1991*ATV Television Star Book* by David Leader, Purnell, 1959

Beat The Clock by Jim Smith, Mayfair Books, 1962

Bruce, The Autobiography by Bruce Forsyth, Sidgwick and Jackson, 2001

Buatier de Kolta: Genius of Illusion by Peter Warlock, 1994

By Royal Command by Bill Pertwee, David and Charles, 1981

Crying with Laughter by Bob Monkhouse OBE, Century Random House UK, 1993

Curtain Up by Lord Delfont, Robson Books, 1989

East End West End by Bernard Delfont and Barry Turner, Macmillan, 1990

Every Night at the London Palladium by Patrick Pilton,
    Robson Books, 1976

From Sawdust to Windsor Castle by Whimsical Walker,
    Stanley Paul and Co., 1922

Funny Way to be Hero by John Fisher,
    Frederick Muller Ltd, 1973

Hengler's Circus by Dr. John M. Turner,
    (a private publication), 1982

Hengler's Circus by Sean McCarthy, The Third Eye
    Centre Exhibition, 1981

Ice Hockey by Major B.M. Patton, Routledge, 1936

Laurel and Hardy: The British Tours, A.J. Marriot,
    1993

Madame Speaker Betty Boothroyd by Paul Routledge,
    Harper Collins, 1995

My Crazy Life by Bud Flanagan, Frederick Muller Ltd,
    1961

My Fabulous Brothers by Rita Grade Freeman,
    W.H. Allen, 1982

Rats, Religion and Royalty by (Wee) Georgie Wood

Sixty Years of Theatre by Ernest Short, Eyre and
    Spottiswoode, 1951

Skaters Cavalcade by A.C.A. Wade,
    Olympic Publications Ltd, 1939

Skating to Antarctica by Jenny Diski, Granta Books,
    1997

Slapstick by Tony Staveacre, Angus and Robinson,
    1987

Stage Struck by Lionel Blair, Weidenfeld and Nicolson,
    1985

Still Dancing by Lew Grade, Harper Collins, 1987

Survey of London Vol XXI, Athlone Press, 1963

Tarbuck on Showbiz by Jimmy Tarbuck,
    Willow Books, 1985

The Autocar

The Bystander

The Crazy Gang by Maureen Owen,
    Weidenfeld and Nicolson, 1986

The Era

The Fool on the Hill by Max Wall, Quartet Books,
    1975

The G.O.W.R: A Legend of Laughter by
    Charlie Chester, W.H. Allen, 1984

The Glorious Deception: The Life of Chung Ling Soo
    by Jim Steinmeyer, Carroll and Graff, 2005
The Golden Jubilee Book of Showbusiness, VABF, 1956
The Grades by Hunter Davies,
    Weidenfeld and Nicolson, 1981
The Graphic
The Great Illusionists by Edwin Dawes,
    David and Charles, 1979
The House of Commons, Houseman
The Illustrated London News
The Journal of the Royal Institution of Cornwall
The Laughtermakers The Story of TV Comedy
    by Anthony Davis, Boxtree, 1989
The Piddingtons by Russell Braddon, Werner Laurie,
    1950
The Sketch
The Stage and Television Today
The World
The World's Fair
Tiller's Girls by Doremy Vernon
Tommy Cooper. Always Leave Them Laughing by
    John Fisher, Harper Collins, 2006
Top of the Bill by Ian Bevan, Frederick Muller Ltd,
    1952
Torville and Dean by John Hennessy,
    David and Charles, 1983
Ulysses by James Joyce, Everyman's Library, 1992
Victorian Arena: The Performers, Volumes One
    and *Two* by John Turner, Lingdales Press, 1995/2000

The London Palladium

SEATING PLAN

UPPER CIRCLE

ROYAL CIRCLE

STALLS

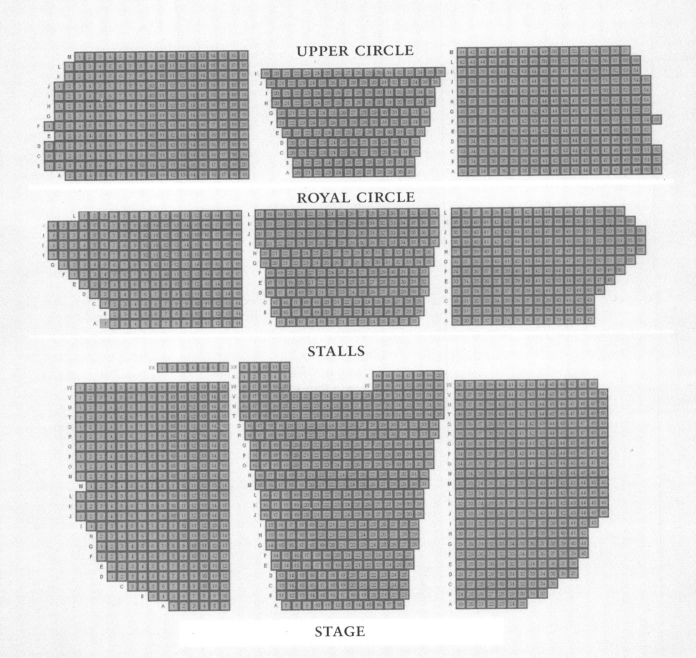

STAGE